The Subversive Tradition
in French Literature
Volume II: 1870–1971

Twayne's World Authors Series

French Literature

David O'Connell, Editor

Georgia State University

TWAS 811

The Subversive Tradition in French Literature
Volume II: 1870–1971

Leo Weinstein

Stanford University

Twayne Publishers
A Division of G. K. Hall & Co. • *Boston*

The Subversive Tradition in French Literature, Volume II: 1870–1971
Leo Weinstein

Copyright 1989 by G. K. Hall & Co.
All rights reserved.
Published by Twayne Publishers
A Division of G. K. Hall & Co.
70 Lincoln Street
Boston, Massachusetts 02111

Copyediting supervised by Barbara Sutton
Book production by Gabrielle B. McDonald
Book design by Barbara Anderson

Typeset in 11 pt. Garamond
by Huron Valley Graphics, Ann Arbor, Michigan

Printed on permanent/durable acid-free paper
and bound in the United States of America

Library of Congress Cataloging-in-Publication Data

Weinstein, Leo.
    The subversive tradition in French literature, 1721–1971 / Leo
Weinstein.
        p.   cm.—(Twayne's world authors series ; TWAS 811. French
literature.)
    Contents: —v.2. 1870–1971.
    Bibliography: p.
    Includes index.
    ISBN 0-8057-8249-4 (v. 2 : alk. paper)
    1. French literature—History and criticism.   2. Protest
literature, French—History and criticism.   3. Revolutionary
literature, French—History and criticism.   4. Opposition (Political
science) in literature.   5. Politics and literature—France.
6. Literature and history.   I. Title.   II. Series: Twayne's world
authors series ; TWAS 811.   III. Series: Twayne's world authors
series. French literature.
PQ145.4.P73W4 1989b   88-28435
                                                               CIP

Contents

About the Author

Leo Weinstein, professor of French, emeritus, at Stanford University, fled his native Germany in 1938, served in the Psychological Warfare Service of the U.S. Army during World War II, and obtained his Ph.D. in 1951 from Stanford University, where he taught French and comparative literature until his early retirement in 1985. He is the co-author of *Ernest Chausson: The Composer's Life and Works* (University of Oklahoma Press, 1955; rpt. Greenwood Press, 1973) and the author of *The Metamorphoses of Don Juan* (Stanford University Press, 1959; rpt. AMS Press, 1967), *Hippolyte Taine* (Twayne, 1972), and articles on Franz Kafka, Stendhal, Flaubert, and Jules Laforgue. He also edited *The Age of Reason: The Culture of the Seventeenth Century* (Braziller, 1965) and translated *Pelé* by François Thébaud (Harper & Row, 1976).

This book represents both the synthesis and the culmination of much of his previous work, since he draws on experience gained in treating large subjects (Don Juan), interdisciplinary study (*The Age of Reason*), and the combination of history and literature employed by Hippolyte Taine.

Preface

To change an existing situation, one must first change minds. This holds true both for those in power and those out of power, those who are trying to get some or all of it. Even the most narrow-minded dictatorships have reluctantly come to that conclusion, because the alternative is the imposition of a political system by means of constant armed force.

The question therefore is, How do you change minds? By propaganda? By rational persuasion? Or by other means? The least effective, at least at the present, is propaganda. It was a powerful weapon in the 1930s, when the unceasing pounding at the German people by its every means, reinforced by brutal force, produced amazing and tragic results. But fifty years later, the posturings by political leaders, the slogans created by speech writers, and the two-minute summations of political and economic policy on television are no longer taken seriously in developed countries, where the people have become more and more cynical about promises and generalities.

Ideally, change ought to be brought about by rational argument. That may still be possible in very small countries with a highly educated population, but it is unlikely to have much of an effect in large nations, where political battles are decided on television and in the press, with victory going to the most telegenic or the most glib.

An appeal to the imagination of the people is lacking in all the above methods. Propaganda operates by the mechanical repetition of slogans; rational arguments are necessarily dry, and judgment based on looks takes advantage of the habit, acquired at an early age, of thoughtlessly staring at a screen. These methods have become so stale that equally unimaginative reformers have come to believe that the only means left to make themselves heard is an act of terrorism, which is effective only in that it turns the people against them.

In the first volume of this study I discussed how great French writers got their message across to readers by means of literary works. And this in spite of difficult and dangerous conditions posed by monarchies—ranging from absolute to constitutional—and by empires, all of which imposed censorship and severe punishment for those who expressed their opposition in terms that offended the rulers or posed a threat to their rule.

During the eighteenth century these writers managed to express their social and political criticism while circumventing censorship and avoiding imprisonment. To a sophisticated and increasingly liberal aristocracy they offered clever satires, thinly veiled exotic tales, or daring but witty plays, which made many of those in important positions laugh and applaud, even against their best interests. Montesquieu's *Lettres persanes,* Voltaire's *Candide,* Crébillon fils's *Ecumoire,* and Beaumarchais's *Mariage de Figaro* formed an important part of the procession that led to the French Revolution, and to the guillotine for more than one of those who had acclaimed their works.

Censorship became even more severe under the Revolution and Napoleon's First Empire. That did not keep André Chénier from filling his poetic pen with poison to be shot at the excesses and the brutalities of the Revolution, but he paid for it with his life. More prudently, Mme de Staël and Chateaubriand voiced timid disapproval of Napoleon by indirect references in some of their works.

Instead of satires, exotic tales, or plays, nineteenth-century authors employed the predominant genres to attack their governments. Béranger and Victor Hugo aimed poetic shafts at the Restoration and the Second Empire, respectively. Stendhal used the novel to show how his young heroes fared during the Restoration, in *Le Rouge et le noir;* during the July Monarchy, in *Lucien Leuwen;* and under an absolute reign, in *La Chartreuse de Parme.*

The attempt to incorporate political views into fictional works is fraught with danger, and it has been severely criticized by both critics and authors, who believe that literature should be pure and not linked to recent or specific events. With the advent of the Third Republic, when censorship was lifted, the temptation to incorporate political views became almost irresistible. Edmond Scherer rightly warned that, in this sort of literature, "the characters are too close to us to permit the use of their names or even to represent them in a manner that would be strictly historical. . . . The author is obliged to attenuate their personality, to modify their character, to distort their looks, frankly speaking, to falsify the historical period in which the novel is set."[1]

Of the many who dared to accept the challenge, only a few, the best, succeeded. Maurice Barrès angrily named those he considered traitors of France and her destiny; Émile Zola accused all over again those who were responsible for the criminal cover-up in the Dreyfus affair; Louis

Aragon and Pierre Drieu la Rochelle described in vivid colors contemporary politicians and generals; and James Jones had us witness the May '68 follies. Yet all of them steered their works safely past the lurking reefs, because they were masters of their craft. Two other great writers, Jean-Paul Sartre and Jean Anouilh, were not able to name their enemies, because they were writing during the German occupation of France. They had to resort to the method of their eighteenth-century predecessors by veiling their attacks under the guise of modernized versions of Greek tragedies.

Thus it is through great authors that we shall watch French history of the past one hundred years go by, and for each portion of that history one or two writers will represent the opposition to the government or to popular opinions they consider to be false or unjust. The result is likely to be a new way of judging French history since the Third Republic, or at least a modification of the French history we were taught in school. To paraphrase Rousseau, if this view of French history is not better, at least it is different.

There is much of interest in all of this to students of American literature. There similar attempts have been made, but a tradition has not been established. Although Harriet Beecher Stowe's novel *Uncle Tom's Cabin* (1852) had a great influence on the abolitionist movement, it is difficult to point to other, similar successes. Certainly, there has been no Béranger, who defied the July Monarchy; no Victor Hugo, who acted as a one-man government in exile during the Second Empire; no Zola, who reversed the condemnation of Dreyfus.

Critics have little praise for the American social or political novel.[2] Although the Vietnam War inspired a rash of novels and short stories, most of them relate personal experiences, leading critics to conclude that "the literary quality of many Vietnam War novels is not particularly high,"[3] or, somewhat more charitably, that "though adding nothing new to the art of the novel, the books provide insight into how a heterogeneous aggregation of authors deals with the peculiar relationship between fiction and the historical, continuing war with which each artist was imaginatively involved."[4]

Obviously, American writers do not enjoy the same admiration as their colleagues in France, where authors have for over a century taken an active part in politics and where a literary dispute makes front-page news. Nevertheless, much can be learned from the French experience both in literature and in history.

Although quite different in most ways, the two countries have been exposed to similar challenges in the past one hundred years: the two world wars, the threat of communism, attempts to cover up illegal acts by government officials, war in Vietnam, to mention only the most important. And there is no reason that one country cannot learn from the successes or failures of the other.

Reference to such parallels is made primarily in end notes. While the reader may not always agree with the subjective judgments expressed, this study is an exercise in comparative history, which I hope will stimulate reflection and widen what is often a provincial presentation, by the media, of American history and current events.

Enough of prefatory remarks; it is time to join the action. France has just been defeated in the Franco-Prussian War, leading to the fall of Napoleon III's Second Empire. Victor Hugo has returned from self-imposed exile, and a republic has been proclaimed. As the curtain rises, we are in 1871. A new era is about to begin in French history.

Unless otherwise indicated, all translations into English are mine, for better or for worse. As a rule, French quotations are cited only for primary sources.

Leo Weinstein

Stanford University

Acknowledgments

Grateful acknowledgment is made to the following for permission to quote previously published material:

Les Beaux Quartiers by Louis Aragon. Copyright © 1936 by Editions Denoël.

La Comédie de Charleroi by Pierre Drieu la Rochelle. Copyright 1934; and *Gilles* by Pierre Drieu la Rochelle. Copyright 1939 by Editions Gallimard.

Sartre on Theater by Jean-Paul Sartre. Documents assembled, edited, introduced, and annotated by Michel Contat and Michel Rybalka. Translated from the French by Frank Jellinek. © 1976 by Pantheon Books, a Division of Random House, Inc.

La Foire d'empoigne by Jean Anouilh, in *Pièces costumées*. © 1960; *Pauvre Bitos* by Jean Anouilh, in *Pièces grinçantes*. © 1961; and *Antigone* by Jean Anouilh, in *Nouvelles Pièces noires*. © 1967 by Les Editions de la Table Ronde.

Catch as Catch Can from *Seven Plays,* volume 3 by Jean Anouilh © 1967 by Hill & Wang. Reprinted by permission of Hill & Wang, a division of Farrar, Straus & Giroux, Inc.

Poor Bitos by Jean Anouilh (New York: Coward-McCann). Translated by Lucienne Hill. © 1964 by Jean Anouilh and Lucienne Hill. Reprinted by permission of Methuen, London.

Antigone by Jean Anouilh, in *Five Plays* (New York: Hill & Wang). Adapted and translated by Lewis Galantière. © 1958 by Random House, Inc.

Un Allemand à Paris by Gerhard Heller. © 1981 by Editions du Seuil.

The Merry Month of May by James Jones. © 1970, 1971 by Delacorte Press. Reprinted in arrangement with Delacorte Press.

The Comedy of Charleroi by Pierre Drieu la Rochelle. Reprinted from *The Comedy of Charleroi and Other Stories* by Pierre Drieu la Rochelle. Translated with an introduction by Douglas Gallagher. © 1973 by Rivers Press Ltd.

Grateful acknowledgment is made to the following for permission to reproduce photos:

Bibliothèque Nationale, Paris: Georges Boulanger, Charles de Gaulle, Alfred Dreyfus, Maurice Barrès, Anatole France, Émile Zola, Louis Aragon, Henri Barbusse, and Pierre Drieu la Rochelle.

AGIP, PARIS: Jean-Paul Sartre, Jean Anouilh, André Stil, and Robert Merle.

MAGNUM: James Jones. © Marc Riboud/MAGNUM.

Part 1
The Third Republic

Chapter One

Seven Characters in Search of a Republic

The Third Republic: The Early Years, 1871–94

If history were written in plain language, it would state that the raison d'être of the French Revolution was to establish a lasting republic for the French people. Measured in these terms, one must perforce conclude that, except for two very brief periods, the Revolution was a failure for eighty-two years. And, to add insult to injury, it must be recognized that the republic which was finally to provide the French people with Liberty, Fraternity, and Equality was produced by Prussian troops and by a French military defeat.[1]

The loss of the Franco-Prussian War spelled the end of the Second Empire and led to the election, on 8 February 1871, of an Assembly with a strong majority of monarchists. It in turn elected two republicans, Grévy and Thiers, as president and premier, respectively.

The greatest obstacle the budding Republic had to face was not Prussian troops but the Paris Commune, which was made up of groups of revolutionaries who opposed the government of monarchists and republicans and who wanted to revive the Commune of year eleven of the Revolution. As the fighting between the government forces and those of the Commune became more intense, atrocities were committed on both sides. Prisoners and hostages were killed, and, although the struggle only lasted two months (March–May 1871), the government forces lost some one thousand men while the Communards suffered probably around twenty thousand lives lost. During the last day of fighting, on 28 May 1871, 147 Communards were shot against a wall of the Père-Lachaise cemetery, a continuing reminder of this fratricidal conflict that has left deep scars in the French political system.

After the bloody suppression of the Paris Commune, the monarchists were in a position to set up yet another royal reign, or even an empire. But the petty quarreling among legitimists, Orleanists, and Bonapartists, compounded by the blind pride of the candidates for power, rendered any such effort ineffective; these rivalries led, in fact, to the election of a republican majority of life-appointed senators in 1876.

Favorable economic conditions enabled Thiers to pay off the huge war reparations to Prussia. Nevertheless, the monarchist majority replaced his administration by choosing Marshall MacMahon as president. The Third Republic did not have a complete constitution but was governed by a series of constitutional laws. As the election results shifted in favor of the republicans, MacMahon and the monarchists made one last desperate attempt to retain power by dissolving the Chamber on 16 May 1877. But the following election swept the republicans into power with 326 seats, against 207 for the Right. MacMahon resigned and was replaced as president by Grévy.

Despite their name, the republicans were not a unified party. Control was exercised by the center group, called the Opportunists; those to the left called themselves Radicals; and beyond these were a small group of Socialists and even fewer Marxists. To the right of center were conservative republicans who, along with the monarchists, were referred to as the Conservatives.

The lack of clearly defined parties and the reduced, largely ceremonial role of the president contributed much to the image we have kept of the Third Republic: a tiresome succession of ephemeral governments playing the game of musical chairs with revolving premiers and cabinet ministers. Until the Dreyfus affair only two names stand out: Gambetta, a liberal republican, who died at the age of forty-four; and Clemenceau, whose time was yet to come.

In addition to the constant problem of revision of the constitutional laws, the republicans proposed the separation of church and state, liberty of the press and of meetings, gratuitous and compulsory education, and the lifting of restrictions on labor unions. Amnesty was granted to prisoners of the Commune in 1880.

The measure that created the most intense controversy was the educational reform, which secularized education by virtually excluding the religious orders, which had enjoyed a near monopoly in this field. The resulting struggle and a growing left wing disunited the republicans and led to the renewed strength of the monarchists, who by 1883 had only one candidate left: the Orleanist count of Paris. In the 1885 elections the monarchists obtained 3,500,000 votes to the republicans' 4,100,000; and it required a concerted republican effort on the second ballot to secure 383 seats for the republicans against 201 for the Conservatives.

The Boulangist Movement (1886–89)

With the urging of Clemenceau, the incoming government appointed a republican general by the name of Georges Boulanger as war minister in January 1886. The youngest French general at forty-nine, blond and handsome, looking stately on his black horse, Boulanger captured popular imagination when he refused to have his soldiers break a strike. "Perhaps, at this very moment, each soldier is sharing his soup and ration of bread with a miner," he declared.[2] To prove his republican loyalties, he replaced many of the monarchist officers and proposed a series of military reforms.

It did not take long for politicians out of power to realize that here was a man who could catapult them into power: he could be all things to all people. Untainted by any previous political alliances, he was touted as a man above parties and a symbol of national unity. He satisfied the liberal republicans by his acts as war minister, he appealed to national pride by his potential for avenging the defeat in the Franco-Prussian War, and he was viewed by monarchists as able to prepare for the return of royal rule to France if constitutional reforms could cast him in the role of a strong president of the Republic. Honesty in government became another issue when it was revealed that President Grévy's son-in-law, Wilson, had been selling decorations and other favors.

All these scandals led to an increasing discontent that favored the rise of a popular leader. By May 1887 Boulanger had turned into a national figure and the Opportunists feared him enough to remove him from the office of war minister. Appointed division commander at Clermont-Ferrand, Boulanger was scheduled to leave the Gare de Lyon on 8 July 1887 at 8:00 P.M. A large crowd tried to prevent his car from reaching the station where some twenty thousand people had gathered. Only by agreeing to ride out of the station secretly on a locomotive that would take him to another train was Boulanger able to leave for his new post.

It is more accurate to speak of a Boulangist movement than party, for this movement contained elements of the Left and extreme Left as well as conservatives and monarchists—in short, all those who were dissatisfied with the ruling centrists. Strange bedfellows they made, indeed: on the extreme Left, the journalist Henri Rochefort, and former Communards, such as Henri Michelin; on the extreme Right, the nationalist Paul Déroulède, the anti-Semite Edouard Drumont (who did not officially join the movement, because it contained Jews, but who sympathized strongly with it), the Jewish Orleanist journalist Arthur Meyer, and his Bonapartist colleague Georges Thiébaud.

The effective leaders of the Boulangist movement were Alfred Naquet, a Jew; Georges Laguerre; and Count Arthur Dillon. Naquet, a Radical dissident, was elected in 1871 to the Assembly, and later to the Senate, where he authored the divorce law. Laguerre was a leftist deputy, while Dillon's position was not well-defined. He probably leaned toward monarchism and conceived of Boulanger's role as that of strong leader, if not dictator. As the propagandist in the movement, it was Dillon who made the deal with Arthur Meyer that brought the Orleanists into the movement, to fight the common adversaries.

Made up of such heterogeneous elements, the Boulangist movement was characterized by two inevitable features: (1) almost all its members used the general to achieve their particular goals and left the movement once it no longer served their purposes; (2) its program was always vague.

Both extremes were opposed to parliamentarianism and to the maneuvering of do-nothing party politics. Constitutional revisions were to give Boulanger strong executive powers as president of the Republic. Honesty in politics, military strength to thwart a possible new Prussian attack or even to avenge the recent defeat, and social and economic justice—for various reasons and with different motives, all the malcontents could unite behind such a vague program.

On the advice of Thiébaud, Boulanger's name was entered in seven by-elections on 26 February 1888. Since as an army officer he was ineligible to hold political office, printed ballots with his name were distributed to voters, who were asked to vote for him on the first ballot only. Although he ran last in all but one of the elections, he received a total of about fifty-five thousand votes. Despite his official dissociation from his candidacy, Boulanger's approving messages to Dillon had been intercepted by the government, and the general was dismissed from active duty—not for his political activity, but ostensibly for having made three unauthorized trips to Paris.

A protest committee was formed, with Naquet as its president. Free to campaign now, Boulanger was entered in a series of by-elections, in which he won impressive victories. Although the Boulangist movement remained substantially leftist, its principal financial support came from wealthy Orleanists, especially the duchesse d'Uzès, who contributed several million francs to his campaigns. His greatest victory was scored in the department of the Nord, where on 15 April 1888 he garnered 172,853 votes, against 75,901 for his closest rival. As deputy of the Nord, on 4 June 1888 Boulanger introduced a bill to revise the Constitution. Vague in details but providing for a constitutional assembly, Boulanger's proposal called for a powerful executive, a Senate elected by universal suffrage, and a referendum on important issues—a program very close to that of a future, and more successful, general.

On 12 July Boulanger proposed that the Chamber vote its own dissolution, not only because it was guilty of misconduct but also because, he warned, the monarchists were awaiting their chance to regain control of the government. He called for a new National Republic to be formed. Since, as expected, the deputies refused to disappear, Boulanger resigned from that body, after an exchange of insults with Premier Floquet.

The altercation led to a duel on 14 July. Boulanger, overanxious, stormed into the sword of the nearsighted parliamentarian and was wounded in the neck. Imagine a general being defeated in a duel by a myopic politician! Although the ensuing ridicule set back the Boulangist movement, the general's popularity was so great that he not only survived the effects of the duel but won several by-elections, and a resounding victory in the Paris elections of 27 January 1889, defeating his closest challenger with 244,700 votes, a plurality of 81,550.

On that day, French history could have changed radically, with many of his followers repeatedly urging him to seize power, shouting, "To the Elysée!"[3] In any event, it is quite possible that he could have marched on the presidential palace without much resistance in a bloodless coup d'état.

Why did Boulanger not seize power when his movement had reached its zenith? In spite of appearances, he seems to have been rather timid, especially for a general. He also had been impressed as a young man when his father read him Victor Hugo's condemnation of Napoleon III's coup d'état, and he consistently maintained that he was a republican willing to come to power only via the ballot box. Finally, *cherchez la femme.* Boulanger, although married, lived with his mistress, Mme de Bonnemains, whose love he valued more than anything else. It may have been a banal choice between spending the night with her or marching on the Elysée Palace that caused him not to act.

Now the pendulum swung, as the administrations of Floquet and, later, Tirard took the initiative. The voting system was changed to their advantage, outdoor political demonstrations were banned, and conservatives were courted by permitting the exiled duc d'Aumal to return to France. Closer to Boulanger, Déroulède's Ligue des patriotes was declared a secret society and its leader, along with Laguerre and Laisant, brought to trial. Although the charge was dismissed, the defendants were each fined a hundred francs for belonging to an unauthorized society.

Fearing imminent arrest, Boulanger fled to Belgium on 13 March 1889, but he returned two days later when it turned out that no warrant for his arrest had been issued. But a change of chief state prosecutor on 1 April prompted Boulanger to flee again to Belgium with his mistress.

The government's case against Boulanger was weak in all respects: applying laws dealing with plotting against the state and with attempting to seize power, the Senate illegally assumed the powers of a high court. Boulanger, Dillon, and Rochefort were found guilty on both counts and sentenced to a penal colony.

Despite the absence of its titular head and some defections (Thiébaud and Michelin), the Boulangist movement did not disappear into thin air. This is an indication not only of its popular support but also of the absence of any other leader who could unify so many disparate groups. But an exiled leader and the new voting system proved to be too much even for the Boulangist movement. In the 1889 general elections the republicans obtained 363 seats, the conservatives 167, and the Boulangists a mere 38. The general himself won on the first ballot in Clignancourt, but the government declared his candidacy illegal and awarded the victory to his opponent. With Boulanger now on the island of Jersey, his followers began to quarrel amongst themselves. After electing only one candidate in the Paris city council elections on 27 April and 4 May 1890, the National Committee was formally dissolved.

Meanwhile, Boulanger became increasingly despondent, as his mistress suffered from tuberculosis. In May 1891 he returned with her to Brussels, where she died in July. Unable to console himself, he committed suicide at her grave on 30 September.

With the Republic more or less safe, the politicians went back to doing the only thing they are really good at: politicking. The greatest challenge the new government had to face was the Panama scandal in November 1892. Ferdinand de Lesseps, after successfully building the Suez Canal, had formed a company to do the same in Panama. But estimates turned out to be vastly inferior to the real costs, and the company was forced to issue new shares by lot. This received the required approval from Parliament, but despite these efforts, the company went bankrupt.

Issues of parliamentary bribery and Jewish financing were seized on by Maurice Barrès and Paul Déroulède, who wanted to destroy the parliamentary system, and by the anti-Semitic Edouard Drumont. Certain sums had been dispensed to members of Parliament, who were called *chéquards,* by Baron Reinach, who, in turn, had been blackmailed by a mysterious adventurer, Cornelius Herz, born in France but by then an American citizen.

Violent scenes took place in Parliament, accusations were leveled, defenses were expounded; finally a judicial inquiry cleared all but six of the accused. Still, reputations suffered, particularly those of Floquet and of Clemenceau, who was accused not only of corruption but also of having served as an English agent.

The republicans weathered the crisis. In the elections of August 1893, some 310 moderate republicans formed the majority, along with 150 radical republicans. But a small number of revolutionary Socialists on the extreme left and violence by anarchists on the right, who saw no hope of gaining power after the demise of Boulangism, were to plague the Republic for several years. The anarchists' first notable victim was President Sidi Carnot, assassinated in June 1894.

Chronology

1871: Election of Assembly; government of Grévy and Thiers; (March–May): Paris Commune insurrection.

1873–1879: MacMahon, president; end of Prussian occupation.

1875: Constitutional laws passed.

1877: Republican victory in elections.

1879–1887: Grévy, president.

1879–1882: Educational reforms of Ferry.

1880: First ministry of Ferry.

1881: Protectorate over Tunisia; ministry of Gambetta.

1883: Second ministry of Ferry.

1884–1885: Campaign in Far East; Tonkin annexed.

1886–1889: Boulangist movement.

1887–1894: Sidi Carnot, president.

1892: Panama scandal.

1894: Assassination of Sidi Carnot.

Maurice Barrès

Les Déracinés

The Boulanger affair and the Panama scandal provide more than just the background of Maurice Barrès's *Roman de l'énergie nationale*. They constitute the main subject of this trilogy of novels: *Les Déracinés* (1897), *L'Appel au soldat* (1900), and *Leurs Figures* (1902).

Intimately involved in these historical crises, Barrès, who was elected deputy of Nancy in 1889 and had a long political career, supplies us with an invaluable historical document, the sort that transcends the dry facts of history to become what the French call a *témoignage,* the often impassioned account of an eyewitness to history-making events. So engaged is he in the political conflicts that he showers us with minute details, and rather than speak here of politics in the novel, one is tempted to refer to his trilogy as the novel in politics.

Continuing the trend of recounting the experience in Paris of provincial young men, set by Balzac and Stendhal,[4] Barrès goes them one (or even several) better: instead of one hero, he sends seven young men from Lorraine to Paris. While this may sound like a bargain, it remains to be seen whether massive Balzac ("du Balzac au kilo") is preferable to lean Balzac, so to speak.

Les Déracinés (The Uprooted) opens in October 1879 at the lycée of Nancy, where a new professor has arrived. His name is Paul Bouteiller[5] and he preaches a Kantian doctrine while indoctrinating his students with their duty to serve the young Republic. Taken by themselves, these views are fine and good, but the new professor from Paris had not taken the trouble to inform himself of the peculiar nature, conditions, and interests of Lorraine or of his students.

Among these students, seven are called to our attention. François Sturel closely resembles Barrès himself. His father died when François was small, and he has been raised by his mother and two very Catholic aunts. Maurice Roemerspacher has a good, solid mind and has been influenced by the good sense of his grandfather. Henri Gallant de

Saint-Phlin is a provincial noble who is heir to an important domain and lives with his grandmother. Georges Suret-Lefort is a social climber. These are the more or less solid citizens of Lorraine. They are joined by three lower-caste students. Honoré Racadot is a descendant of slaves and serfs, who can expect a small inheritance. Alfred Renaudin and Antoine Mouchefrin are poor and on scholarships.

Bouteiller in time is transferred to Paris, but his influence over his students is such that the seven decide to seek their fortunes in Paris before they have obtained an understanding of their native province.

In Paris they enroll in the university, but only Roemerspacher (history) and Suret-Lefort (law) will carry their studies to a meaningful conclusion. Sturel will become absorbed by politics, Saint-Phlin will return home to his domain, Renaudin will turn to journalism, Racadot will lose his inheritance as owner of a newspaper, and Mouchefrin will continually hover at the starvation level.

But first the seven (not from Thebes but from Lorraine) go through many experiences that shape them, make them, or break them. Roemerspacher is marked by his meeting with the philosopher, historian, and critic Hippolyte Taine,[6] who shows him a plane tree that has become a symbol of life for him. What Roemerspacher learns from Taine is that philosophy is not the Kantian abstraction that Bouteiller had taught, but a dynamic experience; that we have to accept the conditions of life; and that nations and institutions behave like living organisms.

"This tree," Taine tells him, "is an image that expresses a beautiful existence. It does not know what immobility is. From the beginning its young, creative strength implanted its destiny in it and moves unceasingly inside." Taine goes on to describe the development of the plane tree according to its own laws rather than the symmetrical nature of French logic. He then points out the obstacles the tree has encountered in the shadow cast by nearby buildings and how it has adjusted to them.

That powerful mass of green obeys a secret reason, the most sublime philosophy, which is the acceptance of the necessities of life. . . . And now that tree, which confidently increased each day the treasures of its energies, is going to disappear, because it has attained its perfection. Nature's activity, without ceasing to support the species, refuses to do any more for that individual. My beautiful plane tree will live no more. Its destiny thus is bounded by the same laws that, after having seen to its birth, will now lead to its death. It was not born in one

day, it will not disappear in an instant. . . . Already certain parts in me are
becoming undone, and soon I shall fade away; my generation will accompany
me, and a little later will come your turn and that of your comrades.

[Cet arbre est l'image expressive d'une belle existence. Il ignore l'immobilité.
Sa jeune force créatrice dès le début lui fixait sa destinée, et sans cesse elle se
meut en lui. . . . Cette masse puissante de verdure obéit à une raison secrète, à
la plus sublime philosophie, qui est l'acceptation des nécessités de la vie. . . .
Et maintenant, cet arbre qui chaque jour avec confiance, accroissait le trésor de
ses énergies, il va disparaître parce qu'il a atteint sa perfection. L'activité de la
nature, sans cesser de soutenir l'espèce, ne veut pas en faire davantage pour cet
individu. Mon beau platane aura vécu. Sa destinée est ainsi bornée par les
mêmes lois, qui, ayant assuré sa naissance, amèneront sa mort. Il n'est pas né
en un jour, il ne disparaîtra non plus en un instant. . . . Déjà en moi des
parties se défont et bientôt je m'évanouirai; ma génération m'accompagnera, et
puis un peu plus tard viendra votre tour et celui de vos camarades. (Les
Déracinés, 199–200)][7]

Like most symbols, Monsieur Taine's tree can be interpreted in
different ways. Simply stated, it crystallizes many of Taine's ideas:
before writing a constitution for the French, we must first determine
what the French character actually is; if we ignore these factors, deal in
abstractions, and fail to apply scientific and experiential evidence before
making decisions, the result will be like trees that develop sideways
because we have put obstacles in their way and they must spend most of
their energy adjusting to them.

Barrès chooses from this symbol only what suits his purposes: by
Taine's law of motion Barrès condemns the immobility caused by parliamentary partisanship; the French character is defined by Barrès's intu-
ition (which differs markedly from Taine's definition of it); and the
natural process of generational succession is turned by Barrès into an
ancestral cult.

The second important experience for our seven provincials in Paris
also originates from Taine. Opposed to the all-powerful state and in
favor of groups of association, Taine approves that the seven from
Lorraine have continued their friendship in the capital. To cement their
association into something more meaningful, Roemerspacher and
Sturel arrange a meeting of the group at Napoleon's tomb in the
Invalides on 5 May 1884, the anniversary of his death.[8]

They are not the first to be inspired by the emperor. Stendhal's
Julien Sorel and Fabrice del Dongo were influenced by him; the former

took him as a model who rose from humble origins to become the most powerful man in the world, and the latter was drawn to the emperor in youthful enthusiasm.

The seven from Lorraine are seeking his political guidance. And so they meet at the Invalides to bask in the emperor's glory and to draw strength from this "Professor of Energy," as Sturel calls him. In a manner reminiscent of the recital of Napoleon's glory in Balzac's *Le Médecin de campagne,* Sturel recounts the stages in Napoleon's life that led to his accomplishments. Sturel praises him particularly for having found "a goal for his soul. . . . It was his ability to conform himself always to his destiny . . . that makes Napoleon a magnificent lesson for us." [Trouver un but à son âme. . . . C'est pour avoir su toujours se conformer à sa destinée, . . . que Napoléon nous est un magnifique enseignement (*Les Déracinés,* 229–30).] He gave up his former idols, Paoli the Corsican and Rousseau, because he realized that France, his former enemy, had become his destiny.

And there, on Napoleon's tomb, they swear to be men and leaders. But that is more easily sworn than done. What can seven young students from Lorraine do to lead France in 1884? They find it impossible to adhere to the existing political parties. Renaudin, already a journalist, suggests that France needs a likable hero to satisfy its need for romantic adventures, but who could this be? The army is out of the question for them.

The solution comes not from the respectable members of the group but from the least fortunate: Racadot, the descendant of slaves (as Barrès never lets us forget) and Mouchefrin, whose ancestors are probably unmentionable. Racadot risks his small inheritance to found a newspaper and Mouchefrin does all the legwork and the dirty work. "We shall be your stepping stones, gentlemen," Racadot concludes prophetically. "Later, don't forget us." [Nous serons vos marchepieds, messieurs: plus tard ne nous oubliez pas (*Les Déracinés,* 249).]

The only contribution to this risky enterprise by the privileged members of the group (Sturel, Roemerspacher, Saint-Phlin, and Suret-Lefort) consists of articles they take the trouble to write. Given that none of them has any journalistic experience and that they probably do not have much to say that will attract readers (Barrès carefully avoids quoting any of their writing), it comes as no surprise that *La Vraie République* never gets off the ground and drives Racadot into ever greater debt.

At various times, members of the group visit their former professor, but Bouteiller shows no more than polite interest in their problems. Thanks to his services rendered to Gambetta and the influence of the financier Reinach, he has become a deputy, and he devotes his energy to making the parliamentary Republic safe from its enemies. Approached by Racadot for help, Bouteiller declares himself unable to do anything. But since all parties support newspapers financially, hope appears for a subsidy from the government.

It is Sturel who ruins this prospect for reasons of pure vanity. He has been flirting with a respectable but capricious girl from Lorraine, Thérèse Alison, who is also courted by the baron de Nelles. One evening Nelles mentions that the Foreign Ministry seems prepared to grant *La Vraie République* the subsidy it has asked for. Embarrassed in front of Thérèse, Sturel denies all knowledge of this matter and asks Nelles to use his influence to refuse the request. "I must point out to you," Roemerspacher remarks as they are walking home, "that you did not have the right to be delicate in his [Racadot's] place. You can quit his newspaper, but why wreck the subsidy?" [Il faut avouer . . . que tu n'avais pas le droit de faire le délicat en son lieu et place. Tu pouvais quitter son journal; mais pourquoi anéantir sa subvention? (*Les Déracinés,* 363).]

The result is only too tragic. To take care of his sexual needs, Sturel has let himself be seduced by Astiné Aravian, an Armenian woman, much traveled and very liberated. She disappears for a while, but Mouchefrin notices her one day and renders her some services. When Racadot and Mouchefrin reach the starvation stage and receive no help or hope from anyone, including their Lorraine comrades (what happened to the oath at Napoleon's tomb?), they decide in utter despair to strangle Mme Aravian in order to steal her jewelry. Racadot is eventually brought to justice and executed, while Mouchefrin remains free—and poor, because the stolen jewels have been recovered by the police.

Sturel is a circumstantial witness, because he has seen his comrades and the Armenian woman together on the night of the murder. His delicate conscience makes him consult Suret-Lefort, now a lawyer, and the two look up Mouchefrin, who lives in a hovel with Racadot's mistress Léontine and a street urchin by the name of Fanfournot. The newly baked lawyer plays a cruel joke on his poor comrade by knocking at the door and shouting that it is the police. They make Mouchefrin admit his crime by claiming that Racadot has spilled the beans. "I shall defend you," Suret-Lefort promises. "Well, well," Léontine replies, "our misfortune will be of some use for these gentlemen." [— Je te défendrai, ajouta Suret-Lefort.— Voilà! dit la Léontine, notre malheur servira à quelque chose pour ces messieurs (*Les Déracinés*, 455).]

L'Appel au soldat *and* Leurs Figures

L'Appel au soldat deals primarily with the Boulangist movement, in which Sturel actively participates. He travels in Italy and on his return exchanges impressions with Roemerspacher, who has studied in Germany. While Roemerspacher, the historian, keeps his distance from the political fever that sweeps over France, Sturel and Renaudin become not only associates of the general but are swept into Parliament on his coattails. There they are joined by Suret-Lefort, who has been more circumspect in his political adherence, and by the baron de Nelles, now Thérèse's husband. He neglects his wife, and Sturel becomes her lover. But he, in turn, neglects her in favor of his political passion. She will eventually divorce the baron and marry Roemerspacher, who will bring out her true nature as a woman from Lorraine.

Sturel returns to Lorraine to visit Saint-Phlin, who has arranged a trip through his region that makes his friend recognize the character and the richness of his native soil. But he returns to Paris and stands steadfastly by Boulanger, even through the general's exiles, until his death and burial.

Leurs Figures is devoted almost entirely to the Panama scandal. It even contains entire pages of parliamentary debate. We learn that Suret-Lefort has become a successful deputy. He obtains the nomination of Roemerspacher as professor at the Ecole des Hautes-Etudes, authors a law for increased regional education, which Saint-Phlin has suggested, and finally replaces Bouteiller, who has become implicated in the scandal, as leader of the reigning party. Despite these real accomplishments, Barrès has only contempt for this social climber, who nonetheless has done far more for his comrades, and even for the cause of Lorraine, than Sturel.

As for the latter, he has only one aim left, now that he has resigned from Parliament and Boulanger is dead: to avenge the general and destroy the parliamentary Republic. He travels to England and manages to obtain an interview with Cornelius Herz, the intriguing intrigant of the scandal. Sturel returns to France with a list of *chéquards,* those deputies who have taken bribes, and threatens to publish the names. He is not swayed by the pleadings of a now humbled Bouteiller or by those of Suret-Lefort. But Thérèse, whose husband is threatened by Sturel's revelations, implores him to desist from his plan, and because of his past love of her and friendship with the man she will later marry, he agrees not to publish his evidence.

In a mood of despair, Sturel takes a walk in the gardens of Versailles, where he crosses paths with Bouteiller, who is being hounded by the gardeners, shouting their contempt of him. While moving away from his assailants, the former professor slips, and Sturel takes his arm to help him up. The two then continue each on his own way.

The Myth of True France

Le Roman de l'énergie nationale is not a great novel; it is, instead, a magnificent failure. It has all the ingredients it takes to make a great political novel: a time of crisis and transition, an author intimately involved in it, the theme of provincials trying to conquer Paris, the atmosphere of a corrupt press and parliament, the conflict between love and politics. But just as eleven stars do not make a great football team, so, promising ingredients do not guarantee a great novel.

The greatest handicap of Barrès's trilogy is its unevenness. Of the three parts, only Les Déracinés fulfills the requirements of a novel; L'Appel au soldat, and Leurs Figures even more so, neglect the novelistic plot in favor of long and often tiresome recitals of parliamentary debates and details that can only interest specialized historians. Moreover, Barrès is too passionately involved in what he recounts. Les Déracinés contains a good deal of perspective, quite naturally so because it re-counts the early and formative years of the young men from Lorraine. But as the succeeding volumes move closer to contemporary events, Barrès is no longer a novelist who analyzes but an investigative reporter who admires, accuses, or hates. Novels written in red heat rarely turn out to be successful.

Despite these grave shortcomings, Le Roman de l'énergie nationale merits far greater attention than it has received from literary critics. It not only represents an invaluable inside account of the Boulanger affair but also portrays a state of mind, a political and psychological concep-tion revealed in all its complexity.

All nations have their contradictions, and the French are certainly no exception. All nations also have their myths, and to understand the French better we must at least be aware of their principal ones.

We have already encountered two of these: the Revolution and Napo-leon. It is probably safer to roast a cow in the center of New Delhi than to attack the French Revolution or Napoleon on the Place de la Concorde, but at least these latter have their origin in history, becoming mythic only by added legends and imaginative poetry, or for the purposes of political interests.

By contrast, the third great French myth has no concrete historical basis. It is the concept of what is purely or truly French. Every nation is tempted by that concept. It may find its expression in *vieille France,* or in the Spanish idea of the *cristiano viejo,* in the German *urdeutsch,* in the Argentine *criollo,* or, even in as mixed a country as the United States, in the Mayflower myth. The problem with these concepts is that no authoritative definitions exist for them. Not surprisingly, therefore, the prototype of the "true" French character tends to reflect very closely the person who advocates it. Invariably, partisans for preservation of "true" national features display an extreme nationalism, even a racism, and a hatred of all that is foreign or different.

All supporters of "true" Frenchness would probably subscribe to de Gaulle's laconic dictum, "Il faut que la France soit la France." But what is the real France really like? On that point, views can strongly differ. The best Barrès can do to illuminate us on that matter amounts to vague generalities. In his definition of the true substance of Frenchness he has this to say:

The true substance of the French is a common nature, a social and historical product, possessed in participation by each of us; it is the sum of natures constituted in each order, in the rural class, in the banks and industry, in workers' associations or through religious ideals, and it evolves slowly and continuously.

[Le véritable fonds du Français est une nature commune, un produit social et historique, possédé en participation par chacun de nous; c'est la somme des natures constituées dans chaque ordre, dans la classe des ruraux, dans la banque et l'industrie, dans les associations ouvrières, ou encore par les idéals religieux, et elle évolue lentement et continuellement. (*Les Déracinés,* 241)]

In simple terms, France is the sum of everything that is French. Another essential element for Barrès is respect for one's ancestors—in his case, a kind of ancestor worship.[9] On the other hand, one cannot always be sure whether Barrès is not confusing France and Lorraine. His political program, as vague as Boulanger's, contains this appeal:

There is no longer any coordination among the efforts of the French; we do not know what we are and, consequently, what we are becoming. . . . So I feel in me the lessening, the disappearance of my French nationality, that is, the substance that supports me and without which I would vanish. We must carry on, protect, increase the energy we inherited from our ancestors. And, to do that, . . . I appeal to the good will of all my countrymen.

[Il n'y a plus de coordination entre les efforts des Français; nous ne connaissons pas ce que nous sommes ni par suite ce que nous devenons. . . . Alors je sens diminuer, disparaître la nationalité française, c'est-à-dire la substance qui me soutient, et sans laquelle je m'évanouirais. Il faut reprendre, protéger, augmenter cette énergie héritée de nos pères. Et pour cette tâche . . . je fais appel à la bonne volonté de tous mes compatriotes. (*L'Appel au soldat*, 281–82)][10]

The threat to "true Frenchness" comes from foreigners, Jews, and cosmopolitan Parisians.

It is not only our territory that is being chipped away, but also our mentality. Too many of our countrymen are unaware of their national roots: they play at being Germans, English, or Parisians. The Parisian is artificial, a composite: there is no such thing as Parisian wood, it is dyed wood.

[Ce n'est pas seulement notre territoire qu'on entame, mais notre mentalité. Un trop grand nombre de nos compatriotes ignorent leurs racines nationales: ils font les Allemands, les Anglais ou les Parisiens. Le Parisien, c'est de l'artificiel, du composite; il n'y a pas de bois parisien, c'est du bois teint. (*L'Appel au soldat*, 402)]

This striving for national purity leads inevitably to a feeling of racial superiority and thence to the search for scapegoats.[11] Implied is not only superiority over non-French people but also over one's own countrymen. Racadot is a descendant of slaves and serfs; consequently, he cannot rise or transform himself and he is bound to commit low or even criminal acts. Inferior races are sacrificed without much regret. The best Barrès can say about the assassination of Astiné Aravian, who initiates Sturel into the art of lovemaking, is that such is the fate of an Oriental woman of her sort. He even finds a silver lining in her premature death. "Would she have liked to grow old? Oriental women tend to put on so much weight!" [Mais eût-elle aimé vieillir? Les Orientales s'alourdissent si fort! (*Les Déracinés*, 404).]

The Jews (particularly German or Alsatian Jewish financiers) are singled out as the principal scapegoats by Barrès. The ethnic origins of Lesseps and the *chéquards* are not divulged, but a Jew is never referred to without being identified as such. When the Boulangist cause seems lost, Drumont suggests appealing to the anti-Semites.[12] Boulanger refuses this course of action to the obvious regret of Barrès. "Shall he reply that Boulangism has been too much under the influence of Naquet [who was Jewish] and it must be anti-Semitic for the very reason of national reconciliation?" [Répondra-t-il que le boulangisme a trop accepté l'influence de Naquet, et qu'il doit être antisémite précisément comme parti de réconciliation nationale? (*L'appel au soldat*, 464).]

The character who so lightheartedly dismisses the descendants of slaves, Orientals, and Jews preaches a new type of racial superiority in France. Sturel's ancestors have saved France from nobody, and he himself can point to nothing that would entitle him to any special consideration. The new superior French type that emerges from these views is thus neither a member of an aristocracy of blood (with some illustrious ancestor or ancestors at its origins), nor of an aristocracy of merit, but is the offspring of good and respectable French natives other than Parisians. If it was said of the old aristocracy that "they took the trouble to be born," the same can be said of Barrès's new supermen. This attitude is in keeping with Barrès's evolution from an earlier "ego cult"[13] to a cult of Lorraine and France. Although apparently a radical change from extreme individualism to collectivism, it retains the same egotism that enthrones him as the prototype of the French character.

What makes *Le Roman de l'énergie nationale* such an interesting work is that it contains all three of the great French myths: the Revolution (although Sturel believes in its outcome, the Napoleonic empire, far more than in its principles); Napoleon himself, the great national hero; and the myth of "true" France. The irony in this combination of myths, however, lies in the choice for inspiration: Napoleon can hardly qualify as "pure" or "true" French, and even Lorraine is not exactly the oldest French territory.

If Barrès's program seems vague and his political solutions more emotional than rational, that does not mean that his criticisms are entirely unjustified. Parliamentary party politics, corruption, a greater concern for reelection than for the national interest—these are the ills of republican regimes that lead to the call for a national leader who stands above parties, and to political upheaval and to dictatorships. His plea for regionalism and decentralization is eminently valid. The overpowering position of Paris has resulted in a sad neglect of the provinces and, while matters have improved considerably since 1889, the problem remains far from solved, even today. His criticism of the educational system, which produces far more candidates than there are openings (especially in teaching), rings equally true.

But neither Boulanger nor Sturel are capable of proposing a more promising alternative. We can see a number of interesting analogies between the Boulangist movement and the May 1968 uprising. In both cases the adherents were made up of disparate discontents who formed a temporary alliance for widely varying motives. Boulanger, like the students in 1968, was used by the extreme Left and Right as a means for seizing power from a conservative middle-of-the-road government. Both movements offered but a vague program (constitutional reforms in 1886–1889, university reform in 1968) and no substantial political philosophy. When we consider that the Boulangist movement at least had a titular head and was organized by experienced politicians (Naquet, Laguerre), we realize retrospectively how little chance the May 1968 uprising had of succeeding. Ironically, it would have taken a General de Gaulle to turn the Boulangist movement into a success and a Lenin to prolong the May 1968 events beyond their feverish excitement.

Even more striking is the mood of idealism and excitement that the two movements had in common. Like his intellectual descendants (who would not have approved of him), Sturel is searching for a cause, something that will give direction to his free-flowing energy:

I would like to acquire a conception of the world; but I'll go further, I would like it to be a motive for action for me, to give a direction to the forces that stir within me. No matter what direction, provided it engulfs me in its course and is dearer to me than my own self.

[Je voudrais me faire une conception du monde; mais je vais plus loin, je voudrais qu'elle me fût un motif d'agir, qu'elle donnât une direction aux forces qui sont en moi. N'importe quelle direction, pourvu qu'elle m'entraîne et me soit plus chère que moi-même (*Les Déracinés,* 212).]

Sturel's quest is obviously caused more by biology than by reflection. It cries out: "Give me a cause, quickly, any cause. Excite me, and I shall embrace it with all my being." Eighty years later his outcry was echoed unchanged. There is something deeply moving in this hunger of the young for an ideal, for a cause. Unfortunately, cynical politicians or other opportunists, usually of the extreme Right or Left (for how can a moderate course excite young idealists?), take advantage of these undirected energies and turn the young idealists into shock troops for their own designs.

Moreover, Sturel, living in Paris like an exile from Lorraine, derives from the Boulangist movement the feeling that he is no longer outside the mainstream, that he is part of the people and rubs elbows with them. The leftist intellectuals of 1968 felt the same rub of excitement.

The Character of François Sturel

Barrès can be criticized for a lack of political perspective, but when it comes to his main character, he must be credited with a masterful job. One would expect the author to present Sturel as a perfect model of the "Frenchness" he advocates. Nothing could be further from the truth.

François Sturel is portrayed with an often brutal honesty, which allows much room for ambiguity in interpretation. A rapid reading of the trilogy may leave the overall impression of a handsome, sincere, idealistic nationalist, a loyal friend, a loyal follower of Boulanger, and a ladies' man. But a closer examination reveals a far different character. Barrès repeatedly calls him "nervous," in the sense of frenetic, excitable, slightly neurotic, a trait he inflicts on Thérèse, who regains her natural "Lorraine" character only when she leaves him for Roemerspacher. Sturel is not only an absentminded lover who prefers politics to women; he is also a bad friend, for he never even suspects his enormous responsibility in the crime and subsequent death of Racadot.

A man with only vague political ideas, an eternal disciple, Sturel gives the impression of futile, wasted energy. Other than his nationalistic and regional fanaticism, which bears a certain resemblance to the Nazi *Blut und Boden* slogan, and his personal adoration of Boulanger, Sturel has little to offer that is positive. He is mainly "against": against the parliamentary Republic, against the corrupt politicians, against everything that is foreign or of foreign origin.

Sturel's traditionalism and ancestor worship leave practically no room for change, and in this he is uncompromising. His single-mindedness does not make for effective politics. When he realizes that his political goals are not going to be achieved in Parliament, he resigns his post as elected deputy without any regard for the obligation he has undertaken to represent his constituents, as does Déroulède when he feels disgusted with his colleagues in Parliament.

Being useless as a deputy, Sturel devotes his massive energies to wreaking vengeance on his corrupt colleagues but then decides not to publish his evidence for personal and sentimental reasons. One can hardly blame French voters for preferring tainted but persistent legislators to candidates like Sturel who, blown up by their self-proclaimed moral superiority, have nothing positive or tangible to offer and who bow out at the first setback. Honesty and sincerity are fine virtues, but they do not suffice to govern a nation.

At the end of the trilogy a more mature and tolerant Sturel seems to see in Bouteiller not merely a machine politician but rather the proponent of a different political attitude, a change in view that suggests a secret mutual desire for brotherhood, "which an organized society would have enabled them to enjoy." [qu'une société organisée leur en eût donné la jouissance (*Leurs Figures,* 327).][14] Not only is this an unjustified criticism of society, because their animosities are personal, political, and philosophical, but the novel has in no way prepared us for Sturel's change of attitude. It is revealed suddenly, rather like a pirouette, to provide an impressive and more palatable ending to this long work.

The Disciple Syndrome

One common motif found in rightist novels is the disciple.[15] Drieu la Rochelle's Gilles, whom we shall encounter later on, is a disciple, and so are the seven from Lorraine. Whether the master is approved of, as in Gilles's case, or criticized, as in Barrès's trilogy, the disciple is incapable of freeing himself from the master's influence. There is something pathetic about this, as if the disciple had been hypnotized and left with no will of his own, no judgement of his own, no personality of his own. It is a perfect example of what Sartre calls "bad faith," i.e., shifting responsibility for one's own life and actions to someone or something else. If, indeed, the seven students from Lorraine never succeed in shedding the straitjacket of being disciples, if they never manage to make the transition from disciple to master, they were probably not much to write home about to Lorraine in the first place.

The whipping boy or scapegoat is another natural motif. In this case the teacher plays the role, perhaps a little surprisingly because (1) he is not a foreigner, although a Parisian; and (2) he creates disciples, and those who produce such adherents are usually praised as great teachers. However that may be, the teacher remains an easy and cheap target. If he teaches objectively, he is accused of conveying no sense of morality or patriotism; if he tries to instill these values in his students, he is accused of indoctrinating or of teaching the wrong values. Society finds it difficult to define the teacher's function, especially since the burden that lies properly with parents or family has been increasingly shifted to the schools, which have been weak or foolish enough to accept it as theirs.

Bouteiller, despite his pompousness and a tendency toward dema-gogic indoctrination, seems to be a highly competent and enthusiastic teacher. It is only natural that, being ambitious, he prefers advance-ment in Paris to staying with a devoted group of provincial students, all the more so since he believes in serving the Republic, and Gambetta in particular. Besides, the virtues he preaches (love of country and of the Republic, and no doubt the Kantian categorical imperative) can stand on their own. The fact that three of his students (Sturel, Suret-Lefort, and Renaudin) are elected to Parliament, and a fourth (Roemer-spacher) could have joined them had he so desired, would indicate that he has formed capable students. But as Bouteiller increasingly shows his selfishness and personal lack of dignity, Barrès was apparently tempted to turn him into a sort of Ubu-Roi.[16]

Basically, Barrès criticizes less the professor, whom he calls "an instrument transmitting forces he cannot direct," than the philosophy of humanism and French centralism. But given this traditional trend, which makes of Paris the magnet that attracts ambitious young provin-cials to the capital, it is too much to ask a high school teacher to reverse it. Besides, with or without Bouteiller, the seven Lorraine students would certainly have been tempted by the magic city. Thus the prob-lem is not so much Bouteiller as how to keep them down on the farm once they have heard of Paris.

Barrès and Stendhal

Le Roman de l'énergie nationale has all the makings of a masterpiece but falls short of the mark. We shall understand the reasons for this better by taking Stendhal's political novels as models for comparison. Barrès's trilogy, as we have seen, emphasizes politics to such an extent that it becomes indeed that "pistol shot in a concert" which worried Stendhal so much. Another factor is tone. Barrès has little sense of humor or irony. As he is too close to the events he relates, everything is serious, and his young men are sincere but lack wit. The author's tone is often patronizing, and he never fails to inform the reader of his opinion of a character or an event. And his characters, being disciples and not self-made men (like Julien Sorel), are in no way superior persons (except in their own judgment). This is one reason they accomplish little, if

anything. The most fundamental difference between Stendhal and
Barrès concerns their choice of historical periods. The July 1830 Revolution, which pervades *Le Rouge et le noir,* was an important turning point
in French history, since it marked the end of Bourbon rule and came
close to ending royal government altogether. By contrast, the Boulangist movement was but a moment of excitement.[17]

Barrès, however, had one notable advantage over Stendhal. He not
only held political office, but in his time he exerted an enormous
influence both as a politician and as a thinker. Idealistic young men
flocked to him, and even as intelligent a man as Léon Blum (who,
being Jewish, should have known better) looked to Barrès for guidance
and went so far as to appeal to him to intercede in favor of Dreyfus!

Boulanger as a Stendhalian Character

Most of our attention has been devoted to Sturel, who increasingly
occupies the center of the stage, but we should not forget the personage
who is ever present in Barrès's trilogy and who is the soldier to whom
l'appel au soldat is made.

Historians have not been kind to Georges Boulanger. They cannot
forgive him for failing to seize power when it was his for the marching,
and for giving priority to private over public life. He stands condemned
in their eyes not only as an unsuccessful statesman but as a human
being as well. "Boulanger was to become known to those who met him
personally as a man of few principles but of considerable ambition. His
overriding aim was less to lead men than to win their sympathy."[18]

He does not even receive credit for his insistence on taking power
only by legitimate means and for his respect of the Republic, a most
unusual attitude for a general in 1889.[19] Historians are like movie fans:
they insist on a script that satisfies their expectations.

Under the harsh searchlight of history, these judgments may have a
certain validity, but literature has opened our eyes to the human side of
history. If proof is needed that literature influences history, no better
example can be cited than one of the reasons for Boulanger's refusal to
seize power through a coup d'état: his father had read him Victor
Hugo's invectives against the coup by Napoleon III.[20]

As a human being, Boulanger comes out far better than many statesmen who are admired by historians. A popular hero, his choice of
mistress over might illustrates the popular ditty recited by Molière's

Alceste, where the love of a woman is preferred to the possession of Paris.[21]

Still more interesting are the resemblances between the historical personage and Stendhal's Julien Sorel. Although different both in character and political views, Boulanger illustrated in life Julien's fictional evolution. He was a general (Julien's dream), rose from modest origins to war minister and to candidate for the highest office in France. But in the course of his experiences he realized that for him at least, personal, intimate happiness was more important than public success. He therefore abdicated and chose suicide when he could no longer hope for happiness with the woman he loved.

Who would ever have thought that fiction and history would have this rendezvous, and that General Boulanger would live out what Stendhal's pen had merely imagined?

Chapter Two
And Justice for All

The Third Republic: The Dreyfus Affair,
1894–99 to 1906

The Dreyfus affair is the biggest governmental cover-up in modern history. It makes the Ben Barka case in France (1965) or the Watergate scandal in the United States look like minor events, even though it shares many aspects with them.

As a dramatic event it was written with the worst scenario imaginable for a morality play: the hero has been badly cast and seems to have misread his script; most of the rest of the cast act out of character, doing things contrary to their convictions or interests;[1] and the moral of the story gives rise only to confusion and arguments.

It all started with Mme Bastian, a cleaning woman at the German embassy in Paris. She earned some extra money by delivering what she found in the German wastepaper baskets to the Statistical Section of the French Army. Apparently the only statistics kept by that section were the number of crumpled or torn-up papers Mme Bastian turned over to this counterintelligence agency directed by Commandant Sandherr.

After several years of poring over copies of laundry lists and documents of similar importance, the Statistical Section was shocked out of its half-sleep by a paper Mme Bastian delivered in September 1894. It was an invoice (*bordereau*) which indicated that a spy, obviously a French officer, had supplied the German military attaché, Von Schwarzkoppen, with information about:

1. The hydraulic brake of the 120-gauge canon;
2. the disposition of border troops during mobilization;
3. the fortifications at Madagascar.

The resulting inquiry led eventually to the suspicion that Alfred Dreyfus, a Jewish officer from Alsace, was the author of the invoice. Several handwriting experts were called in, and all but one affirmed that the writing was that of Dreyfus.

One of the "experts," an amateur graphologist, was Marquis du Paty de Clam, the kind of extravagant person who always seems to turn up on the scene in this sort of affair. He conceived the idea of calling in Dreyfus and dictating to him the text of the invoice. "You tremble," Du Paty exclaimed. "My fingers are cold," Dreyfus replied. At the end of the dictation, Du Paty arrested Dreyfus, who proclaimed his innocence.

Dreyfus would probably have been released because of insufficient evidence if the information had not been leaked to the press. Two anti-Semitic papers pounced on it, and henceforth the prestige of the General Staff and the minister of war was tied to the conviction of Dreyfus.

On 19 December 1894, Dreyfus was tried by a court-martial composed of seven officers. The evidence against him amounted to the similarity of handwriting, the assertion that he had trembled when writing the dictated text, and the existence of another note from the German wastepaper basket in which reference was made to a supposed informer identified by the initial "D." Commandant Henry, another bizarre member of the Statistical Section, melodramatically pointed to Dreyfus, shouting, "The traitor is this man." And he added solemnly, "I swear it." Throughout the trial the prosecution maintained that it possessed secret evidence that could not be presented for reasons of national security. While the judges were deliberating, however, an envelope of documents was shown to them. Dreyfus was found guilty and given the maximum sentence: he would be broken in rank and imprisoned for life in a fortress.

On 5 January 1895 Dreyfus went through the ordeal of being broken in rank before four thousand soldiers while the crowd outside demanded his death. It was then that he shouted the words that created a great moment for actors to portray: "Soldiers, an innocent man is being dishonored. Vive la France! Vive l'Armée!"

Actors may find the role of Dreyfus attractive and make the most of it, but this dramatic scene also provides insight into the man. Alfred Dreyfus was a military man through and through; in fact, he sometimes strikes us as the caricature of a French officer. France and the army had unjustly condemned him and yet he shouted, "Vive la France! Vive l'Armée!" He marched to his martydom like a military marionette, and not at all like someone who would revolt against those who made him suffer unjustly; he acted, on the contrary, like an ardent admirer. Until the last possible moment he remained firmly convinced that General Boisdeffre, the chief of staff, was defending his cause, and he was deeply shaken when he realized that his idols were conspiring against him, lying and perjuring themselves to have him condemned.

He had few friends. Distant, cold, often cutting in his remarks, he was unable to strike in people the natural sympathy reserved for the underdog. Yet those closest to him displayed a loyalty such as is rarely met in history. Both his wife and his brother Mathieu, who gave up his business and hurried to Paris, unswervingly believed in his innocence and steadfastly defended him. But the majority of those who would fight for a revision of the court-martial's judgment rallied to his cause rather than to the man.

On 5 April 1895 Dreyfus arrived on Devil's Island to serve a life term. So ended the first phase of the affair. No doubt the fact that Dreyfus was Jewish contributed to the suspicions and the subsequent belief in his guilt, but this phase was primarily concerned with a spy case and punishment of the person generally believed to have been the traitor.

Aware that Mathieu Dreyfus was determined to prove his brother's innocence and was enlisting the help of influential persons, the General Staff charged Commandant Georges Picquart, who had replaced the ailing Sandherr, with the task of gathering all information and documents relative to the case. Picquart had witnessed Dreyfus's degrading ceremony unmoved because of his dislike for Jews. And so he eagerly set out to prove the traitor's guilt beyond any doubt.

But lo and behold! In March 1896 faithful Mme Bastian turned over her usual loot with one interesting item: a *petit bleu,* an express pneumatic message, with a clearly marked address:

> Monsieur le Commandant Esterhazy
> 27, rue de la Bienfaisance—Paris.

Now, without informing his superiors, Picquart began his own investigation about Esterhazy and Dreyfus. He discovered that the latter was well-to-do, had a clean record, with no logical motivation to sell military secrets to the Germans, whereas Esterhazy lived with his mistress, gambled, and was constantly in need of money. Picquart managed to get hold of a sample of Esterhazy's handwriting and was struck by the similarity it bore to that of Dreyfus. Thereupon he informed his superiors of his discoveries, but they showed little interest in them; in fact, after a while Picquart was sent off on inspection trips. He was eventually even jailed for failure to inform his superiors immediately of his findings.

After a long silence, the press finally mentioned Dreyfus again with the false news of his escape from Devil's Island, a report that led to his being tied up in chains every night. Another article revealed the secret document with the reference to a spy with the initial "D." On 16 November 1896 the Dreyfus case was brought up in the Chamber of Deputies. A new phase was about to begin, in which the question would no longer be the innocence or guilt of an individual but rather anti-Semitism.

A formidable array of groups and individuals was lined up against Dreyfus: the successive ministers of war (Mercier, Zurlinden, Cavaignac, Billot, Chanoine); the General Staff, headed by Boisdeffre and Gonse; the Statistical Section, with Sandherr, Henry, and Du Paty de Clam; equally important, most officials of the Catholic Church, and the most vociferous anti-Semitic propagandists of the time, Drumont and Rochefort; finally, a number of writers, the most fanatic of whom was none other than Maurice Barrès, who never gave up his conviction that Dreyfus was guilty.

Compared to this steamroller, the Dreyfus side seemed very weak indeed: his wife, Lucie, and brother Mathieu; his lawyer, Demange; Scheurer-Kestner, an Alsatian and vice-president of the Senate; later, Picquart, Clemenceau, Jean Jaurès, and a number of intellectuals, including Charles Péguy, Anatole France, Léon Blum, and Émile Zola. But the *dreyfusards* were inspired by their faith and conviction that an innocent man was being sacrificed on the altar of national security for individual interests.

Meanwhile Mathieu Dreyfus had learned of the suspicions about Esterhazy and had brought a lawsuit against him. A new and vicious press campaign pro and con broke out. The General Staff stood firmly behind Esterhazy, advising him in melodramatic fashion, with Henry and Du Paty wearing false beards and dark glasses in secret meetings with him.

In January 1898 Esterhazy was brought before a court-martial, and letters were exhibited that shed doubt on his patriotism. But Esterhazy was acquitted, while Picquart was placed under arrest. And during all this time Premier Méline staunchly maintained, "There is no Dreyfus affair."

All hope for Dreyfus seemed to be lost, when Zola entered the fray with his famous article "J'accuse," published in the newspaper *L'Aurore* on 13 January 1898. Zola's enormous contribution lay in his realization that it was of no use to find judicial or technical errors here and there or to file individual lawsuits, but that the entire arsenal at the disposal of the *dreyfusards* had to be combined, not only in Dreyfus's defense, but even more in a frontal attack on those who were responsible for the monstrous cover-up of the truth.

In his article, Zola accused Du Paty of having masterminded the conspiracy against Dreyfus, General Mercier of being Du Paty's accomplice, General Billot of having hushed up proof he had of Dreyfus's innocence, and the court-martial of having received secret material during its deliberations.

Now the government had no choice but to sue Zola for libel, but precautions were taken during his trial to limit debate to only three of Zola's accusations, and every time his lawyer Labori attempted to widen the discussion, the presiding judge cut him off with the phrase that was to be heard again sixty-seven years later in the Ben Barka case: "The question will not be asked." [La question ne sera pas posée.] The officers refused to answer questions on grounds of national security, but Zola's lawyer managed to damage the case of the General Staff by getting Henry to divulge what was in the secret file.

Throughout the trial there were violent demonstrations against Zola, and there is no telling what would have happened if he had been acquitted. As it turned out, he was found guilty of libel and condemned to one year in prison and a three thousand franc fine. On the advice of his lawyer, Zola fled to England.

Zola's intervention constituted the third phase of the Dreyfus affair, because it went beyond the issues of anti-Semitism and the guilt or innocence of an individual, and addressed the moral choice between national security and justice.

Governments succeeded each other, and Cavaignac was appointed war minister. A strong opponent of the revision of sentences, he ordered still another examination of the Dreyfus file. Alerted by a letter from Picquart to the premier stating that he could prove the existence of forged letters, Captain Louis Cuignet, a friend of Henry's who remained an ardent anti-*dreyfusard,* discovered that one of the incriminating letters in the secret file had apparently been forged: the top and bottom were not of the same paper as the portion on which the text was written. It is much to their credit that the officers Buignet consulted, as well as Cavaignac, never hesitated to pass their findings on to their superiors. The effect was dramatic. General Boisdeffre resigned; Henry was arrested and shortly after was found dead in his prison cell—he had cut his throat with a razor.

Far from giving up after these setbacks, the anti-Dreyfus movement turned Henry into a hero, a patriotic martyr who had fabricated false evidence because there were real documents that could not be published for reasons of national security. Still, the Chamber of Deputies decided to have the case reviewed by a Court of Appeals. After much emotional debate and a heated newspaper campaign, it was finally decided to have Dreyfus retried by another court-martial, this time in Rennes to avoid the feverish atmosphere prevailing in Paris.

The trial began on 7 August 1899. Dreyfus, looking like the ghost of his former self but still as military as ever, had been brought back from Devil's Island. The secret file was examined in closed session. Of the witnesses called, Du Paty and Esterhazy did not appear, while the war minister, General Mercier, maintained that Dreyfus was guilty as charged. On 9 September 1899 the accused was found guilty by a five to two vote; the judges, however, unanimously recognized attenuating circumstances and recommended ten years of imprisonment instead of a life sentence.

Dreyfus received a governmental offer of pardon, which his brother and his wife urged him to accept, in view of his failing health. A split now took place in the Dreyfus camp between those who cared primarily for the man and those who cared only for what he represented. Clemenceau, Labori, Picquart, Jaurès, Péguy, and Zola wanted him to refuse the proffered pardon and continue efforts to win his case in the courts. But Dreyfus accepted the offer and was pardoned on 19 September 1899. By the end of the year an amnesty was declared, annulling all previous trials. In 1903 Dreyfus asked for an official revision of sentence in his case; it was granted in 1904, and Dreyfus was reinstated in the army with the rank of commandant. In 1906 he was exonerated by the Court of Appeals. Picquart was promoted to general and later on was appointed war minister.

The Dreyfus affair resulted in political and other changes. As the French people realized that they had been duped by those in power, they voted in favor of a more liberal government headed by Waldeck-Rousseau. And the Catholic Church paid for its blatant interference in the affairs of the state through increased anticlericalism and a law of separation of church and state passed in 1905.

The lessons of the bull *Unigenitus* and of the Dreyfus affair may be of some interest to the United States in the last decades of the twentieth century. They clearly demonstrate that in a republic it is very dangerous for religious groups, even in a country where one religion distinctly dominates, to engage in political infighting, as only professionals stand a chance of leaving the combat unscathed.

The real heroes in the Dreyfus affair were not those who talked the loudest or who occupied center stage, even though they too deserve our admiration. The real heroes were those who pronounced the truth derived from proof, regardless of their political, personal, or racial preferences.

For the French Army the proof that Dreyfus was innocent constituted anything but the defeat seen by the extreme nationalists. To be sure, some of its highest officers turned out to be dupes, liars, or perjurers, but an army that had formed men with the disinterested integrity of Picquart; of Forzinetti (the officer who first jailed Dreyfus); of the two officers who voted in favor of revision at Rennes (Commandant de Bréon and Colonel Jouaust); and of the three officers who discovered the letter forged by Henry and revealed it, even though they still remained convinced of Dreyfus's guilt (Cuignet, General Roget, and War Minister Cavaignac); and most certainly, an army that had formed a man of caliber such as Dreyfus himself, who, like the other officers who were imprisoned or punished, continued to remain a loyal soldier—such an army had every reason to be proud.

The legal profession had its heroes, too: Dreyfus's and Zola's lawyers (Demange, Labori, Hild); Picquart's friend Leblois; and perhaps even more so the judges and legal officials who exposed their findings despite enormous pressures and insults (Ludovic Trarieux, Loew, Mornard, Chambereaud). There was even an unselfish politician, Scheurer-Kestner, the Alsatian who was vice-president of the Senate. Clemenceau, Blum, Jaurès, Millerand, and others rallied to Dreyfus's cause, but often late and in part for reasons of their own. Most of the latter, like Jean Jaurès, wanted Dreyfus to be a means, a symbol of justice and truth, or an arm to attack the institutions of traditional France, the army and the Church, and the nationalists.

Even though he failed to play his role the way it was expected of him, Alfred Dreyfus remains, strangely enough, the greatest hero of his own story, and a far greater hero than historians tend to give him credit for.

He was grateful to all those who had fought to prove his innocence, but he refused to be stamped into a symbol, not even by his most fervent supporters. He steadfastly insisted that he was fighting for his honor and his rehabilitation. Not for the transformation of society, not for the Jews, not against the army or the Church. He had been wronged and he wanted justice—for himself. He told one of his supporters, "I am not a symbol of justice; that Dreyfus is your creation."[2]

He had an equally striking response to those who were distressed by his failure to display strong emotions. Having learned that General Chamoin had written that, at the Rennes court-martial, "Dreyfus was unable to move people, the heart did not speak," he declared at the revision hearings of 22 June 1904: "I am dumbfounded. I believe in reason; I thought that, in matters of this sort, where the meanderings of the heart can contribute no explanation or modification, reason alone ought to guide the judges."[3]

Dreyfus not only reminded the French that their traditional and classical heritage is based on reason; he also expressed the existential attitude that those humanitarians who are willing to sacrifice the individual for the sake of humanity dehumanize all of us, and that justice is not meant to serve abstract purposes but to protect or punish distinct persons in concrete cases.

Chronology

1894:	Dreyfus arrested on spy charges; court-martial of Dreyfus.
1895–1899:	Félix Faure, president.
1896:	Annexation of Madagascar.
1897:	Barrès: *Les Déracinés.*
1898:	Zola's article "J'accuse."
1899:	Court-martial at Rennes; Dreyfus found guilty but pardoned by the government; founding of Action Française; Anatole France: *L'Anneau d'améthyste.*
1899–1902:	Ministry of Waldeck-Rousseau.
1899–1906:	Loubet, president.
1900:	Barrès: *L'Appel au soldat.*
1901:	Anatole France: *Monsieur Bergeret à Paris.*
1902:	Government of Combes; Barrès: *Leurs Figures;* Zola: *Vérité.*

1904: Previous trials of Dreyfus annulled; Entente Cordiale with England.

1905: Law of separation of church and state; resignation of Combes.

1906: Dreyfus exonerated by supreme court of appeals.

Anatole France: The Opinions of Monsieur Bergeret

L'Anneau d'améthyste *and* Monsieur Bergeret à Paris

Although it occupied French attention for more than ten years, the Dreyfus affair did not lead to much important literature during that time. All the works that do in one way or another deal with it appeared after the second court-martial of 1899,[4] but those we shall discuss appeared only shortly afterward, and well in advance of the final judgment by the Court of Appeals in 1906.

Both Anatole France and Émile Zola were deeply involved in the Dreyfus affair, each in his own way: France more intellectually, Zola more emotionally. That does not mean that France felt any less strongly about the injustices committed, only that he expressed his indignation in his particular manner.

The two writers agree that justice should never be sacrificed to anything, not even to national security. To the statement that the reversal of Dreyfus's conviction would lead to war, France's M. Bergeret replies, "The poet Bouchor teaches us that it is better to suffer through a war than to commit an unjust act." [Le poète Bouchor nous enseigne qu'il vaut mieux endurer la guerre que d'accomplir une action injuste (*L'Anneau d'améthyste*, 151).][5] Zola expresses the same view more dramatically: "One single act of injustice may suffice for a whole nation to be stricken with madness and die slowly." [Il suffit d'une seule injustice, pour qu'un peuple en meure lentement, frappé de démence. (*Vérité*, 1143)][6]

Zola and France do not, however, share the same faith in the inevitable triumph of truth over lies, and their differences are expressed by the two principal characters in their respective novels. M. Bergeret, featured in *L'Anneau d'améthyste* (1899) and *Monsieur Bergeret à Paris* (1901),[7] is a university professor of classical literature, while Marc Froment, the hero of Zola's *Vérité*, is an elementary school teacher.

M. Bergeret is urbane, skeptical, and worldly-wise. He rejects the idea that truth contains an invincible force that will bring it to the fore sooner or later. With argumentation worthy of a Jesuit casuist, he supports this point: truth is one and whole, while lies can be multiplied; truth is inert, while lies are flexible; besides, lies appeal to the habits of men, who "have based their ideas of good and evil, and their divine and human laws on the most ancient, the most saintly, the most absurd, the most august, the most barbaric, and the most erroneous interpretations of natural phenomena." [. . . ont fondé leur idée du bien et du mal, leurs lois divines et humaines, sur les interprétations les plus anciennes, les plus saintes, les plus absurdes, les plus augustes, les plus barbares et les plus fausses des phénomènes naturels (*L'Anneau d'améthyste*, 197).]

By contrast, Zola's elementary school teacher is inspired by an unshakable faith in the triumphant march of truth.

Truth, truth! . . . Now, after having seen it so furiously attacked, denied, buried deep under lies, like a corpse that would never revive, he believed in it even more; he felt it was irresistibly possessed of sufficient power to blow up the world, should men again try to bury it underground. It followed its road without ever taking an hour's rest; it was marching on to its shining goal, and nothing could stop it. He shrugged his shoulders in ironic contempt when he beheld guilty men believing that they had destroyed truth, that it lay crushed beneath their feet as if it had ceased to exist. When its time would come, truth would burst forth, quiet and bright, and scatter them like dust. And it was this certainty, to have the truth on his side, ever alive and victorious, even after centuries, that gave him the calm strength to take up his task again and wait cheerfully for its inevitable triumph, even though it might only come after his own lifetime.

[La vérité, la vérité! . . . Maintenant, après l'avoir vue si furieusement combattue, niée, enfouie au plus profond du mensonge, ainsi qu'une morte qui ne se réveillerait pas, il croyait en elle davantage, il la sentait d'une façon irrésistible, capable de faire sauter le monde, le jour où l'on voudrait l'enfermer sous terre. Elle cheminait sans une heure de repos, elle marchait à son but de lumière, et rien ne l'arrêterait. Il haussait les épaules d'ironique dédain quand il voyait des coupables croire qu'ils avaient anéanti la vérité, qu'ils la tenaient sous leurs pieds, comme si elle n'était plus. Le moment venu, la vérité éclaterait, les disperserait en poussière, tranquille et rayonnante. Et c'était cette certitude d'avoir avec lui la vérité toujours vivante et victorieuse, même après des siècles, qui lui donnait cette force tranquille de se remettre à la besogne et d'attendre gaîment, même au delà de son existence, le triomphe certain (*Vérité*, 1377).]

France deals with the Dreyfus affair primarily as a topic of conversation and dispute. The characters do not live it, are not profoundly affected by it. True, M. Bergeret suffers unpopularity and is attacked in a newspaper article for his pro-Dreyfus stand, but his life and his career are never seriously threatened. The tone of *L'Anneau d'améthyste* and *Monsieur Bergeret à Paris* remains always light, almost bantering; in fact, France devotes as much space to the dog Riquet as he does to the Dreyfus affair.

Despite this apparent frivolity there persists a constant undertone. M. Bergeret, and a few artists and intellectuals of the same caliber, make up a tiny island of reason and sanity in a sea of madness that has engulfed the army; the nobility; the Catholic clergy; the nationalists; the monarchists; and even converted Jews such as Mme de Bonmont, whose lover is a violent anti-*dreyfusard,* and her son, whose only concern is to be received in aristocratic circles—in short, all those who are against the Republic—plus the vast majority of the French people.

In these circumstances Anatole France purposely underplays the emotional tragedy of the Dreyfus affair, in order to concentrate his attention on the irrational arguments of those hostile to Dreyfus and the rational examination of these arguments by M. Bergeret. He counters the belief that seven French officers (the military court that condemned Dreyfus) cannot be wrong, by stating that seven or even fourteen officers of any nationality can be wrong.

He deals in the same calm manner with the justification anti-Semites give for their attitude: that they simply don't like Jews and, if they bother to add anything to this irresistible argument, that the Jews remain a foreign element in the nation. He simply replies that he finds it impossible to hate eighty thousand people and that, on the contrary, the facts prove that the Jews assimilate very well.

But M. Bergeret reserves his strongest ammunition for the monstrous cover-up by the army and its protectors. M. de La Barge, a supporter of the three-year compulsory military service for everybody except his own son, claims that the campaign in favor of Dreyfus will weaken the army and its chiefs. M. Bergeret replies:

If the army's prestige suffers by way of some of its leaders, that's not the fault of those who have asked for justice; it's the fault of those who for so long have refused to render it; it's not the fault of those who have insisted that the truth be revealed; it's the fault of those who have obstinately hidden it with an inordinately stupid and atrocious wickedness. And finally, since there have been crimes, the bad thing is not that they should be known but that they have been committed.

[Si l'armée est atteinte dans la personne de quelques-uns de ses chefs, ce n'est point la faute de ceux qui ont demandé la justice; c'est la faute de ceux qui l'ont si longtemps refusée; ce n'est pas la faute de ceux qui ont exigé la lumière, c'est la faute de ceux qui l'ont dérobée obstinément avec une imbécilité démesurée et une scélératesse atroce. Et enfin, puisqu'il y a eu des crimes, le mal n'est point qu'ils soient connus, le mal est qu'ils aient été commis (*Monsieur Bergeret à Paris*, 70–71).][8]

France combines M. Bergeret's linguistic knowledge with current events by having the professor read to his favorite student old texts that are relevant to the Dreyfus affair. One is a Greek text from the Alexandrian period about Hercules Atimos, not the great one but his twin brother, less worthy of praise. He receives from his father, Amphitryon, a bow and arrows that will never fail to kill men or animals. Having promised a cattleman that he will kill a cattle thief, he sees a man who looks to him like the thief, and strikes him with one of his arrows. Pallas Athena, disguised as a servant, informs him that he has been mistaken and that he has killed an innocent man, but Atimos persists in claiming he has killed the thief. Soon thereafter he comes upon the real thief and decides he has to prove that man to be innocent, so as not to hurt his own reputation. So he gives him one of his deadly arrows and promises the thief that he will be honored by all men. Again Pallas Athena, this time disguised as a shepherd, warns Atimos that by absolving the guilty man he has killed the innocent a second time and that he will not enjoy glory among men, but again Atimos curses her and threatens her.[9]

The story breaks off at this point, but the parallel is too clear to need much amplification: those who, by error and for reasons of personal pride, have punished the innocent Dreyfus and are now compounding their error by aiding and shielding those they know to be guilty, will not be honored.

Another old text, this one in French, that M. Bergeret reads to his favorite student dates from 1538 and tells about the Trublions (implied Troublemakers), who, "emitting furious shouts and very insane speeches," were made up of hypocrites, bigots, and impostors, "and had an aversion for, and disgust of, meditation, philosophy, and any argument deduced by good sense and proper reasoning, and any sub-

tle thought, and knew only force, and that only if it was brute."
[. . . faut jeter cris furieux et discours très insanes, . . . avoient pris
en aversion et desgoust la méditation, la philosophie, et tout argument déduict par droit sens et fine raison, et toute pensée soubtile, et
ne cognoissoient que la force, encore ne la prisoient-ils que si elle
estoit toute brute (*Monsieur Bergeret à Paris,* 103, 106).] These misogy-
nist demagogues and xenophobes, believing themselves more patriotic
and useful than productive citizens, burst one day, because they were
full of wind.

The reference to the anti-*dreyfusards* is again obvious, but M.
Bergeret (and Anatole France, as well) did not believe that ignorance
and prejudice would simply disappear like a burst bubble. It would
take a long, long time before a just society would be created. As for the
means of achieving such a society, France believed, like Hugo, in the
power of the word.

"And how can you put an end to iniquity, father? How can you change the
world?"
"By the word, my child. Nothing is more powerful than the word. A solid
chain of reasoning made up of elevated thoughts is a bond that cannot be
broken. The word, like David's slingshot, knocks down the violent and brings
the strong to their knees. It is the invincible arm. Without it the world would
belong to armed brutes. Who keeps them in respect? Only ideas, unarmed and
naked."

[— Et comment la [l'iniquité] faire cesser, mon père? Comment changer le
monde?
—Par la parole, mon enfant. Rien n'est plus puissant que la parole.
L'enchaînement des fortes raisons et des hautes pensées est un lien qu'on ne
peut rompre. La parole, comme la fronde de David, abat les violents et fait
tomber les forts. C'est l'arme invincible. Sans cela le monde appartiendrait aux
brutes armées. Qui donc les tient en respect? Seule, sans armes et nue, la
pensée. (*Monsieur Bergeret à Paris,* 257–58)]

Émile Zola

And Justice for All: Vérité

Émile Zola also believed in the power of the word and of ideas, but
he realized that it would take more than that to bring about the
triumph of truth and social change. It would require action, and he had

proven what courageous commitment could accomplish by his personal intervention in the Dreyfus affair. He also knew that the struggle would be long and that the battle would be not a scrimmage with intellectual arguments but a struggle for the minds of the young for generations to come.

That is why Zola transposed the Dreyfus affair, a temporary scandal with ephemeral players, to the permanent field of education. Just as he had raised the Dreyfus conflict to the moral level, so he moved the arena of his novel from the courtroom to the classroom.[10] His hero, likewise, is not an army officer or a lawyer but an elementary school teacher. And finally, Zola felt that the real threat to the Republic and to justice came not so much from the army as from those who were responsible for the state of mind of the majority, who believed Dreyfus guilty without proof; from those who had formed these minds by their teaching—the Catholic Church.

Doesn't the Catholic Church itself, though based on absurd dogmas, claim to be the only truth? . . . If you tell the son of a peasant or a worker that the earth is round and revolves in space, he will accept that unquestioningly, the way he accepts the fairy tales of the catechism, the Trinity, the Incarnation, and the Resurrection. Experiments have to demonstrate scientific certainty, so that he will be able to tell the difference. All revealed truth is a falsehood, only experimental truth is true, one and whole, eternal. And therefrom stemmed the basic necessity to oppose the Catholic catechism with the scientific catechism, to explain man and the world by science, to restore them in their living reality, their march toward a continuous and ever more perfect future.

[L'Eglise catholique elle-même, basée sur des dogmes absurdes, n'a-t-elle pas la prétention d'être la vérité unique? . . . Un fils de paysan ou d'ouvrier, auquel on dit que la terre est ronde et tourne dans l'espace, accepte cela de confiance, comme il accepte les contes du catéchisme, les trois personnes de Dieu, l'incarnation et la résurrection. Il faut que l'expérience lui en démontre la certitude scientifique, pour qu'il puisse faire la différence. Toute vérité révélée est un mensonge, la vérité expérimentale est seule vraie, une et entière, éternelle. Et de là venait la nécessité première d'opposer au catéchisme catholique le catéchisme scientifique, le monde et l'homme expliqués par la science, rétablis en leur réalité vivante, en leur marche vers un continuel avenir, de plus en plus parfait. (*Vérité*, 1146–47)]

Zola's hero is Marc Froment, an elementary school teacher, trained at the Ecole normale by Salvan, who has undertaken the long and arduous

task of fulfilling one of the goals of the Revolution by making secular
education win out over the still traditional religious schools. One of
Marc's colleagues, a Jewish teacher by the name of Simon, is in charge
of the boys' school in the small town of Maillebois. Happily married
and the father of two beautiful children, Simon has taken charge of his
nephew Zéphirin, a handsome but invalid child, who has converted to
catholicism. One day Zéphirin is found strangled after having been
sexually abused in his room on the ground floor. Marc, who happens to
be in Maillebois, where he is spending his vacation at the home of his
wife's mother and grandmother, rushes to the scene, finding there the
teaching assistant Mignot, Mlle Rouzaire (a religious bigot who is in
charge of the girls' school), and two priests, Father Philibin and Father
Fulgence. The assailant had stuck a newspaper into the victim's mouth
to stifle his cries, and wrapped up in that paper was a sheet of handwriting copy bearing the inscription, "Love each other." [Aimez-vous les
uns les autres.] The upper right corner of the handwriting copy is
missing, but below the text one can detect initials difficult to identify,
because of the victim's saliva and teeth marks.

Simon had returned late that night from a banquet in a neighboring
town and has to be awakened. He testifies that he missed the train and
walked home, a distance of about four miles. Further testimony reveals
that Zéphirin had been at a religious ceremony and that a certain
Brother Gorgias had accompanied some children home while Mlle
Rouzaire led Zéphirin back to his room on the ground floor.

Little by little, the investigation leads to a suspicion that Simon is
the guilty one. He has thrown away his railroad ticket, and nobody in
the small town saw him returning home. Since the kind of handwriting
copy found at the site of the crime is not used in secular schools, the
more liberal people suspect Brother Gorgias of the crime, but the
majority of the population, educated in the religious schools, are convinced that Simon killed his own nephew.

Disturbed by these rumors, Marc Froment sets out to try to find
another copy of the handwriting copy, but runs into the mistrust of the
provincial parents. One boy, the son of a co-owner of a stationery store,
blurts out that his cousin, who attends a religious school, has such a
copy, but his aunt, a religious woman, silences him.

Meanwhile the latent anti-Semitism, kindled by the local paper *Le
Petit Beaumontais,* leads to violent accusations against Simon, claiming he
disliked his nephew because of the child's conversion to catholicism. Simon is arrested and found guilty after a farcical trial, despite the ener-

getic defense of his lawyer, Delbos, who maintains that only a teaching priest could have committed the crime. The jury asks M. Gragnon, the president of the court, to give them information, or perhaps he insists on speaking to them. At any rate, he stays with the jury for an unusually long time, and rumors circulate that some new last-minute evidence has been presented to the jury. Simon is sentenced to life imprisonment and led away shouting: "I am innocent! I am innocent!"

Marc Froment returns to his teaching job, but his former teacher Salvan asks him to take over the position in Maillebois left vacant by the arrest of his friend Simon. He would like to stay where he is, but decides to accept the challenge after witnessing a procession in honor of a religious relic containing a fragment of the skull of Saint Anthony of Padua, claimed to accomplish all sorts of miracles, for which the faithful contribute large sums of money. Marc now realizes that the Church, through its power over the minds of people, has been engaged in destroying the work of the Revolution and turning the France of Voltaire and Diderot into a reactionary nation.

The Jews, as in the Middle Ages, served as a pretext to instill fresh warmth into cooling beliefs, to exploit an ancestral hatred and sow the horrid seeds of civil war. And beneath this vast movement of reaction there was the stealthy labor of the Church, taking advantage of the historical moment in order to try to regain the ground it had lost when the old world broke up, toppled by the liberating breath of the French Revolution. It was the spirit of the Revolution the Church strove to kill by regaining control over the bourgeoisie, which had been brought to power by the Revolution and had now decided to betray it in order to retain this illegitimate power, for which it had to render account to the people.

[Les juifs, comme au moyen âge, servaient de prétexte à rechauffer les croyances tièdes, monstrueuse exploitation d'une haine ancestrale, semence atroce de guerre civile. Et il n'y avait, au fond de ce vaste mouvement de réaction, que le sourd travail de l'Eglise, profitant de l'heure historique pour tâcher de regagner le terrain perdu par elle jadis, dans la débâcle du vieux monde sous le souffle libérateur de la Révolution. C'était l'esprit de la Révolution qu'il fallait tuer, en reconquérant la bourgeoisie portée par elle au pouvoir, résolue maintenant à la trahir, afin de conserver ce pouvoir illégitime, dont elle avait à rendre compte au peuple. (*Vérité,* 1170)]

Marc's first act in his new post is to do away with the religious prayer that has been practiced in secular schools. "Sit down, children," he

says. "You are not here to say prayers. You can say them at home if your
fathers and mothers so desire." [Asseyez-vous, mes enfants. Vous n'êtes
pas ici pour dire des prières. Vous les direz chez vous, si vos papas et vos
mamans le désirent (*Vérité,* 1141).] Through his patient and dedicated
work he gains the confidence and affection of his students, and after
two years he dares to take down the cross hanging on the classroom
wall. But the reaction from the clergy and the population is terrible.
Worst of all, Marc loses his beloved wife, Geneviève, who has never
shaken off her religious education and who leaves him to live with her
mother and her bigoted grandmother because of his refusal to have their
daughter receive her First Communion.

A long and bitter period begins now for Marc, who lives alone with
his daughter, Louise, who eventually leaves him and joins her mother.
But Marc shares the faith of Simon's wife and brother, David, and is
sustained by the certainty that his struggle is just and necessary, all the
more so since France is no longer the generous and just country he had
always believed it to be.

So his France had been changed? Was it no longer the liberator? Since the
country knew the truth at present, why did not the people rise as one, instead
of continuing to be an obstacle, a blind and deaf multitude barring the road?
And he always returned to the point he had started out from, when the
necessity of his task as a humble schoolmaster had dawned on him. If France
was still sleeping in its profound sleep of unawareness, it was only because it
did not know enough yet. A shudder ran through him: how many generations,
how many centuries would it take for a people, nourished with truth, to
become capable of justice?

[On lui avait donc changé sa France? elle n'était donc plus la libératrice?
Puisqu'elle savait à cette heure, pourquoi donc ne se levait-elle pas en masse,
au lieu de continuer à être l'obstacle, la foule aveugle et sourde barrant la
route?
Et il retournait toujours au point d'où il était parti, lorsque la nécessité de
sa besogne d'humble instituteur lui était apparue. Si la France dormait
toujours son lourd somme d'inconscience, cela venait simplement de ce que la
France ne savait pas encore assez. Un frisson le prenait: combien de généra-
tions, combien de siècles fallait-il pour qu'un peuple, nourri de vérité, devînt
capable de justice? (*Vérité,* 1284)]

A sign of the success of his teaching appears when the stationery
store owner's son, now his pupil, spontaneously confesses that he had

been forced to retract his statement about his cousin having a handwriting copy in his possession. Marc gets hold of this precious piece of evidence when the mother, feeling that she is being punished by her son's serious illness, hands it over to him. It does, indeed, contain the stamp of the religious school. Simon's lawyer, Delbos, now influential in French politics, has an unexpected search made at the religious school, which turns up the missing corner of the copy found in the victim's room: Father Philibin had torn it off and kept it in his files. Armed with this new evidence and the disclosure of what had taken place in the jury room when M. Gragnon talked to the jurors, Delbos manages to get the case reopened by the Court of Appeals in Beaumont. After nine years in prison, Simon is brought back for the new trial.

It seems to be an open-and-shut case, because the president of the first trial had presented a clearly forged letter to the jury and all evidence points to Brother Gorgias as the guilty person, but the new court, although more correct in procedure than its predecessor, makes no more of an effort to get at the truth. The jurors, influenced by the religious pressure groups, return a majority verdict of guilty with attenuating circumstances. To the consternation of his friends and supporters, Simon is sentenced to ten years in prison. Marc's only consolation is a letter from his now-estranged wife, who tells him that she has followed the trial, that she knows now Simon is innocent, and that a monstrous crime has been committed by the court. Bothered by their consciences, the jurors unanimously sign a petition that Simon be pardoned, and the petition is granted. Since he cannot very well live in Maillebois, Simon joins his brother in a deserted valley of the Pyrenees, where they take over a marble quarry.

The religious party has triumphed, and Father Cabot, the brains behind all its machinations, has the priests who were involved disappear in foreign monasteries. But time is on Marc's side in the terrible war "between two camps forever enemies: authoritarian men, defending a rotten edifice of the past, and the men of freedom of thought, on the move toward the future." [. . .entre les deux camps éternellement ennemies, les hommes autoritaires, défendant l'édifice pourri du passé, et les hommes de pensée libre, en marche vers l'avenir (*Vérité*, 1329).] This war the latter are bound to win. Geneviève and Louise return to live with Marc and bring with them his young son, Clément. Marc is transferred back to his original post, an apparent demotion, but one he accepts as a fortunate challenge, since, working behind the scene, the school supervisor places trustworthy teachers in the schools. Joseph,

Simon's son, marries Louise; and his sister Sarah marries Sébastien, the son of the stationery store owner. As succeeding generations are educated, the power of the Church diminishes. One day Brother Gorgias reappears. Angry at his superiors, who are tied to him by a shady deal that led to a will in favor of the religious establishment, but who refuse to supply him with any more money, he practically confesses his crime. Delbos, now a powerful politician, submits a new file on Simon's case and the Court of Appeals reverses the original decision in a brief statement declaring Simon to be innocent.

Back in Maillebois, the new generation, mostly Marc's students, have decided to build a house for Simon and to have him come back to live among them. During the moving ceremony celebrating Simon's return, Brother Gorgias appears and, in a scene similar to the confession in *The Scarlet Letter,* admits his guilt in a rambling speech. Marc and a few others barely save him from being lynched by the furious crowd. Marc, blessed with longevity, sees the generations succeed each other and experiences the happiness of seeing his dream fulfilled: one France, one education, separation of church and state, and the triumph of reason, truth, and justice.

Zola's Novel and the Dreyfus Affair

Zola's *Vérité* is obviously a general adaptation of the Dreyfus affair and, although the roles do not always neatly correspond, one can readily recognize the parallel characters. Naturally, Simon represents Alfred Dreyfus; David, his brother, Mathieu. Brother Gorgias corresponds to Esterhazy, while Brothers Fulgence and Philibin represent Du Paty de Clam and Colonel Henry, respectively. The lawyer, Delbos, takes the place of Fernand Labori, and Marc Froment is a kind of Zola turned into a teacher. The circumstances, although changed in kind, are the same in nature as in the Dreyfus affair. The invoice (*bordereau*) has been replaced by the handwriting copy, the military court by a provincial one. There are also forgeries, cover-ups, anti-Semitism, and a bizarre criminal, as in the Dreyfus case.

We have already seen that Zola's transposition of the affair is not gratuitous. He attempts to come to grips with the most profound issues raised by the affair. Why are the French people incapable of reacting when an obvious miscarriage of justice has taken place? Why have the French such deep-seated prejudices? Why have some of the essential goals of the French Revolution not been realized after more than one hundred years?

All the answers point to two principal factors: the education the French have received in Catholic schools, and the betrayal by the bourgeoisie of the Revolution that brought them to power. The success of secular schools, thanks to the efforts of dedicated teachers, such as Marc Froment, and of the succeeding generations of students instructed by them, will accomplish Zola's dream of a just society. Marc uses a teaching method which he sees as leading to that goal. First, he removes all religious emblems and all pictures and books that deal with miracles, war, or brutality. Next, he replaces these harmful influences by positive teaching.

> He emphasized especially lessons of civic morality, striving to make of each child a citizen who would be very much informed about his country, able to serve it and to love it enough so as not to separate it from humanity. France should no longer dream of conquering the world by arms, but by the irresistible force of ideas, by so much liberty, truth, and fairness that she would liberate all nations and enjoy the supreme glory of founding with them the great confederation of free and fraternal peoples.

> [Il donna surtout de l'importance aux leçons de morale civique, s'efforçant de faire de chaque enfant un citoyen très renseigné sur son pays, capable de le servir, de l'aimer assez pour ne pas le mettre à part de l'humanité. Ce n'était plus par les armes que la France devait rêver de conquérir le monde, mais par l'irrésistible puissance de l'idée, par tant de liberté, de vérité et d'équité, qu'elle délivrerait toutes les nations et qu'elle aurait la suprême gloire de fonder avec elles la grande confédération des peuples libres et fraternels. (*Vérité*, 1387)][11]

Émile Zola's *Vérité* has not been applauded by the critics, and for good reasons. The novel suffers from a number of shortcomings. Marc Froment is too perfect. He is a perfect husband, a perfect father, a perfect friend, and a perfect teacher. He lives for years separated from his wife, who has left him, without ever abandoning the hope of an eventual reunion of his family, and without taking a mistress. Readers of Zola had been accustomed by the author to less perfect heroes: drunkards, violent people, prostitutes, and crooks, subject to the irresistible forces of heredity. They were certainly not prepared to accept Marc Froment any more than the idyllic ending.

At the same time, Zola remains true to his manner of portraying real people in their environment. The narrow-minded and prudent spirit of the provinces that cuts across social classes, the realistic dialogues, and the great scenes (Marc's first day in class at Maillebois, the procession of the saintly relic, the confrontation of Marc's wife with her mother and grandmother, Brother Gorgias's public confession) are typical of the great naturalistic author. And the four generations that pass by represent not only the effects of Marc's teaching but also the changes that gradually took place in French society.

The Dreyfus affair presented "committed" writers with a difficult challenge because of the emotionally charged atmosphere it had created in France. That is probably the reason so few works about it were produced during that period. One can write about religious quarrels, governmental mismanagement, bad diplomacy, or corruption with a certain detachment and irony. But during the affair nobody could forget that there was an innocent human being rotting away in a prison on a far-off island.

It is remarkable that Anatole France was able to detach himself sufficiently, at least as an author, to write two lighthearted novels with thin plots in which the affair occupies an important place. But he very likely had an effect only on intellectuals, most of whom needed no further convincing.

Zola, by making his readers sense all the suffering caused by a deliberate miscarriage of justice, and by raising the issues to the highest level, no doubt exerted a far greater influence on the French people.

Both authors thus played their part in helping to bring about a radical change in French attitudes toward the affair. It seemed as if the clean air of idealism was sweeping over France, idealism that would prevail and inspire its youth to face the trials and sufferings of the First World War.

Chapter Three

How to Become a Communist

The Third Republic: The Dawning of War, 1906–14

Once the Dreyfus affair was resolved, French attention was mainly occupied by foreign affairs, and particularly the expansion of its colonial possessions. To Algeria and Tunisia had been added Madagascar, Guinea, the Ivory Coast, Dahomey, and Senegal, but French intervention in Morocco had produced an international crisis. Foreign Minister Delcassé wound his way through this labyrinth by a Franco-Russian defensive alliance (1894), a secret understanding about African possessions with Italy (1900), and an Entente Cordiale with England (1904).

Relations remained strained, however, with Germany, which insisted on maintaining its interests in Morocco. Delcassé's insistence on a rejection of German claims was not supported by the Chamber of Deputies and he resigned. But an international conference in 1906 recognized the primary role of France in Morocco. Between 1905 and 1911, several crises threatened war between France and Germany, but a compromise, in which Germany recognized a French protectorate over Morocco in return for receiving a part of Cameroon from France, averted hostile action.

Still, relations between these two countries remained strained. To balance German military power, the French government introduced a motion to extend compulsory military service from two to three years. Despite strenuous opposition from the Left, led by Jean Jaurès, this measure was passed in August 1913. While the country was swinging to the Left in the general elections and the Chamber was struggling over an income tax, the fateful assassination of Archduke Francis Ferdinand of Austria and his wife occurred in Sarajevo on 28 June 1914. As one crisis led to another, French troops were massed near the German border, Germany invaded Belgium and declared war on France, Britain declared war on Germany, and the great slaughter was ready to begin.

Chronology

1906:   International conference recognizes French role in Mo-
         rocco.

1906–1913: Fallières, president; government of Clemenceau.

1908:   *L'Action Française* becomes a daily newspaper.

1909:   Wave of strikes.

1912:   Government of Poincaré.

1913:   Law of three-year military service passed.

1914:   Assassination of Austrian archduke and wife; Germany
         declares war on France.

Louis Aragon

Le Monde réel

The four novels that make up Louis Aragon's *Le Monde réel* and its
continuation, *Les Communistes,* have not enjoyed a good press.[1] Critics
point an accusing finger at the lack of psychological depth in many
characters, their black/white depiction as all bad or all good, and the
evident prejudice of the author against the bourgeoisie and in favor of
organized labor and communism, as only the most glaring defects. A
good deal of this is valid, but Aragon must also be credited with a
courageous pioneer effort in a number of areas, and his shortcomings
become more understandable and less serious, once his aim is fully
understood.

Converted from surrealism to communism, Aragon wanted to depict
a mass movement; hence individuals often had to give way to multi-
tudes.[2] Depicting a foreordained course of history, he does not have to
adhere to the traditional requirements of the novel (logical plot, dramatic tension, freedom and development of characters, etc.). Conflict
of interest is no longer that of individual versus individual or of individual versus society, but that between social classes. Above all, Aragon
wanted to reveal the "real world" to his readers: one in which, behind
the pretense of altruism and patriotism, events are determined by
financial interests, international cartels, and power-hungry groups

working together for their own benefits and against those of the people, that is, the workers.[3]

Such a conception may not make for a great novel, but at least it had the merit of novelty and experiment. Whereas most committed novelists depict the effects on the main characters of social and political conditions caused by persons we rarely or never see, Aragon shows us those who are responsible for France's plight, and the revolt of the workers against them and their class.

Given this theoretical background, one might expect a series of populist novels with nearly anonymous characters and an oversimplified psychology. Fortunately, Aragon is at least as much an artist as a political thinker; beyond that, he is a poet who feels a profound empathy with people, even those he dislikes, and he loves Paris as deeply as he loved his wife, Elsa Triolet.

As it turns out, *Le Monde réel* tells us far more about those nasty but fascinating capitalists, greedy bourgeois, unproductive Don Juans, and meandering husbands and wives than about the virtuous, unselfish, self-sacrificing militants who have seen the light and have become union activists or members of the Communist party. It is like those religious novels where sin deliciously occupies the lion's share of the novel and punishment or conversion arrive only in the last few pages.

The Story of Two Women: Les Cloches de Bâle

Occasionally Aragon realizes the dangers of focusing on evil and is overcome by remorse, as at the end of *Les Cloches de Bâle* (1934), where, after devoting 334 pages to the story of two bourgeois women who spend a great part of their time on their backs, he appends a two-page epilogue praising the German militant Clara Zetkin as the ideal to strive for.

The first of these two women is Diane de Nettencourt, a beautiful, frivolous woman, who falls in and out of love with charming and alarming alacrity, and eventually marries Georges Brunel, a wealthy but shady businessman, whose doubtful dealings get him into trouble. The military is represented by General Dorsch and the de Sabran brothers, captain and lieutenant, respectively. The latter commits suicide, and we realize after a while that Georges Brunel is responsible for it; in fact, we realize that people like Brunel and the car manufacturer Wisner are responsible for quite a few things.

These captains of industry and their subordinates have created a state within the state, above the law. Wisner explains to an open-mouthed Brunel:

When I say "France," that is a simplified way of saying "we," a certain group of common interests. It is nonetheless true that, once you accept the rules of the game, we are in the process of transforming a wild, unproductive region into a kind of terrestrial paradise, where it will be quite an experience to walk ten or fifteen years from now.

[Quand je dis *la France,* c'est une façon de parler très simple, pour dire *nous,* un certain groupe d'intérêts communs. Il n'en est pas moins vrai que, la règle du jeu une fois admise, nous sommes en train de transformer une région sauvage, improductive, en une espèce de paradis terrestre, où ça sera curieux de se promener dans dix, quinze ans. (*Les Cloches de Bâle,* 87)]

The "we" who make up Wisner's France include men like Joseph Quesnel, who in 1908 organized a taxi operation controlled by a consortium. Through agreements with Standard Oil, with French and German banks, and with petroleum operators in Rumania and Russia (the Simonidzé wells), Quesnel created a monopoly that enabled him to set the price his taxi drivers had to pay to buy gasoline for their cars.

These then are the people who are part of the real world. Who are they?

The Wisners, the Rockefellers, the de Wendels, the Finlays, the Krupps, the Poutilovs, the Morgans, the Joseph Quesnels, [who] move in a higher sphere, closed to the common man, where the destiny of the masses is decided. Figures are being written on blackboards. Ticker tape unwinds in automatic machines. War. War is being prepared.

[Les Wisner, les Rockefeller, les de Wendel, les Finlay, les Krupp, les Poutilov, les Morgan, les Joseph Quesnel s'agitent dans un monde supérieur, fermé aux foules, où se joue le destin des foules. Des chiffres s'inscrivent à des tableaux noirs. De petits rubans perforés se déroulent dans des appareils automatiques. La guerre. La guerre se prépare. (*Les Cloches de Bâle,* 352–53)]

And, set against those powerful forces, there is only the ringing of the bells of Basel, where, in 1912, a meeting for peace is taking place, and the inspiring words of the French Socialist leader Jean Jaurès seem like mere hollow echoes. Yet "ideas are like songs in the Cathedral of

Basel," and Jaurès announces future revolutions. "Governments should remember, when they evoke the danger of war, how easy it would be for the people to make the simple calculation that their own revolution would cost them fewer sacrifices than the war of others." [Les idées sont comme les chansons dans la cathédrale de Bâle. . . . Les gouvernements devraient se rappeler, quand ils évoquent le danger de guerre, comme il serait facile pour les peuples de faire le simple calcul que leur propre révolution leur coûterait moins de sacrifices que la guerre des autres (*Les Cloches de Bâle*, 352–53).]

The international conspiracy of high finance is exemplified by Wisner, who has financial interests not only in Morocco but also in the Balkans, consisting of mines, not cars.

Much of the plot of *Les Cloches de Bâle* is told in a purposely flippant tone, since events are often seen from the perspective of frivolous Diane. Aragon proves to be a master of style in his narration. Speaking of the Serbian visitors and embassy staff, he offers this Voltairean view:

They had all more or less assassinated Queen Draga and her husband. One of them had been in prison during their reign. In a sort of pit, it seems. Diane was flirting a little with a secretary of the embassy named Milan something or other, a kind of very handsome hussar with large black eyes. Apparently he was the one who had thrown the queen out of the window. He skated very well.

[Ils avaient tous plus ou moins assassiné la reine Draga et son époux. L'un d'eux avait été en prison sous leur règne. Dans une espèce de puit, paraît-il. Diane flirtait un peu avec un secrétaire d'ambassade qui s'appelait Milan quelque chose, une sorte de hussard très beau, avec de grands yeux noirs. Il paraît que c'est lui qui avait jeté la reine par la fenêtre. Il patinait très bien. (*Les Cloches de Bâle*, 49)]

The second woman in *Les Cloches de Bâle* might easily have lived the same frivolous and opportunistic life, since she had many of the same advantages as Diane de Nettencourt. Although not noble, Catherine Simonidzé is the daughter of the Russian petroleum magnate who does business with Quesnel's taxi consortium, and she receives her regular check from Baku. But Catherine, although no less reluctant to go to bed with men than Diane, gradually develops a social conscience.

Two factors contribute to her awakening: her revolt against the subordinate condition of women, and her involvement in strikes. At first she attends meetings of a group of anarchists led by Albert

Libertad, the director of an anarchist paper, who eventually will be brutally killed by the police. She also helps out during a strike of taxi drivers caused by the exorbitant price they have to pay the Quesnel consortium for their gasoline. There she meets Victor, a simple but determined union militant, who opens her eyes to the plight of the workers.

But the real shock occurs unexpectedly during a trip with one of her lovers. At Cluses, in 1904, they witness what happens during a strike of watchmakers, who had been forbidden by their bosses to present a list of workers at an election. Little by little, both sides become more adamant. The factory owners arm themselves, and when the strikers march on the factory, a young worker gets killed by two bullets.

It is the view of the dead body of the nineteen-year-old that has a profound effect on Catherine. It forces her to compare what she is witnessing—another example of the real world—with her own world in the small but cozy apartment at the rue Blaise-Desgoffe. Only later, while walking aimlessly along the Seine at the Pont Mirabeau, does she realize that

it was then that something in her had been irreparably broken, there in the crowd scurrying in all directions, while the wounded were lying in the dust, the soldiers were moving with their guns in the direction of the burning house, and the sun was dancing on a little yellow dog.

[. . . c'était alors que quelque chose en elle s'était irrémédiablement brisé, là dans la foule agitée en tous sens, tandis que les blessés étaient dans la poussière, que les soldats se portaient vers la maison en flammes avec leurs fusils, et que le soleil dansait sur un petit chien jaune. (*Les Cloches de Bâle*, 227)]

Les Cloches de Bâle seems disjointed at first reading. Obviously, the evolution of two women is compared, with Clara Zetkin thrown in for good measure at the very end. But, in the framework of *Le Monde réel*, this first of the four novels establishes a great deal. It exposes the men who run the show, and the brutal police who carry out their orders—only the politicians will appear in the later novels. It raises the basic question of who wants war, the war that will be known as World War I, which hovers already over Europe; and it insists on the error of anarchists, such as Libertad and Bonnot, who deny the division of the world into social classes.

Aragon sums up one of his principal intentions. "In *Les Cloches de Bâle* I wanted to show most of all the passing over of a part of the bourgeoisie into the camp of the workers, or at least the desire to pass over, that is, how, historically, that desire first appeared. I had been struck by a phrase in the [*Communist*] *Manifesto* of Marx and Engels saying that a moment will come when the best part of the bourgeoisie will pass over to the side of the working class."[4]

Equally important, *Les Cloches de Bâle* introduces some of the characters who, like Wisner and Quesnel, will have major roles in the novels to come, or who, like Diane de Nettencourt, will reappear but remain in the background. Most of the reappearing characters, however, whom we shall encounter throughout *Le Monde réel,* and as late as his six-volume *Les Communistes,* are introduced in *Les Beaux Quartiers.*

The Story of Two Brothers: Les Beaux Quartiers

Les Beaux Quartiers (1936) opens at Sérianne-le-Vieux, a rather small provincial town in southern France. The extramarital affairs, the petty politicking, and the fiery temperament of its inhabitants recall *Les Scandales de Clochemerle,* except that some of the characters are destined to have important careers in Paris.

One of these is the mayor, Dr. Philippe Barbentane, who will later become a senator. His two sons go in entirely different directions: Edmond, the older, leaves to study medicine in Paris, but he never practices. Instead, this handsome seducer has affairs with his professor's wife and with Carlotta, Joseph Quesnel's mistress, before marrying Quesnel's daughter Blanche and all her wealth. Armand, the younger son, vacillates in his choice of profession. Preparing himself for the priesthood at first, flirting with the theater later, he impetuously leaves Sérianne one day, after an argument with his father, shows up at his brother's flat in Paris, and soon experiences starvation, factory work, and strikes. In *Les Communistes* he reappears as a journalist for the Communist newspaper *L'Humanité* and finally ends up in the French Army during World War II.

We also meet Adrien Arnaud, the only son of the owner of a department store. Adrien organizes Pro Patria, a rightist group of young militants designed to keep the Italian workers at the local chocolate factory in their place. Once Edmond Barbentane takes over Quesnel's enterprises, Adrien becomes his timid right-hand man, who actually runs the business. And when Edmond's wife, Blanche, finally can no longer put up with her unfaithful husband, Adrien Arnaud marries her, while Edmond rejoins his only real love, Carlotta.

Most of *Les Beaux Quartiers* deals with the rise of handsome and opportunistic Edmond Barbentane from an obscure provincial medical student to the inheritor of Quesnel's enormous business and wealth. At the same time, we follow the rise of Edmond's father from provincial mayor and doctor to senator in Paris and candidate for a cabinet post. But in the long run, the evolution of Armand Barbentane, from confused young idealism, through loss of religious faith, to final conversion to communism, may be the most important aspect of the novel, at least from the author's point of view.

Throughout the novel we are constantly reminded of the political issues of the early twentieth century, the most important of which was the law to increase compulsory military service from two to three years (*la loi des trois ans*), which was adopted in August 1913 under the presidency of Poincaré. Aragon sees in this measure the decisive victory of those who wanted war, and he therefore devotes much space to this matter. As World War I is thus being prepared, the politicians, who are judged as harshly by Aragon as they had been by Barrès, continue to play their game of party politics while being themselves the playthings of the great financiers and industrialists.

All these strands come together at the gambling casino, called "The Passage Club," where the financiers, the criminals, the politicians, and the brutal police combine in sordid schemes.

Despite its many incidents and characters, *Les Beaux Quartiers* is primarily the story of two brothers. By the end of the novel Edmond Barbentane has clearly been more successful than his brother Armand, at least in material terms. But in the process Edmond has sold his soul to the greedy capitalist system; whereas Armand will become a true Aragonian hero, for he will find the right way, the road to communism.

The Infernal Machine: Les Voyageurs de l'impériale

With *Les Voyageurs de l'impériale* (1942) we return to a more private sphere. This novel recounts the story of Pierre Mercadier, born in 1856, a high school (lycée) history teacher, who has inherited a fair amount of money with which he speculates in the stock market—in short, a perfectly useless man, at least in Aragon's eyes. If only, at least, he had a political conscience! But no such luck; Mercadier is politically indifferent. "I am convinced that he is innocent," the history teacher says of Dreyfus. "But, after all, . . . I am not Jewish; it does not concern me." [Je suis persuadé de son innocence. Mais, au fond, . . . je ne suis pas juif, cela ne me concerne pas (*Les Voyageurs,* 240).] His only redeeming feature is a sense of adventure. "He was a sentimental soldier who had gotten lost in books. A switching error." [C'était un soldat sentimental qui s'était perdu dans les livres. Une erreur d'aiguillage (*Les Voyageurs,* 19).] This is how Aragon describes the false situation of a man whose temperament inclined him to be a soldier or a sailor but who finds himself married, a father, and a lycée teacher. And he cares less and less about his nagging wife and his annoying children; he has never cared for his boring and unmotivated students.

Still, Pierre Mercadier has obtained a certain reputation for his writings about seventeenth-century England; he has even been awarded a prize for a work about Charles I. He is now working on a study about John Law, the Scotsman we encountered before who introduced the use of paper money in France during the Regency with disastrous results. Here is where Aragon introduces his political theme, because he interprets Law's economic system as an essential step in the process that transformed coin money into paper money and thus made possible the formation of international finance, which now controls the destiny of Europe and the world.

By contrast, the selfish Pierre Mercadier is fascinated by a far different aspect of Law's system. The Scotsman symbolizes for him the possibility of getting rich quick through speculation, and he judges him as "one of those rare men who changed the course of the world—*he* was not a top-deck passenger." [. . . l'un des rares hommes qui firent dévier le monde. Il n'était pas, lui, un voyageur de l'Impériale (*Les Voyageurs,* 567).]

Which brings us to the admirable political symbolism of the title. The *impériale* is the upper deck of a bus, and, transposed into political terms, those who ride there "are carried along without knowing anything about the machine that is transporting them," as distinguished from those who run the machine and "know the mechanism of the monster, and who play and tamper with it." [. . . ceux qui pareils aux gens de l'impériale sont emportés sans rien savoir de la machine qu'ils habitent, . . . et les autres qui connaissent le mécanisme du monstre qui jouent à y tripoter (*Les Voyageurs,* 566).]

It seems strange that Pierre Mercadier, a seemingly hopeless tourist who looks at political life from the upper deck of a moving bus, should have had these thoughts. The explanation lies in his sense of adventure, a desire for freedom, even if it is only personal freedom he seeks. And suddenly, one day, Mercadier cashes in what is left of his unsuccessful speculations and, leaving home, wife, children, and job without a word, disappears into the blue.

That blue is actually Venice, where a mysterious girl turns out to be common blackmail bait; and eventually Monte Carlo, where he lives the life of an elegant gambler, a sort of minor modern-day John Law. Here he meets and falls in love with a truly mysterious woman: Reine de Bercy, the former wife of an important politician and now mistress of a German diplomat.

After spending all his money, Mercadier returns to Paris, where he is taken in as a teacher by Georges Meyer, a former colleague who has opened a private school. Meyer, a Jew with whom Mercadier used to play chess and discuss music, considers the man who had received him in his home without prejudice a genius, and describes the projected work on Law in such glowing terms that its author attains a local notoriety.

But Mercadier is worn out by now. Difficult times, cold quarters, unappetizing food, and lack of money take their toll on the professor, who by now looks more and more like Emil Jannings in the late stages of the film *The Blue Angel*. His only pleasure consists in his frequent visits to a café that serves as a front for a bordello. In time Mme Tavernier, as dilapidated as her establishment, falls in love with this strange old man and finally whisks him away to her run-down country home, where he will die in her arms. In the last years of his life Mercadier has developed a curiosity to see his grandson, Jeannot, and he does so secretly with the help of the child's nurse.

The end of the novel is rather contrived. Mercadier, upon his death, can only utter one word: "Politics." His son, Pascal, a ladies' man, upon learning of the suicide of his mistress Reine de Bercy (she certainly gets around!), decides to enroll in the army to fight the last of all wars, so that little Jeannot won't have to go through that horrible experience.

And now the moral of the story comes at us thick and heavy. "It is the end of the individual, that phantom, and his errant freedom." [C'en est fini de l'individu, ce fantôme, et de sa liberté errante (*Les Voyageurs,* 620).] And Pascal, scarcely a model of political consciousness, accuses his father and the latter's generation. "They are the ones who have gotten us to where we are, our fathers, with their blindness and their haughty disdain of politics, their way of dragging their feet while leaving the others in a mess." [Ce sont eux qui nous ont menés là, nos pères, avec leur aveuglement, leur superbe dédain de la politique, leurs façons de se tirer des pieds toujours, en laissant les autres dans le pétrin (*Les Voyageurs,* 626).][5]

This undisguised message is fortunately limited to the last pages of the novel, which otherwise makes for fascinating reading because it describes one of Aragon's great creations: a complex character who goes from irritation to revolt and from riches to rags, one who, like other great characters (one thinks here of Julien Sorel), was meant to lead one sort of life but lives another, who gambles, has great enjoyments and great sorrows, and finishes life in misery.

To those who have read the two preceding volumes of *Le Monde réel* with at least some attention, Aragon does not have to spell out the moral of Mercadier's erroneous ideal. For even though the individual volumes of this collective work present different heroes, the author could have chosen the title Jean-Paul Sartre used later for his unfinished series of novels: *The Roads to Freedom (Les Chemins de la liberté)*. The underlying theme in all of them is freedom or, perhaps, ways of liberation.

The path to freedom may be a false one because entirely egotistical (Pierre Mercadier). It may be only partially valid (Blaise the painter), linked more to an escape through art than to political commitment. Or it may be ideal (Armand Barbentane and others we shall encounter in *Les Communistes*), devoted entirely to social progress. Yet, in the final analysis, even the ideal choices exchange one sort of restraint (the family, bourgeois life and mores) for another (the party); and of all of Aragon's heroes only Pierre Mercadier, albeit for only a short time, experiences total freedom. He may have been totally wrong, but even Aragon cannot help but feel some grudging admiration for this adventurous egoist—and perhaps even secretly envy him a bit.

A Love Story: Aurélien

Aurélien (1944), listed by Aragon as the last in the series of *Le Monde réel,* can be considered either an interlude or an afterthought. It makes little difference, actually, because the total work (which would be completed anyway by *Les Communistes*) was not conceived in strictly chronological terms. The earliest action in any of the novels goes back to 1889, at the opening of the Paris World Fair in *Les Voyageurs de l'impériale,* and *Aurélien* takes place in the 1920s, jumping at the end to 1940 during the fall of France.[6]

Of the four novels collectively entitled *Le Monde réel, Aurélien* is the least political, and the most traditional in the sense in which we tend to think of novels. It is a love story.[7] Aurélien, a ladies' man, falls desperately in love with Bérénice, the provincial cousin of Blanchette Barbentane, and his fascination for her is as profound as Tristan's for Isolde and as incomprehensible as Swan's for Odette in Marcel Proust's *Un Amour de Swan*. For Bérénice is less desirable than almost any other woman of importance in the novel. She is less sophisticated, less beautiful, less elegant, less witty, less wealthy, and yet Aurélien, who did not find her attractive at first, becomes obsessed with her. The only distinction she seems to possess is an air of mystery, the sort one finds in André Dhôtel's women of Greek origin, a kind of Russian unpredictability but without the grandeur that makes Dostoevski's women interesting.

In his infatuation Aurélien accepts what might be called the reverse double standard: Bérénice, who is married to a one-armed pharmacist, can of course inhabit the marital bed whenever she has to or wants to; whereas Aurélien, whom she grants no favors, is expected to be faithful to her. And when he spends one night with a prostitute and misses her unannounced and unexpected visit at his apartment, he accepts guilt and begs forgiveness—which she refuses to grant him! Instead, she decides to run off with an insignificant young would-be poet, whom she obviously does not love.

Aurélien does see Bérénice once more, nineteen years later, when, married and once again serving in the French Army during the World War II debacle, he happens to pass through the provincial town where she lives. But after a brief moment of recalling the past, she is killed by a German bullet while they are taking a ride together.

Just why is theirs an impossible love? Somehow it seems that the circumstances, the conditions, and the timing are never right. One has the feeling that, if Aurélien only said the right words or made the right gesture at the right time or if he were at the right place at the right time, then perhaps something marvelous might develop. But he has not been granted amorous grace any more than political grace. Politically, Aurélien is empty, and perhaps Bérénice senses that a meaningless bourgeois life cannot satisfy her. By contrast, Jean and Cécile, the ideal lovers in *Les Communistes,* although facing far greater obstacles, will be united, because they have both been converted to communism.

Politics is not altogether absent in *Aurélien,* but it remains in the background. An officer in World War I, disoriented on his return to civilian life, Aurélien might have become another Gilles, the protagonist in Drieu la Rochelle's novel, which will be discussed later.[8] But that would have required a much greater social consciousness, perhaps a master to indoctrinate him, and far less wealth. In the course of the action Aurélien meets a young worker with whom he has a drink. The young man's remarks about his condition as an unproductive inheritor of wealth make him feel uneasy, but matters do not go any further. Political commitment and the conversion to communism in Aragon's novels resemble religious grace. Some seize the opportunity, like Catherine Simonidzé; others let it go by, like Pierre Mercadier or Aurélien. But all suffer the consequences of politics, and that is why even unpolitical people like Aurélien have to fight in two world wars and watch helplessly while those they love get killed.

How to Become a Communist

Le Monde réel, completed by *Les Communistes,* covers fifty-one years of French history, thus continuing the tradition established by Balzac, Zola, and Proust. Like his prestigious predecessors, Aragon parades an impressive number of characters before the reader's eyes. Among these, some are remarkable and memorable creations. That, in itself, is not so surprising as the fact that they are, almost without exception, evil capitalists or social good-for-nothings.

Using the symbolism of the "top-deck passengers," one can divide these characters into three large groups: those who know the machine and manipulate it, those who are carried along by it without any knowledge of its mechanism; and finally those who have seen the light and fight the mechanics.

The first group is dominated by the captains of industry and finance, and while Aragon underlines their evil doings and their international cartels and accuses them of being warmongers, he does not portray them unsympathetically. Wisner is obviously a competent, imaginative automaker who enjoys life, women, and good food and has a good deal of grandeur and patronizing joviality about him.

The most remarkable in this group, however, is Joseph Quesnel, the head of the taxi consortium. In *Les Beaux Quartiers,* Quesnel turns into a tragic figure. Superior and intelligent, he is a man of culture and philosophy, but, ill and grasping at life, he gives up all dignity in his love for the much younger Carlotta. Although knowing her to be unfaithful, he does not want to give her up and even goes so far as to provide Edmond Barbentane, her lover, with money and the succession to his business.

At the next level are the important politicians: Clemenceau, Poincaré, Caillaux, in *Le Monde réel;* later Daladier and Reynaud, in *Les Communistes.* Even though of different parties and divergent views, they serve not the people but special interests. The same holds true for the generals in the military.

Next in importance in this first group of mechanics are the opportunists, such as Edmond Barbentane and Adrien Arnaud, who rise through the influence of women and take over wealth they have not created. Stendhal's Julien Sorel comes to mind, but the comparison falls short, because Aragon's young opportunists have no ideal, no class consciousness, and no capacity for love. But they are energetic, ambitious, and skillful in their quest for success.

Still further down, rank the lesser politicians, such as Dr. Philippe Barbentane or Monzie (in *Les Communistes*), and the lower military officers, who turn the wheels but can only guess the direction in which the machine will go. On the very bottom of the power structure but in direct contact with the people are the police, the *flicaille,* as Aragon calls them. Brutal, vulgar, using agents provocateurs, cowardly attacking in groups perhaps only one person—the author cannot find words deprecating enough to spit at the hated cops. In fact, the most sinister figure in the entire work is Inspector Colombin, who may well be another disguise of Brunel, sunk ever lower. By blackmailing women (including Carlotta), he forces them to submit to his vicious pleasures until Charles Leroy, a simple croupier who is in love with one of the abused women, strangles this beastly creature in what amounts to a symbolic murder.

The only opposition to these groups of social mechanics and tamperers can be found in the Communists and their friends or allies. The great opposition leaders will not appear until *Les Communistes,* and then only indirectly. But Armand Barbentane will rise to the position of editor of *L'Humanité,* and a friendly lawyer, Watrin, who has access to ministers, also knows what the score is. Behind them are gathered humble but eager and dedicated workers, who, not unlike petty politicians, do the necessary chores without seeing the entire picture.

But the subordinate position of these simple party members should not make us overlook an important aspect of Aragon's work. If Drieu la Rochelle's novel *Gilles* could be subtitled *How to Become a Fascist,* Aragon's *Le Monde réel* teaches us how to become a Communist. And the difference between the two is remarkable. Whereas Drieu la Rochelle's (and similarly Maurice Barrès's) young heroes need a spiritual and political master to turn them into fascists or chauvinists, Aragon's "chosen characters" become Communists after undergoing shattering experiences (Catherine Simonidzé), after watching a popular demonstration against injustice (Armand Barbentane), or by verbally agreeing, without thinking, to join the party (Jean de Moncey in *Les Communistes*)—by virtue of what may be called an act of political grace.

By now we have come to understand what Aragon means by *Le Monde réel*. Obviously, if one speaks of the real world, by implication there exists also a world of illusion, created by the politicians, industrialists, and financiers, who hide their real goals (power, wealth, pleasure) behind a facade of patriotism and social usefulness. And Aragon's symbols underline the illusions of those who know not where they are being led (*Les Voyageurs de l'impériale*), and the self-delusions of those who believe they can achieve peace by meetings and by rousing speeches, while ignoring the class struggle (*Les Cloches de Bâle*). The real decisions are made elsewhere, in private meetings of the politicians and in the luxurious homes of *Les Beaux Quartiers*.

The Double Men of Capitalism

It is obvious where Aragon's sympathies lie, but he is not so simple-minded as to pretend that those who run France are inhuman, devoid of emotions or personal tragedy, ever cold and calculating. His greatest character, Joseph Quesnel, is haunted by a sense of unreality, as if he were two persons, one public and the other private.

While discussing important transactions with Joris de Houten, a younger man, Quesnel muses:

Now, here we are, and we are having a chat. And all that seems to you very important. But you are in a hurry. Your head is elsewhere. You are younger than I. Someone is waiting for you. Don't protest. The careful way you dress is not only intended for embassies. Come now! You are perhaps happy. Or unhappy. As for me, I am talking to you. My lips are moving. I too have my light and my dark moments. I too am surrounded by a dead world. The government, business matters, figures, all that is but a deceptive setting. I am thinking of things I am not saying. We are both hiding what is probably a similar reality. Don't interrupt me: for a moment, I am speaking in a sincere vein. We are, like the others, double beings. We are living in a historical period that will perhaps some day be characterized as the time of double people. I have always divided my life into two parts.

[Voilà. Nous sommes ici, et nous bavardons. Et tout vous a des airs d'importance. Mais vous êtes pressé. Votre tête est ailleurs. Vous êtes plus jeune que moi. On vous attend. Ne protestez pas. Le soin que vous donnez à votre toilette n'est pas seulement destiné aux ambassades. Allons donc! Vous êtes peut-être heureux. Ou malheureux. Moi, je vous parle. Mes lèvres vont. J'ai aussi mes lumières et mes ombres. J'ai aussi avec moi tout un monde mort. Le gouvernement, les affaires, les chiffres, tout cela n'est qu'un décor menteur. Je pense à ce que je ne dis pas. Nous cachons tous deux une réalité proba-blement semblable. Ne m'interrompez pas: pour un instant, je suis en veine d'être sincère. Nous sommes, comme les autres, des êtres doubles. Nous vivons à une époque historique qui se caractérisera peut-être un jour par là: le temps des hommes doubles. J'ai fait toujours deux parts de ma vie. (*Les Beaux Quartiers*, 269–70)]

Joseph Quesnels's confession reveals the sickness of the capitalist system, whose inhumanity splits people into two parts, the business half and the private half; and since the first half is inhuman, the capitalist cannot develop a harmonious, unified personality.[9] The an-swer to the drama of the divided, schizophrenic, and incomplete man is implied and clear. It is adherence to the Communist party, where the private and the public man can achieve unity in the fusion of individual and collective goals.

Thus, by reappearing characters and the complex phenomenon of reality / unreality / illusion, Aragon joins individual and collective experience and gives unity to what otherwise would have been dis-jointed, individual stories. In political terms, the same unity asserts itself: the capitalists have wanted war and the success of their efforts has resulted in World War I. Still not satisfied, they have prepared a Second World War and again they have succeeded against the wishes of the people. While World War I receives only brief treatment (in *Aurélien*), World War II will be the subject of *Les Communistes,* which we shall discuss later.

Chapter Four
War is Hell
The Third Republic: World War I, 1914–18

Both sides believed that this would be a short war, and both felt that offensive strategy would succeed. The war created national unity in France, but the Germans were once again more efficient and advanced close to Paris, until Galliéni counterattacked in September and saved the capital in the Battle of the Marne. Gradually politics surfaced again and the costly defense of Verdun in 1916 was more a necessity for Briand's political survival than for that of France. This battle also helped to create the reputation of General Pétain. As prolonged trench warfare without results led to disillusionment, Briand was replaced by Ribot. But the senseless offensive of Nivelle led to an enormous loss of life and caused the appointment of Pétain and Foch at the head of the French Army. They succeeded in stopping mutinies that had broken out and followed a more prudent course.

Faced with demands for a negotiated settlement from the Socialists and pressured by the Right to fight to the end, Poincaré reluctantly appointed the militant Clemenceau to the premiership. By that time the situation had become desperate for France. Although the United States had entered the war, American troops were slow to arrive, and personal haggling between England's General Haig and Pétain prevented a united Allied command being formed. As German onslaughts continued, Foch was finally named supreme commander. He patiently withstood the German attacks and then drove them back with a counteroffensive in July. On 11 November 1918 the Armistice was signed.

The great relief and joy of a victorious end to the long war was soon followed by a mood of pessimism. France had lost some 1,250,000 soldiers and half a million civilians, and 750,000 men were permanently injured. Large amounts of territory were devastated and the national debt surpassed anything previously imagined.

Chronology

1914:   (July): Jaurès assassinated; (August): Germany declares
        war on France; French defeat in Ardennes; (September):
        Battle of the Marne.

1915:   Briand ministry.

1916:   Battles of Verdun and the Somme; Henri Barbusse: *Le
        Feu*.

1917:   Ministries of Ribot, Painlevé; appointments of Foch and
        Pétain; Clemenceau government.

1918:   German offensive led by Ludendorff; Foch counteroffen-
        sive; (November): Armistice signed at Compiègne.

Henri Barbusse

Le Feu

Along with Remarque's *All Quiet on the Western Front,* Henri
Barbusse's *Le Feu (Under Fire)* is justly considered the best novel to have
come out of World War I. Published in 1916, it received the Prix
Goncourt the following year and sold five hundred thousand copies,
thus becoming, for that time, a notable best-seller in France.

The war experience leaves its mark on men in different ways. For
some, it is the revelation of their virile strength and leadership capacity, of heroism, of glory, of patriotism, of the community of comrades;
for others, it signifies sheer hell, degradation, the successive loss of
one's humanity. In between is the great majority of those who, if they
survive unscathed, return to civilian life, readjust, and tell their war
stories until they no longer elicit any interest from a new generation.

Reactions to the War Experience: Drieu la Rochelle

It is, of course, those with extreme reactions who transform their
experiences and visions into artistic works. One extreme view on war is
expressed by Pierre Drieu la Rochelle, whose novel *Gilles* will be discussed in the next chapter.

And then, all of a sudden, something quite extraordinary took place. I had
stood up, stood up among the dead, among the living dead. I discovered the

meaning of the words grace and miracle. There is something human in those words. They mean exuberance, exultation, culmination, before meaning effusion, extravagance, intoxication.

All of a sudden, I found myself, I found my life. This was what I was, this strong man, this free man, this hero. So, this was my life, this sudden joyous surge that would never ever stop.

Ah! at certain moments I had felt this effervescence of young hot blood—the puberty of virtue; I had been conscious of some prisoner pulsing within me, ready to spring forth. A prisoner of the life which had been imposed on me, which I had imposed on myself. A prisoner of the crowd, of sleep, of humility.

What was it that suddenly sprang up? A leader. Not just a man. A leader. Not only a man who gives, but a man who takes. A leader is a man in his prime, a man who gives and takes in the same ejaculation. . . .

Everything depended on me, the whole of this battle—and tomorrow's battles, tomorrow's revolutions—rested on me, summoned me, begged me, sought its resolution in me. Everything depended on me. I had only to will, and everything immediately became clear, everything became possible, everything had a meaning. . . .

I held victory and liberty in my hands—liberty. Man is free; man can always do what he wants. Man is a fragment of the world, and each fragment is able, in a moment of paroxysm, in a moment of eternity, to realize within itself everything that is possible. Victory.[1]

[Alors, tout d'un coup, il s'est produit quelque chose d'extraordinaire. Je m'étais levé, levé entre les morts, entre les larves. J'ai su ce que veulent dire grâce et miracle. Il y a quelque chose d'humain dans ces mots. Ils veulent dire exubérance, exultation, épanouissement—avant de dire extravasement, extravagance, ivresse.

Tout d'un coup, je me connaissais, je connaissais ma vie. C'était donc moi, ce fort, ce libre, ce héros. C'était donc ma vie, cet ébat qui n'allait plus s'arrêter jamais.

Ah! je l'avais pressenti à certaines heures, ce bouillonnement du sang jeune et chaud—puberté de la vertu; j'avais senti palpiter en moi un prisonnier, prêt à s'élancer. Prisonnier de la vie qu'on m'avait faite, que je m'étais faite. Prisonnier de la foule, du sommeil, de l'humilité.

Qu'est-ce qui soudain jaillissait? Un chef. Non seulement un homme, un chef. Non seulement un homme qui se donne, mais un homme qui prend. Un chef, c'est un homme à son plein; l'homme qui donne et qui prend dans la même éjaculation. . . .

Tout dépendait de moi, toute cette bataille—et les batailles de demain, les révolutions de demain—pesait sur moi, me sollicitait, me suppliait, cherchait sa résolution en moi. Tout dépendait de moi. Il me suffisait de vouloir et tout se précipitait en un point, tout se réalisait, tout se signifiait. . . .

Je tenais dans mes mains la victoire et la liberté. La liberté. L'homme est libre, l'homme peut ce qu'il veut. L'homme est une partie du monde, et chaque partie du monde peut, à un moment de paroxysme, à un moment d'éternité, réaliser en elle tout le possible. La victoire.]²

The Soldiers of the 231st Infantry Regiment   What would the members of Barbusse's squad have said if someone had read them Drieu la Rochelle's ode to war? Probably the same as what that wounded soldier said when Paradis told the story of a woman who thought attacks were beautiful: "Beau! Ah! merde alors!"³

For the members of Barbusse's squad, belonging to the 231st Infantry Regiment, the war they fight in the trenches of the Soissonais, in Argonne and Artois, in 1915, is sheer hell. Prolonging the inarticulate phrase of Paradis, "That's war. . . . It's not something else." [c'est ça, la guerre. . . . C'est pa'aut'chose], the author defines what this "glorious" war experience means to them.

More than the charges that look like reviews, more than the visible battles unfolding like decorative banners, more even than the hand-to-hand fighting, where you struggle, shouting—this war is that horrible and supernatural fatigue, and the water up to your waist, and mud, and garbage, and foul filth. It's mildewed faces and flesh in tatters and cadavers that don't even look any more like cadavers, floating up on the voracious earth. It's that, that never-ending monotony of drudgery, interrupted by intense dramas; it's that—not the bayonet shining like silver, nor the bugle sounding like the cock crow in the sunlight.

[Plus que les charges qui ressemblent à des revues, plus que les batailles visibles déployées comme des oriflammes, plus même que les corps à corps où l'on se démène en criant, cette guerre, c'est la fatigue épouvantable, surnaturelle, et l'eau jusqu'au ventre, et la boue et l'ordure et l'infâme saleté. C'est les faces moisies et les chairs in loques et les cadavres qui ne ressemblent même plus à des cadavres, surnageant sur la terre vorace. C'est cela, cette monotonie infinie de misères, interrompue par des drames aigus, c'est cela, et non pas la baïonnette qui étincelle comme de l'argent, ni le chant de coq du clairon au soleil! (*Le Feu,* 330)]

Gradually, these soldiers suffer the loss of their humanity, the loss of their former identity. They can no longer communicate with those who have not shared their life and their experiences.

Even if you tried to tell, you know, people wouldn't believe you. Not because they're evil or because they wouldn't give a damn about you, but 'cause they just couldn't. If you would say later on, if you're still alive, just to get a word in: "We worked at night, we were groggy, we nearly sank into the mud," they'd reply: "Oh!" or perhaps, "You must have had a bad time of it." That's all. Nobody will know. Only you.

[T'auras beau raconter, s'pas, on t'croira pas. Pas par méchanceté ou par amour de s'ficher d'toi, mais pa'ce qu'on n'pourra pas. Quand tu diras plus tard, si t'es encore vivant pour placer ton mot: "On a fait des travaux d'nuit, on a été sonnés, pis on a manqué s'enliser", on répondra: "Ah!"; p'têt qu'on dira "Vous n'avez pas dû rigoler lourd pendant l'affaire." C'est tout. Personne ne saura. I'n'y aura qu'toi. (*Le Feu*, 332)]

To them at least, war does not unify a nation—it splits it into two parts. "There is not one single country. . . . There are two. I say that we have been split into two countries foreign to one another: at the front, all the way down there, where there are too many unhappy people; and the rear, here, where there are too many happy ones." [Y a pas un seul pays. . . . Y en a deux. J'dis qu'on est séparés en deux pays étrangers: l'avant, tout là-bas, où il y a trop de malheureux, et l'arrière, ici, où il y a trop d'heureux (*Le Feu*, 303).]

The Members of the Squad

And yet, these men are very ordinary Frenchmen, not the special race whom Barrès wrote about and whom Drieu la Rochelle eulogizes, but the usual mixture one finds in any army of volunteers and conscripts.

They are of all ages: the oldest could be the fathers of the youngest. They are of all races: blond, dark-skinned, light-skinned, Bretons, Parisians, northerners, southerners, peasants from Poitou. They come from all walks of life: farmworkers, miners, deliverymen, innkeepers, factory workers, salesmen of all sorts. The narrator, whose name is never revealed, is obviously the only intellectual in the group.

Despite the diversity of age, race, and professions, these mud-spattered men have been melted into a uniform pattern because of their closed-in existence, which has given them

the same manners, the same habits, the same simplified character of men who have reverted to the primitive state.

The same way of talking, made up of a mixture of the slang of workshops and barracks, and of dialect, seasoned with neologisms, blends us, like a sauce, into a dense mass of men who, for several seasons now, have been draining out of France to accumulate in the Northeast.

[. . . les mêmes moeurs, les mêmes habitudes, le même caractère simplifié d'hommes revenus à l'état primitif.

Le même parler, fait d'un mélange d'argots d'atelier et de caserne, et de patois, assaisonné de quelques néologismes, nous amalgame, comme une sauce, à la multitude compacte d'hommes qui, depuis des saisons, vide la France pour s'accumuler au Nord-Est. (*Le Feu*, 17)]

Out of this mass of dirt-covered men, seventeen individuals emerge, one by one: Lamuse, the farmhand, who is in love with a girl who loves not him but Farfadet; Poterloo, the miner, who has seen his wife—through the window, smiling in the company of German officers; Eudore, the innkeeper, who could only spend one night of his leave with his wife due to red tape, and that in the company of people they are lodging because of a storm; Cocon, the walking calculating machine, who used to work in a hardware store; Corporal Bertrand, the factory foreman, who speaks little and is a model soldier admired by all; and the others, Volpatte, le père Barque, the brothers Mesnil, Bécuwe . . . , names not recorded in history but that Barbusse has immortalized.

They pass like shadows and die like flies, one after the other, even Corporal Bernard. It is unbelievable, but it happens so frequently that the heart can no longer pour forth emotions, and so the unbelievable becomes routine.

Monotony and Death

While they live as soldiers, they wait: for the chow to come, for the mail, for the night when they are on duty, for those rumored, marvelous leaves that never materialize, and for death, which comes to nearly all of them.

Barbusse conveys the monotony and the banal atmosphere of the squad's existence by his frequent use of the present tense, which expresses duration as effectively as Flaubert's imperfect tense. The eternal present fading into eternal death. The only events that interrupt the drudgery are short stays in filthy barns during a move, the recitals of those who have come back from leave, and combat. But fighting is not glorious. They are as lost as Stendhal's Fabrice del Dongo was at the battle of Waterloo, but they share none of his enthusiasm. They are not idealistic noblemen from Italy fighting for an emperor; they are just ordinary Frenchmen trying to survive.

Ordinary they may be, but not unworthy. Volpatte takes one last look at Cocon, dead, disfigured, almost unrecognizable. He comments, "You can't imagine it," and the narrator orchestrates his poor words into a hymn of admiration.

No, you can't imagine. All those disappearances together wear out your mind. There are just not enough survivors. But you feel a vague notion of the grandeur of these dead. They gave everything; they gave, little by little, their strength, and then, finally, they gave themselves all in one heap. They went beyond life; their effort contains something superhuman and perfect.

[Non, on ne peut pas se figurer. Toutes ces disparitions à la fois excèdent l'esprit. Il n'y a pas assez de survivants. Mais on a une vague notion de la grandeur de ces morts. Ils ont tout donné; ils ont donné, petit à petit, toute leur force, puis, finalement, ils se sont donnés, en bloc. Ils ont dépassé la vie; leur effort a quelque chose de surhumain et de parfait. (*Le Feu*, 268)]

The War Profiteers

The soldiers certainly do not profit from the war, but others do. The profiteers who overcharge the soldiers, like the one who has already piled up fifty thousand francs. They learn the truth from a child's mouth during a halt in a small town.

"Fifty thousand francs! That can't be!"
'Oh, yes," the child insists. "He said so to mother. Pa would like it never to end. Ma, she's not so sure because my brother Adolphe is at the front. But they'll get him out of there, and then the war can just keep going on."

[— Cinquante mille francs! C'est pas vrai!
—Si, si! trépigne l'enfant. Il a dit ça avec maman. Papa voudrait qu'ça soit toujours comme ça. Maman, des fois, elle ne sait pas, parce que mon frère Adolphe est au front. Mais on va le faire mettre à l'arrière, comme ça, la guerre pourra continuer. (*Le Feu*, 74)]

Barbusse cries out against those who favor, and profit from, the war: financiers, small and big operators, militarists, "who get drunk on military music, . . . the dazzled, the feebleminded, the fetishists, the savages," those who live in the past, the traditionalists, the priests who promise paradise, the lawyers who spout theoretical verbiage,

who proclaim the antagonism of national races, when each modern nation has only an arbitrary geographical unity within the abstract lines of its frontiers and is a mixture of races; and who, dubious genealogists that they are, fabricate false philosophical diplomas and imaginary titles of nobility for ambitions of conquest and spoils.

[Ceux qui s'enivrent avec la musique militaire, . . . les éblouis, les faibles d'esprit, les fétichistes, les sauvages. . . . Il y a des avocats . . . qui proclament l'antagonisme des races nationales entre elles, alors que chaque nation moderne n'a qu'une unité géographique arbitraire dans les lignes abstraites de ses frontières, et est peuplée d'un artificiel amalgame de races; et qui, généalogistes véreux, fabriquent aux ambitions de conquête et de dépouillement, de faux certificats philosophiques et d'imaginaires titres de noblesses. (*Le Feu*, 345)]

These supernationalists and profiteers are the real enemies, much more so than the German soldiers, who are also duped in the same way. The simple soldiers of the squad have no idea what Germans are like.

"Well, old man," says Tirloir, "people talk about the bloody Kraut race. As for the ordinary soldiers, I don't know whether it's true of them or whether it's all made up too, and if, basically, they're not men more or less like us."

["Ah! mon vieux, dit Tirloir, on parle de la sale race boche. Les hommes de troupe, j'sais pas si c'est vrai ou si on nous monte un coup là-dessus aussi, et si, au fond, ce ne sont pas des hommes à peu près comme nous." (*Le Feu*, 32)]

Corporal Bertrand's Vision of the Future

The only one in the squad who has a philosophy of sorts is the taciturn Corporal Bertrand, an admirer of Liebknecht. In a rare moment of expansiveness, he proclaims his faith in what is to come.

The future! The future! The work of the future will be to wipe out this present, to wipe it out much more than we may think, to wipe it out as something abominable and shameful. Still, this present was necessary! Shame on military glory, shame on armies, shame on the task of the soldier, which changes men in turn into stupid victims and vile henchmen. Yes, shame on it all. It's true, but it's too true, it's true in eternity, not yet for us. Let's be careful about what we're thinking now! It will be true when there will be a true Bible. It will be true when it will be written among other truths, which the purification of the mind will enable us to understand at the same time. We are still lost and exiled far from those times. At the present, in these moments, that truth is almost an error, that holy word is but a blasphemy.

[L'avenir! L'avenir! L'oeuvre de l'avenir sera d'effacer ce présent-ci, et de l'effacer plus encore qu'on ne pense, de l'effacer comme quelque chose d'abominable et de honteux. Et pourtant, ce présent, il le fallait, il le fallait! Honte à la gloire militaire, honte aux armées, honte au métier de soldat, qui change les hommes tour à tour en stupides victimes et en ignobles bourreaux. Oui, honte: c'est vrai, mais c'est trop vrai, c'est vrai pour l'éternité, pas encore pour nous. Attention à ce que nous pensons maintenant! Ce sera vrai, lorsqu'il y aura toute une vraie bible. Ce sera vrai lorsque ce sera écrit parmi d'autres vérités que l'épuration de l'esprit permettra de comprendre en même temps. Nous sommes encore perdus et exilés loin de ces époques-là. Pendant nos jours actuels, en ces moments-ci, cette vérité est presque une erreur, cette parole sainte n'est qu'un blasphème! (*Le Feu*, 259)]

Corporal Bertrand will not live to see that wonderful future, but the narrator, one of the few survivors, echoes his hopes among the wounded. He foresees a revolution greater than the one of 1789, when people will realize that liberty and fraternity are mere words, but that equality is real; "the principle of the equality of the rights of every created being and the sacred will of the majority . . . will bring with it all progress." [Le principe de l'égalité des droits de chaque créature et de la volonté sainte de la majorité . . . amènera tous les progrès (*Le Feu*, 341).]

An Exceptional War Novel

There are few great war novels, and Barbusse's *Le Feu* is among that small number. It is unusual in that it does not tell of heroism but of misery, not of heroes but of ordinary men lost in the immenseness, the brutality, the filth, and the drudgery of World War I.

While Barbusse has strong opinions, he never preaches. He lets the soldiers and the facts speak for themselves, and only at the end of the novel do the results of those experiences burst spontaneously out of the mouths of those who are wounded and those who are about to die after so many who have gone before them.

The author succeeds admirably in making his characters speak their language—not the horrible jargon Balzac throws at the reader in the speech of Baron Nucingen, but natural argot and patois. The narrator stays in the background, never talks about himself; in fact, he is defined only by what his comrades say to him. For a militant communist, such as Barbusse was to become, that is no small accomplishment.

Obviously, *Le Feu* is not an objective work. It makes its point, and it makes it unmistakably. But where Barrès uses bombast and pages of rhetoric, Barbusse appears restrained, classical, almost chaste. Quite remarkably for a war novel, no salacious stories are told, no sexual scenes take place. These men, although bored with their long hours of drudgery, talk very little of women.

The only woman of any importance in the novel is Eudoxie, a mysterious, frail, blond girl who follows Farfadet, her lover. Big Lamuse lusts after her, but she refuses him indignantly. She does finally come to him, but what he holds in his arms is a rotting corpse killed some time earlier in a bombing attack and falling on him from a beam in a house. "She tried to fall on me with all her weight," Lamuse recounts. "You know, she wanted to be in my arms and I didn't want her, it was awful." [Elle essayait d'me tomber d'ssus de tout son poids. Mon vieux, elle voulait m'embrasser, je n'voulais pas, c'était affreux. (*Le Feu,* 197–98)]

Le Feu ends on a hopeful note. Symbolically, Barbusse expresses the conviction of those who have suffered, that their sacrifice will lead to a better future.

And while we prepare to join the others to get back to the war, the black sky, overcast until then by storm clouds, opens up gently above our heads. Between two masses of gloomy clouds, a calm flash of light appears, and that luminous line, so confined, so mournful, so pitiful that it seems to be a reflection, nonetheless proves that the sun exists.

[Et tandis que nous nous apprêtons à rejoindre les autres, pour recommencer la guerre, le ciel noir, bouché d'orage, s'ouvre doucement au-dessus de nos têtes. Entre deux masses de nuées ténébreuses, un éclair tranquille en sort, et cette ligne de lumière, si resserrée, si endeuillée, si pauvre, qu'elle a l'air pensante, apporte tout de même la preuve que le soleil existe. (*Le Feu,* 349)]

World War I left deep scars on those who fought in it and lived through it. Victory after so much suffering created hopes and expectations that turned out to be illusory. The world had not been made safe for democracy, nor was this the last world war, nor was prosperity around the corner. When these sad facts became evident, the veterans accused those they felt were responsible for their disappointment: the capitalist system and the kind of government they lived under.

Chapter Five
How to Become a Fascist
The Third Republic: Between the Wars, 1919–39

The Treaty of Versailles, signed on 28 June 1919, restored Alsace and Lorraine to France, provided for a limited occupation of bridgeheads on the Rhine river, an Anglo-American guarantee of assistance against future German aggression, and a demilitarized zone in the Rhineland. But the United States soon repudiated its commitment, followed by Great Britain; and France was saddled with a large repayment of debts to America, thus exacerbating the already huge national debt. The resulting inflation was to haunt future governments.

The Treaty of Versailles was probably one of the worst settlements of war in modern times. Its framers were looking to the past instead of the future. They seemed to be ignorant of the only possible justification for all-out war, namely, the goals to be achieved in the postwar period. Principal among these goals are two that are preferably reached jointly: (1) placing the defeated nation in a position such that it either cannot or does not desire to start another war; (2) turning the former enemy nation into a future ally. Neither of these desiderata resulted from the treaty, and it may be claimed that the seeds of World War II were contained in that failure.

With the war over, politics in France returned to normal, that is, to the seesaw pattern from right to left and left to right. In the November 1919 elections the conservative Bloc National won 433 seats to only 86 for the Radicals and 104 for the Socialists. The new Chamber, with a majority of practicing Catholics, drew closer to the Vatican. With Millerand as president and later Poincaré as premier, mutual assistance treaties were concluded with the new Balkan nations and Poland. To help the latter resist Soviet forces, General Weygand was dispatched to fight the battle of Warsaw. Poincaré attempted to collect reparations from Germany by sending French troops into the Ruhr territory, but passive resistance and the collapse of the German mark put an end to that plan.

In 1924 the pendulum swung to the left with the election of a Cartel des gauches. Led by Herriot, the parties of the Left were again unable to function in unity. What complicated matters even more was the split of the Socialist party into socialist and communist factions. Soon thereafter the trade unions experienced a similar division. Although faced with communism on the Left and militant catholicism on the Right, the greatest problem of the Cartel des gauches still remained finances. Confidence in the franc was restored by the appointment of Poincaré, who was empowered to formulate financial policy by decree.

Just when economic prosperity was beginning to make its appearance in France, the Wall Street crash in October 1929 crushed hopes of financial stability. And international stability, which Foreign Minister Briand had labored for in his attempts of reconciliation with Germany, received a fatal blow when 107 Nazi members were elected to the Reichstag in 1930.

In 1932 the parties of the Left (Radicals and Socialists) were returned to power only to face an unprecedented economic crisis. The deterioration of the world economy left France with 1,300,000 unemployed, and not only were there no German reparations in sight but France was obliged to continue paying its war debt to the United States. As cabinets succeeded each other at a dizzying pace, the Stavisky scandal, a shady financial affair in which influential politicians were involved, broke out. Compared to the Panama affair of 1892, this was a relatively small matter, but the Right seized on it to force compromised ministers and Premier Chautemps out of office.

The new premier, Daladier, began by dismissing the Paris chief of police, who was known to sympathize with the Right. He even went so far as to dismiss the director of the Comédie Française for having staged the antidemocratic play *Coriolanus*. These moves, and perhaps the fear of a reputedly strong premier, induced groups of the extreme Right to stage a coup on 6 February 1934. Led by the Action Française and inspired by the model of Fascist Italy, the march on the Chamber of Deputies was joined by other organizations, such as the Jeunesses Patriotes of Pierre Taittinger, the Croix de Feu of de la Rocque, and the Francistes of perfume millionaire Coty. Even the Communist-controlled Association Républicaine des Anciens Combattants joined in this attempt to overthrow the Third Republic. During several hours of street fighting, the demonstrators suffered fourteen dead and some two thousand injured, while the outnumbered police counted one dead and about a hundred wounded.

But this uprising, on which Drieu la Rochelle had placed so much hope, resulted only in bloody heads. The groups responsible for it had no program and were united only in their hatred of the Republic. They, as those who would make similar attempts later, failed to understand that the majority of the French people would rather put up with unstable governments and doubtful politicians than give up their Republic.

Calm was restored with the resignation of Daladier and the appointment of former president Doumergue as premier of a cabinet of national unity. But when Doumergue called for constitutional changes to increase the power of the premier, he too went the way of his many predecessors and was replaced by a rightist cabinet under Pierre Laval.

The 6 February riot and the threat posed by fascism finally brought about the union that the parties of the Left had been unable to form on their own. With the Communists joining in, a program of the Popular Front was hammered out, and the 1936 elections gave them 380 seats against 237 for the Right. The new Léon Blum government was immediately confronted by an unexpected crisis: strikes by aircraft factory workers who expected to take over their factories. These were followed by other sit-down strikes. An agreement was signed on 9 June that granted workers a twelve percent wage increase, paid vacations, and a forty-hour week. The armament industry was to be nationalized and the government would regulate the Bank of France.

The Popular Front had to defend itself from attacks on all sides, even from its own allies. The inflation caused by wage increases and lower production led to a devaluation of the franc, and in March 1937 Blum suggested a pause in the reforms. By June he had to resort to laws by decree, but when the Senate excluded exchange control from the decrees, Blum resigned.

On the surface, France had devised a more coherent foreign than domestic policy. Briand's efforts for reconciliation with Germany were at first continued by his successor, Laval. When Hitler came to power in Germany in 1933, France signed the Four-Power Pact, which intended to give France, England, Italy, and Germany control over European affairs. But when Germany walked out of the disarmament conference, Barthou, the new foreign minister, undertook the formation of an alliance to contain possible new German aggression. It might have succeeded if Barthou had not been assassinated, along with King Alexander of Yugoslavia, by a Macedonian terrorist in October 1934.

This brought Laval back to the Quai d'Orsay. He continued Barthou's negotiations for a Franco-Soviet pact, which was ratified only in 1936 by the Popular Front. But blindness on the Left, sympathy with fascism on the Right, constant miscalculations by the French General Staff, and British treachery permitted Nazi Germany and Fascist Italy to succeed in aggressive acts and treaty violations that could have been easily prevented or crushed. The Socialists opposed extension of military service to two years on the wishful conviction that the French workers would rise as one man to defend their country; the Right opposed any sanctions on Italy for blatantly invading Abyssinia; France remained neutral in the Spanish civil war; and the French General Staff, led by Pétain, believed only in the defensive strategy behind its Maginot line. Meanwhile England had signed a naval treaty with Germany without consulting her allies.

The year 1936 was a fateful period, during which inexcusable errors were committed by Allied statesmen. Thus one may claim that World War II began not in September 1939 but on 7 March 1936. That was the day Hitler decided to remilitarize the Rhineland with a small force of German troops. This was a clear violation of both the Versailles treaty of 1919 and the Locarno Pact of 1925, which had guaranteed the demilitarization of the Rhineland. Being a schoolboy in Germany at the time, I remember distinctly that everybody looked at the sky that day for the inevitable French and British warplanes—which never came. The slightest show of force would have called Hitler's bluff and possibly put an end to German military and territorial ambitions. Unfortunately, at that time the French were having one of their periodical government crises and an interim government, headed by the Radical Sarraut, lacked the power to act decisively. Great Britain, however, consulted by France and unwilling to move, had no excuses. Apparently, German schoolboys knew more about historical moments of truth than French Commander-in-Chief Gamelin, Marshall Pétain, the French Right, and especially Britain's Lord Halifax.

This criminal failure to act not only led to the abrogation by Germany of the Versailles treaty on 16 March 1936, and to the introduction of conscription in Germany, but also spelled the end of the French system of alliances, since no one could trust the French any more to stand up to Germany. The Franco dictatorship in Spain, the *Anschluss* of Austria, the annexation by Germany of the Sudetenland of Czechoslovakia, the pathetic Munich agreement, held up triumphantly by Daladier and Chamberlain as a guarantee of peace, and the equally meaningless Declaration of Friendship, signed by German Foreign Minister Von Ribbentrop in Paris—all these were inevitable consequences of the failure to act at the critical moment.

And World War II, which just as inevitably broke out in 1939, with its millions of victims, is to be blamed as much on those French and British statesmen who failed to react to blatant provocations as on the insane minds of the Nazi leaders.[1]

While, of course, every effort must be made to avoid unnecessary wars, that historical experience and its horrifying consequences should make us remember that the most elementary rule of medicine holds true also of politics: that an ounce of prevention is worth a pound of cure.

Chronology

1920: Deschanel defeats Clemenceau for presidency; government of Millerand; Socialist Congress at Tours.

1922: Government of Poincaré.

1923: Occupation of Ruhr territory.

1924: Resignation of Millerand and Poincaré.

1924–1931; Doumergue, president; government of Herriot.

1925: Evacuation of Ruhr territory; Locarno agreement.

1925–1932: Briand, foreign minister.

1926–1929: Poincaré's National Union for Defense of the Franc.

1928: Military service reduced to one year; decision to build Maginot line.

1930: French evacuation of Rhineland.

1931: Doumer elected president.

1932: Assassination of Doumer.

1932–1940: Lebrun, president.

1932: Success of Cartel des gauches in elections; Herriot government.

1933: Daladier government; Stavisky scandal.

1934: (6–7 February): Riots in Paris, attempted coup of rightist groups; coalition government under Doumergue; Barthou assassinated at Marseilles; Aragon: *Les Cloches de Bâle;* Laval, foreign minister; fall of Doumergue.

1936: Fall of Laval; Aragon: *Les Beaux Quartiers;* Germany remilitarizes the Rhineland; Popular Front wins majority

in elections; first Blum cabinet; Franco-Soviet pact ratified; devaluation of the franc; Spanish civil war breaks
out.

1937:   Blum defeat in Senate.

1938:   Second Blum ministry; Daladier, prime minister; (September): Munich Agreement; Reynaud, finance minister; Ribbentrop visits Paris; friendship declaration.

1939:   Drieu la Rochelle: *Gilles*.

Pierre Drieu la Rochelle: *Gilles*

Pierre Drieu la Rochelle's novel *Gilles* was written from 1936 to
1939. It covers the period between 1917 and the early part of the
Spanish civil war, about 1936–37, thus offering a panorama of France
between the two world wars. To a great extent the novel is autobiographical, but it would be erroneous to substitute the author for the
protagonist at all times, for a character in a novel always escapes his
author's grasp. Proust said this emphatically in his tirade against
Sainte-Beuve, and Drieu la Rochelle makes the same observation in his
preface.[2]

Nevertheless, there are obvious resemblances between Gilles and his
author. Drieu la Rochelle was very much a ladies' man. He had associated with the dadaists and the surrealists; in fact, he had been very close
at one time to André Breton and Louis Aragon, but he did not follow
Aragon on his road to communism. Instead he turned to fascism, and
during the German occupation he assumed the editorship of the important *Nouvelle Revue Française* (NRF) while collaborating with the German authorities. He committed suicide in March 1945 when it was
evident that Germany had been defeated. He is probably best known in
the United States, at least indirectly, by way of Louis Malle's film *Le
Feu follet* (1963), based on one of Drieu's novels, which deals with the
problem of suicide.

Gilles opens in 1917 with Gilles Gambier's arrival in Paris during a
leave from the front, where he has been wounded by a bullet in his arm.
After spending the night with a couple of floozies, he visits the
Falkenbergs' home. The two sons of the family, members of his regiment, have been killed in the war, but the real purpose of his visit is
not to talk about them but to obtain money from this wealthy Jewish

family. He is met by Myriam Falkenberg, who falls in love with him. Although at first attracted to her, he soon decides that only her money interests him, and he makes her suffer a great deal before finally marrying her, strictly again for her money. His avowed desire to return to the front does not prevent him from using Myriam's relations to obtain a pleasant job at the Foreign Office and to remain in Paris, where he divides his time between prostitutes and several affairs. He eventually divorces Myriam and marries Pauline, formerly a kept woman, who has a miscarriage and dies.

An orphan who does not know who his parents were, Gilles is profoundly influenced by his guardian, Carentan, who indoctrinates him with a reactionary political view that looks back to a mythical time in the Middle Ages as an ideal and despises everything that is modern, such as republics, liberalism, America, and Jews. Gilles tries to find a political faith in existing parties, and for a while he flirts with a group, led by the charlatan Caël, that calls itself Révolte, but he soon becomes disenchanted with its lack of substance. Forced to earn his own living as the money obtained from his divorce runs out, he founds a publication, *Apocalypse,* with Lorin, a knee-jerk Marxist, and Preuss, a Jew he knew at the Sorbonne. They place their hopes in Clérences, the son-in-law of a former president of the Republic and a deputy of the governing Radical party who is in disagreement with his fellow politicians.

Their great opportunity arrives on 6 February 1934, when, after the Stavisky scandal, an antigovernment demonstration, supported mainly by right-wing groups, offers the possibility of a revolution such as France actually experienced in 1830 and 1848, and could have during the Boulanger movement in 1886. But Clérences, despite Gilles's supplications, refuses to act and Gilles loses all hope for France. After Pauline's death, we discover Gilles in Spain during the civil war, on Franco's side, of course. Having assumed the name Walter and braving danger every day, he at last finds fulfillment through the realization of his ideal: war, virility, a return to medieval catholicism, and the politics of fascism.

Comparisons with Characters in the Past

While reading *Gilles,* a number of comparisons with past works inevitably come to mind. One thinks of Rousseau's *Confessions,* because of the confessional nature of the novel; of Stendhal's *Le Rouge et le noir,* because we follow the education and the evolution of a young man who improves his situation thanks to women; and of Benjamin Constant's *Adolphe,* because a part of the novel deals with the problem of how to break with a woman one no longer loves.

Gilles contains, indeed, the confessions of a young man who seems to bare his heart without any concern for how it makes him appear.[3] But, like Rousseau's, his confession is an apology, and he finds excuses for his inexcusable behavior by blaming factors outside himself. One reads *Gilles* with the fascination of disgust. It is almost like a good pornographic novel. But instead of describing the disorder of the senses, it expresses the disorder of the heart and the mind: it could have borne the subtitle Crébillon fils chose for his best-known novel: *Les Egarements du coeur et de l'esprit.*

What fascinates the reader is the apparent frankness and cynicism with which Drieu exposes the behavior and motives of Gilles. Like Crébillon's Versac or Diderot's nephew of Rameau, Gilles is depicted as a character who hides none of his despicable traits: an egotist, a sycophant, a heartless dowry chaser, a man incapable of loving a woman, a man who prefers spending his time with prostitutes or tarts, a racist who is at the same time attracted to Jews, a political activist who courts failure in all his enterprises, Gilles combines Versac's seductiveness and Rameau's unabashed frankness.

But whereas Versac and Rameau, while severely criticizing their times, assume full responsibility for their actions and openly avow their motives, Gilles declares himself to be what his country and society have made of him, that is, he refuses to consider that in a free country a person can rise above these circumstances by swimming against the stream.

Stendhal's Julien Sorel has to face more difficult challenges than Gilles, but he has that peasant energy to rise above his condition and to act. Julien's dream is to be a heartless seducer like Gilles, but his heart keeps getting in his way, for he loves and loves deeply. In a period of reaction he constructs for himself a model of action, and his education is his own, based on his readings and his experiences.

Benjamin Constant's *Adolphe* comes to mind in Gilles's occasional bouts with a bad conscience for his treatment of Myriam Falkenberg, whom he is planning to marry but does not love. Just like Adolphe, he shies away from pronouncing the brutal truth every time it threatens to pass his lips, by pretending that he does not want to hurt her. This behavior in Adolphe comes close to being credible, since he does not derive any material benefits from his relationship with Léonore, and, in

General Georges Boulanger,
14 July 1986.
Reproduced from the portrait
by Debat-Ponsan.

Charles de Gaulle

Alfred Dreyfus

Émile Zola

Maurice Barrès. By Nadar.

Anatole France. By Nadar.

Louis Aragon

Henri Barbusse, 15 August 1928.

André Stil

Pierre Drieu la Rochelle

Jean Anouilh

Jean-Paul Sartre

Robert Merle

James Jones. Photo by Marc Riboud.

fact, is seriously harming his career. Gilles, however, can claim no such mitigating circumstances, as he is primarily interested in Myriam's money.

By comparing Gilles with characters of the past, one comes to realize the appalling degeneration of the modern hero, who blames society, historical conditions, his parents, or his teachers for what he is, but who never has the courage to take a good look at himself. Like Rousseau, Gilles maintains throughout his inconsistent and vile actions a sense of moral superiority. He looks down contemptuously on his country and his countrymen, in whom he condemns softness, a lack of virility, and degeneration.

Yet what is he? A dilettante, a man who has apparently read quite a bit, including Pascal at the front, but who is competent at nothing; a potential writer who has no confidence in himself and whose complete works consist of scribbled notes; a political thinker who spits at politicians of all colors but who has no political philosophy of his own; a philosopher whose thoughts have been gleaned from a lonely misanthrope whose views seem to come out of his pipe instead of his head. The resulting incoherent brew can only produce a nihilist. Where will he end up? Nihilists tend to drift or jump. If they drift, they end up violently, victims of their own bombs or policemen's guns. If they jump, they are likely to fall into one of three nets: religion (it is no accident that Carentan is writing a book on the history of religion, which he will never finish), communism, or fascism. Whatever differences there may be among religion, communism, fascism, and nihilism, for a man like Gilles they all possess the attraction that he does not have to devise an independent philosophy. Nihilism has none, and the other three are ready-made. The choice, in his case, finally narrows down to religion or fascism, for Carentan has cluttered his mind with a mixture of medieval fiction and racial mysticism that communism cannot satisfy: Notre-Dame and Nuremberg are naturally more impressive than a May Day parade in Moscow.

Master and Disciple

If one reads Drieu la Rochelle's novel closely, one realizes that the education Gilles has received from his adored guardian, Carentan, and his unquestioned acceptance of it are far more responsible for his behavior than the conditions in France during the interwar years.

The least that can be said of the lessons Gilles drinks greedily off

Carentan's lips is that they render him unfit to live in the twentieth century. Carentan instills in him his ill-humored dislike of all that is modern and an ideal based on a highly questionable concept of what life was like in the Middle Ages—attitudes that could at best fit a sort of Don Quixote. But Gilles is not even a Rastignac capable of resisting the temptations of this fascistic Vautrin, nor can his ideal man, a failure in almost every sense, compare with Julien Sorel's Napoleon. Gilles accepts Carentan's guidance and theories not only because his spiritual father has influenced him from his early days on, but because they suit him, since they provide ready-made excuses for his lack of origins and of enterprise, as well as for his despicable behavior toward people who have shown him nothing but affection and generosity.

Gilles, who does not know who his parents were,[4] acquires via Carentan's confused theories a sense of racial superiority and a sense of belonging to that undefined but marvelous group of "superior" beings. When he needs a justification for his cruelty to Myriam Falkenberg, Carentan reassures him.

If you hesitate with that woman, you will not hesitate with the next one. Many people will have to suffer because of you. . . . You are like me, a spiritual ascetic, but not one of life. Wolves will always eat lambs. I have been one in my way; be one in yours. I have done some pretty nasty things in my time to take care of my old age.

[Si tu hésites devant cette femme, tu n'hésiteras pas devant la suivante. Il y a beaucoup d'êtres qui doivent souffrir par toi. . . . Tu es comme moi, un peu ascète de l'esprit, mais pas de la vie. Il faut faire la part du loup. Je l'ai faite à ma manière, fais-la à la tienne. J'ai fait d'assez vilains coups dans mon temps pour m'assurer un magot. (*Gilles,* 157)]

One problem with being a disciple is that one rarely does better than the master, and Carentan, regardless of all his virile talk, has been a failure. He has retired from French modern society, not like a world heavyweight champion at the height of his career, but as someone who has never gone into the ring. Incapable of overcoming his initial upbringing, Gilles himself turns out to be a failure at every level: as a lover, as a husband, as a friend, in his professional endeavors, and in his political activities.[5] Like his tutor, Gilles is a loser. Incapable, therefore, of winning by his own merit and effort, he has to throw himself into a large movement where he merely has to obey and where success or failure becomes collective.

One can scarcely expect more from a young man whose spiritual father is Carentan, who "has imposed his weight on him with all his might" (*Gilles,* 154). A brief conversation between the two strikes us like the exchange of vows between a naive Boy Scout and his scoutmaster. The old man, blowing smoke out of his pipe, begins:

"I am a fanatic."
"Yes, but a fanatic of a kind of male liberalism. Nothing is more liberal than virility. Soldiers who fight well have a magnificent indulgence."
"Not for cowards. I hate cowards of the mind."
"So do I. Do not fear. I shall always be decisive."
"That is our motto: Always clear and decisive."

Everything is guts. Gut philosophy, gut reactions. Carentan's explanation of why he dislikes Jews illustrates this attitude.

"I am not an anti-Semite, because I abhor politics. . . . Anti-Semitism is one of those elementary mishmashes like all 'isms.' But then there is experience, what our contact with people teaches us. Now, I can't stand Jews, because they are, par excellence, the modern world that I abhor. . . . For me, a provincial, a country bourgeois, who by instinct is bound to a complex and old world, a Jew is horrible, like a graduate from the Polytechnical School or from the Ecole normale."

[— Je suis un fanatique.
—Oui, mais fanatique d'une espèce de libéralisme mâle. Il n'y a rien de plus libéral que la virilité. Les soldats qui se battent bien ont une indulgence magnifique.
— Pas pour les lâches. Je hais les lâches de l'esprit.
—Moi aussi, n'aie pas peur: je trancherai toujours.
—Voilà notre devise: tranche toujours. (*Gilles,* 154–55)

—Je ne suis pas antisémite parce que j'ai horreur de la politique. . . . L'antisémitisme, c'est donc une de ces ratatouilles primaires, comme tous les ismes. Passons. Reste l'expérience, ce que nous enseigne le contact avec les personnes. Eh bien! moi je ne peux pas supporter les juifs, parce qu'ils sont par excellence le monde moderne que j'abhorre. . . . Pour moi, provincial, bourgeois de campagne, qui, par l'instinct et par l'étude, me rattache à un univers complexe et ancien, le juif, c'est horrible comme un polytechnicien ou un normalien. (*Gilles,* 158–59)]

Carentan is, undeniably, clear and decisive, but that does not make him a profound thinker. Translated into simple language, here is what

he states: "I am not an anti-Semite. That is a political attitude and I
hate politics. My attitude is personal: I simply can't stand Jews." And
for him all Jews are alike; they are all modern. There are no craftsmen,
no rabbis; he certainly had never met, or heard of, Orthodox Jews in
caftans who are further removed from the modern world than any
French country squire. For Carentan, all Jews go to the Sorbonne and
are representatives of the modern world that he hates. It's as simple as
that.

Having done such diligent research in the formation of his beliefs,
Carentan naturally feels the necessity of indoctrinating his ward with
them, and he has encountered fertile soil. Like Maurice Barrès's young
provincials, Gilles is a natural disciple, and there is nothing more pathetic in the intellectual realm than a disciple who can never let go of his
master's shirttail. He will remain a pitiful adolescent all his life. Spiritual fathers are far more difficult to shake off than natural ones, especially
when they are imbued with Carentan's philosophy of education.

We are not, neither of us, half-wits, the sort of pale, anemic rationalists who,
like Pontius Pilatus, wash their hands and say, "I don't want to force any ideas
on my son; he'll choose for himself later on." You can't bring up your child in
a vacuum; you'll only produce a spineless person. Whether you like it or not,
you fill his head with many things and shape his character substantially.
So? . . . I have exerted pressure on you with all my might, right? I am your
spiritual father. Don't ask of me any more. That's the only thing that matters.

[Nous ne sommes ni l'un ni l'autre de ces imbéciles, de ces pâles navets du
rationalisme, de ces Pilates qui se lavent les mains et qui disent: "Je ne veux
rien imposer à mon fils; plus tard, il choisira." On ne peut pas faire le vide
autour de son enfant, on peut tout au plus faire du mou. Qu'on le veuille ou
non, on bourre son esprit d'un tas de choses et on donne de sérieuses
pichenettes à son caractère. Alors? . . . J'ai fait pression sur toi de toutes mes
forces, hein? Je suis ton père spirituel. Ne m'en demande pas plus. Il n'y a que
ça qui compte. (*Gilles*, 154)]

It is never even remotely clear what Carentan's political philosophy
is, but we discover in him again a version of that *Vieille France* myth
that Maurice Barrès had espoused earlier (see chap. 1,). In both cases,
the attitude is reactionary[6] and antievolutionary, namely, the view that
at some time in the past the evolution of France reached its ideal state
and no changes should be made in it. But while Barrès fabricated a
composite image of this concept, Carentan supplies a precise time

element: the Middle Ages. He has just returned from a propaganda trip through Canada.

Do you know what I told these good Canadians? There are still Frenchmen, beings of flesh and blood, and soul, who are not made only of books and newspapers. I am calling on you in the name of these Frenchmen. . . . Aside from that, it is curious to see Frenchmen who have not been affected by 1789, nor the 18th century, nor even by the 17th, nor even by the Renaissance and the Reformation; those are Frenchmen completely raw and alive.

[Tu sais ce que je leur ai dit à ces braves Canadiens: il y a encore des Français, des êtres de chair et de sang, et d'âme, qui ne sont pas faits uniquement de livres et de journaux. C'est au nom de ces Français-là que je viens vous appeler. . . . A part ça, c'est drôle de voir des Français, sur qui n'est pas passé 1789, ni le XVIIIe, ni même somme toute le XVIIe, ni même la Renaissance et la Réforme, c'est du Français tout cru, tout vif. (*Gilles,* 161)]

Although the romantics held up the Middle Ages as a model for literary reasons,[7] Carentan proclaims that France should actually turn its back on all that had changed in nearly three centuries and return to the Middle Ages. In that attitude he is both a parody of the *Vieille France* school and a reactionary in the practical and pejorative sense.

Gilles's Politics

The confused ideas and virile negativism of Carentan condition Gilles's political views and actions. Disappointed at first, and finally revolted by the charlatanism he observes in the Révolte group he has associated with, he founds his own publication, appropriately called *Apocalypse.* Disgusted with party politics and judging that "France was nothing more than a vast academy of weak-minded and perverse old people, where words were understood only as words, . . . Gilles's pen expressed grating exasperation. He denigrated everything in France with increasingly pitiless violence." [La France n'était plus qu'une vaste académie, une assemblée de vieillards débiles et pervers où les mots n'étaient entendus que comme des mots. . . . Sa plume s'exaspérait, grinçait. Il dénigrait tout en France avec une violence de plus en plus inexpiable (*Gilles,* 574, 572).]

Clérences, the dissident deputy of the Radical Party, remains his only hope for forming a new party. Just what will it be like? "A party that will be national without being nationalist, that will break with all

prejudices and routines of the Right on that matter, and a party that
will be social without being socialist, one that will boldly reform but
without falling into the rut of a doctrine." [Un parti qui serait national
sans être nationaliste, qui romprait avec tous les préjugés et les routines
de la droite sur ce chapitre, et un parti qui serait social sans être
socialiste, qui réformerait hardiment mais sans suivre l'ornière d'aucune
doctrine (*Gilles*, 537).]

For a man whose motto is to be always clear and decisive, this
political credo appears not only vague but messy. Even if Gilles were to
call his dream party by the unoriginal name of National Socialist, the
concept would not be any clearer. And neither does his involvement in
the Spanish civil war on Franco's side clarify his thoughts. To a comrade in arms, an Irishman, he explains why he is in Spain: "Virile
catholicism, the one of the Middle Ages." And later on, he muses, "He
was on the road of Joan of Arc, a Catholic and a warrior." [C'est aussi
exactement la raison pour laquelle je suis ici. Le catholicisme mâle,
celui de Moyen Age. Hein? . . . Il était sur le chemin de Jeanne d'Arc,
catholique et guerrier (*Gilles*, 658, 677).] Gilles repeats Carentan's
lessons very much as Sganarelle repeats Dom Juan's apology for his
inconstancy in love to Elvire in Molière's play.

With such a mishmash of political mysticism, our Joan of Arc has, of
course, no definite ideas to offer when, on 6 February 1934, a popular
antigovernment demonstration seems to provide Clérences with a
unique opportunity to assert himself.

"What do you propose?"
"Open at once a bureau to recruit combat sections. No manifesto, no
program, no new party. Only combat sections that will be called combat
sections."
. . . .
"And then what?" Clérences asked gently.
"With the first section formed, do anything at all."
"Anything at all, that's great."
"Attack Daladier or take up his defense, but by actions that are completely
concrete. Invade in turn a newspaper of the Right and one of the Left. Have
somebody or other be beaten up at his home. At any price, get out of the
routine of the old parties, manifestos, meetings, articles, and speeches. And
you will immediately have a tremendous power of attraction. The barriers
between Right and Left will come down forever, and waves of life will rush in
every direction. Don't you feel this moment of enormous flooding? The wave

is right before us: we can cast it in any direction we want, but we must do it at once, at any price."

[— Qu'est-ce que tu proposes?
—Ouvre un bureau immédiatement pour recruter des sections de combat. Pas de manifeste, pas de programme, pas de nouveau parti. Seulement des sections de combat, qui s'appelleront des sections de combat. . . .
—Et alors? demanda doucement Clérences. . . .
—Avec la première section formée, fais n'importe quoi.
—N'importe quoi, c'est bien cela.
—Attaque Daladier ou défends-le, mais par des actes qui soient tout à fait concrets. Envahis coup sur coup un journal de droite et un journal de gauche. Fais bâtonner à domicile celui-ci ou celui-là. Sors à tout prix de la routine des vieux partis, des manifestes, des meetings et des articles et des discours. Et tu auras aussitôt une puissance d'agrégation formidable. Les barrières seront à jamais rompues entre la droite et la gauche, et des flots de vie se précipiteront en tout sens. Tu ne sens pas cet instant de grande crue? Le flot est là devant nous: on peut le lancer dans la direction qu'on veut, mais il faut le lancer tout de suite, à tout prix. (*Gilles*, 599)]

This is the street fighter's credo. Gilles could be a Communist just as readily as a Fascist; in fact, he is prepared to march with anyone who will overturn the government. "Now I will march with any guy who will get rid of this government, with anyone, no matter what the conditions may be." [Maintenant, je marcherai avec n'importe quel type qui foutra ce régime par terre, avec n'importe qui, à n'importe quelle condition (*Gilles*, 600).] But there is more in Gilles than just the street fighter. Even above his insensate directives there hovers a naive ideal: the virile, energetic nation led by men who are no party men and who will unite the country in a political life that has neither right nor left wings.

Gilles is a poet who did not make it in poetry, for "the secrets of religion and philosophy, as those of poetry, were nearly closed to him; having given up hopes to penetrate them, he had to resign himself to venerate them in their social context, to spell them out by means of political syllables." [Les secrets de la religion et de la philosophie, comme ceux de la poésie, lui restaient à peu près interdits; n'espérant plus les pénétrer, il devait se résigner à les vénérer dans leur contour social, les épeler au moyen de syllabes politiques (*Gilles*, 512).]

In characterizing Napoleon's master faculty, Taine speaks of "the constructive imagination of an artist locked up in politics."[8] Alas,

Gilles Gambier is no Napoleon. Like his author, he will at best make a collaborator once the German Nazis occupy France.

Gilles's Contradictions and Sex Life

The blatant contradictions between Gilles' avowed beliefs and his actions illustrate perfectly what Jean-Paul Sartre called bad faith. He tacitly concurs with Carentan's dislike of Jews, yet greedily accepts money and favors from them; he proclaims to anyone ready to listen that his greatest wish is to return to the front, yet immediately accepts Myriam's help to get a soft job in Paris; he rails against Paris yet clings to the city as if it were a drug. One could easily add to these examples. It will not do to explain these contradictions away as a love-hate relationship, because in his inconsistencies Gilles is consistent in one respect: he usually chooses the easy way out, and this "spiritual ascetic" loves nothing more than luxuries for which he does not have to work.

Gilles is a very modern figure, the sort of protester one finds throughout much of the rest of the the twentieth century. He wants to change his society, but he is unwilling to turn his task into a full-time vocation, unwilling to sacrifice his pleasures, his indolent desire for luxury, his self-indulgence. He wants to be a master before going through the drudgery of apprenticeship. He dreams of an elevated ideal and cannot find enough contempt for his contemporaries, but his own behavior is even more contemptible than what he condemns. For one cannot speak of the grandeur of evil in a man who seeks out weak victims, such as masochistic Myriam, who literally asks to be destroyed. Nor does a man change society in the boudoirs of prostitutes. Unable to show the way by thought or behavior, he takes refuge in holding his society responsible for what he is. But regeneration and virility require more than pointing an accusing finger outward.

Gilles is obviously a ladies' man, a sort of Don Juan. Just how he seduces women is not entirely clear. He is blond, blue-eyed, with white teeth, and despite a somewhat round nose, he seems to be attractive to women who quickly fall for him.[9] Most of them are older than he: an American nurse; a French nurse; and Dora, an American woman—married and the mother of two children—ten years older than he, whom he loves desperately and who eventually leaves him to return to America with her family.

One need not necessarily condemn Gilles's relations with women. If Gilles prefers prostitutes, where the preliminary period is reduced to zero, or the Austrian woman, with whom he does not have to talk, that is his business. A person's sexual life is a private manner, into which neither the state nor courts have any right to stick their noses, and each person is entitled to his or her preferences.

If we want to probe more deeply into Gilles's particular case, one may suggest that the absence of a mother (or a sister) in the life of this orphan probably contributed to his sexual formation. The reference to Oedipus, tempting but all too brief, as representing the history of sin (*Gilles,* 163) is certainly not gratuitous, nor is Gilles's preference for older women.

Gilles's sex life is interesting, but it stops there. As a modern Marquis de Sade, he might have been a fascinating case; but, being subject to qualms of conscience, he falls into disappointing mediocrity. For, if he does not love the timid, pure, intellectual Myriam, for whom he experiences sudden gusts of admiration and tenderness mixed with pity, he is incapable of rising to the level of satanic grandeur. In fact, Myriam is avenged by Dora, who makes him suffer in his turn and weep, yes weep, the way Myriam had suffered and wept because of him.

How to Become a Fascist

Most important perhaps of all, *Gilles,* thanks to the frankness of Drieu la Rochelle, reveals why certain types of persons drift into totalitarian movements. Lonely, vaguely idealistic, intelligent but unable to devise a philosophy of their own, egotistic and with a high opinion of themselves, but unsuccessful in their social and professional contacts, they long to belong. A totalitarian party offers them a simple and simplistic fulfillment, complete with vague but vigorous slogans that express their own vague and unexpressed ideas.[10] And the uniform, the military maneuvers, provide them with the comradeship that satisfies both the lonely loser and the war veteran who has been unable to digest his war experience. And soon they are on their way, behind a leader who represents for them strength, virility, courage—and who will lead them right to their death.

Gilles was not the only one of his generation to grasp at the straw of totalitarianism. André Breton, Louis Aragon, and the surrealists, Jules Romains and his idea of unanimism, Malraux and his heroic revolutionaries, were just some of the manifestations of the malaise during the interwar years.

Had he lived later in the century as a young man, Gilles would have mounted the barricades in Paris during May 1968. Older, and perhaps a bit wiser, he would have hitched his star to de Gaulle. Like Malraux.

What Drieu la Rochelle's novel reveals is that people are not born Fascists but become Fascists, and that they do so in several stages. First, they need to be so disgusted with the present state of political affairs that they will join any movement that seeks to overturn the existing government or governmental system. Next, they need to feel a personal desire to lose themselves in a mass movement. At this stage they may become either Communists or Fascists. The reasons for choosing one or the other may vary: the influence of a master, which is frequently the case with those who become Fascists; the prestige of other systems in power (Mussolini in Italy, Hitler in Germany, or Stalin in the Soviet Union, for example); or the effectiveness in recruiting by the totalitarian party in their own country.

The Lesson of Gilles

If *Gilles* is hardly "one of the greatest novels of the century," as Gaëton Picon claims,[11] it is nevertheless a significant illustration of a general mood in France during the interwar years. The feeling that a civilization was coming to an end, that the only way to overcome a decadent society was to find a new energy, a revitalized virility, such as the war experience had revealed, was indeed prevalent in many quarters. And by steering a careful course that avoids the pitfalls of presenting a model hero, Drieu created a successful political novel—highly readable although stylistically not flawless—that mixes personal and political life.

On a more general level, *Gilles* describes the experience of the returning war veteran. He is not the same man who left civilian life. He has looked death in the eye and his vision will never be the same. Like the soldiers in Barbusse's *Le Feu,* he is shocked by the contrast between the seriousness of warfare and the frivolity and lust for luxury of those at home, especially in Paris. One does not easily step without transition from army life at the front into elegant drawing rooms. Most of all, the returning veteran finds it difficult to accept business as usual. He thinks that the deaths of his comrades and his own sacrifices had some purpose, that things will be different, that governments will be run with the same dedication to the country as the soldiers offered. And when he realizes the disorder and instability, the cynicism and the greed, the lack of attention to the general welfare by the government at home, he wants to go to war all over again, but with his gun pointed the other way.

Gilles is a novel that every partisan of democratic government should read and reread. It not only describes the making of a Fascist but deals with some deeper and ominous warnings and a lesson to be learned by heart: that the principal cause for the rise of totalitarian regimes is the incompetence, the blind party politics, and the corruption of weak democratic governments. It is their inability to deal with challenges such as inflation and unemployment, their lack of farsighted leadership, their appointment of unqualified cabinet officers and governmental officials, their lack of imagination, their pandering to press and television, their preoccupation with reelections, and their scandals that bring about their downfall—and not the pathetic Gilles Gambiers.

What Drieu la Rochelle has to say about the Third Republic during the interwar years may be more than just past history.

Part 2

From World War II to the Fifth Republic

Chapter Six

The Phony War

The Third Republic: World War II until the Fall of France, 1939–40

The Second World War turned out to be a disaster for France. Ignoring the modernization of warfare and warnings from a young general by the name of Charles de Gaulle, the General Staff believed the country to be safe behind its Maginot line. Inside France there was much division over resistance to the German threat. The Socialist party was split on the issue, with its secretary general, Paul Faure, leading the pacifist wing. Within the government, Minister of Foreign Affairs Georges Bonnet opposed any action against the Nazis, and, of course, the extreme Right, led by the Action Française, joined these antiwar groups because of its fascist sympathies. Only the Communist party denounced the Munich agreement at the time.

When Germany climaxed its aggression by invading Poland on 1 September 1939, Great Britain and France had no choice but to declare war on 3 September. Poland, however, fell before the Allies could take any action. The division of Poland, the result of a secret clause in the German-Soviet pact, caused strong resentment against the Communists in France. The party members were split on the issue of war, and, although their deputies voted in favor of the miltary expenses, the government dissolved the Communist party on 26 September 1939, prohibited its publications, and in January 1940 deprived the remaining Communist deputies of their seats. [1]

As in World War I, the French believed the war would not be of long duration and could be won without major sacrifices. During the winter very little action took place, as the French Army waited to be attacked in what has been called the phony war [*drôle de guerre*]. In March 1940 Daladier was replaced by Paul Reynaud but remained in the government as minister of war.

On 10 May 1940, Germany invaded Holland and Belgium, which were quickly overrun. The heaviest fighting in France took place at the

Meuse, near Sedan, and by 15 May the French Army was in full retreat. In despair, Reynaud recalled General Weygand from Syria, but the general judged the situation to be hopeless. Allied forces were defeated in the Low Countries and had to be evacuated at Dunkirk. On 10 June the French government left Paris for Bordeaux, and on 14 June the Germans entered Paris.

The rest we recall only too well from film clips: the tears of humiliation running down their cheeks as powerless Parisians watched their city being taken over by the Nazis, and Hitler's jig on 22 June 1940, when the French capitulation was signed at Compiègne in the same railroad car in which the 1918 armistice had been signed.

For France, World War II had been lost in one month. It was the most humiliating defeat the country had suffered in its history.

Chronology

February 1939:	France recognizes Franco government of Spain.
March 1939:	Germany occupies Czechoslovakia; Anglo-French guarantee to Poland.
August 1939:	Russo-German pact, supported by French Communist party.
1 September 1939:	German invasion of Poland.
3 September 1939:	Great Britain and France declare war on Germany; Russian invasion of Poland.
26 September 1939:	Government dissolves French Communist party.
March 1940:	Daladier resigns; Reynaud takes over.
10 May 1940:	German invasion of Low Countries.
13–14 May 1940:	French front broken at Meuse; Reynaud assumes post of minister of national defense in place of Daladier; General Gamelin replaced by General Weygand; General Pétain enters government.
21 May–4 June 1940:	Dunkirk evacuation of Allied troops; Italy enters war.

10 June 1940:   French government leaves Paris for Bordeaux.
14 June 1940:   German troops enter Paris.
22 June 1940:   Capitulation signed at Compiègne.

Louis Aragon

Les Communistes

Les Communistes (1949–51) constitutes the continuation and conclusion of Louis Aragon's work to which he gave the collective title *Le Monde réel*. In six volumes, dated chronologically from February 1939 to May/June 1940,[2] the author traces the events immediately leading up to World War II—the *drôle de guerre,* that lull during the winter 1939–40 when the French maintained their illusions of security behind the Maginot line—and the German blitzkrieg, which led to the inglorious defeat of the French Army and the last-minute evacuation of English and French troops at Dunkirk.

Les Communistes might have been for World War II what Barbusse's *Le Feu* had been for World War I; in fact, Aragon's depiction of the drudgery, the filth, the inhumanity, and the horrors of war rival, and at times surpass, that of his predecessor.[3] Furthermore, we encounter at various times characters reappearing from the volumes of *Le Monde réel:* Wisner, Armand Barbentane, Aurélien Leurtillois, Pierre Mercadier's grandson Jeannot (who now calls himself Jean-Blaise), and others. Consequently, these characters, representing the second and third generations of families known to the reader, possess a greater depth than those of Barbusse.

Had he limited himself to the war alone, Aragon might indeed have been the great World War II novelist of France.[4] But the author pursued more far-reaching goals, and if the work is judged a failure, then it is a grandiose one, due not so much to the novelist's inability as to the inadequacy of the novelistic form to express the ambitious design of the artist.

The Levels of War Recital

Barbusse viewed World War I from the ground level. His soldiers have no idea of what the overall strategy of the generals is; they simply carry out orders and most of them get killed in the process. Aragon, too, shows us the ground level of war. Lieutenant Armand Barbentane and his squad, Jean de Moncey and his ambulance unit, know no more about the why, when, and where of what is going on than Barbusse's sheep for the slaughter.

But Aragon adds two more levels to the ground level of ignorance: the government chiefs and the generals. We attend cabinet meetings and listen in on private conversations, so that Daladier, Reynaud, cabinet ministers, and deputies reveal to us their plans and their innermost secrets. Likewise, the generals pass in review: Grandsard, Baudet, Billotte, Corap, Gamelin, Weygand, Pétain, and others. We follow their catastrophic strategy, their quarrels, their occasional acts of heroism, but, above all, their incompetence. The much ridiculed Colonel Avoine, who has his men dig fortifications inside France, shows much more foresight than the generals, because his strategy can serve the cause of the Resistance against the superior German army, which cannot be kept out of France by the Maginot line.

Aragon not only cuts like a mad film editor from level to level, but in the war episodes, which take up close to one-half of the six volumes, he flits, often with blinding speed, from one military unit to another, or from battleground to cabinet meetings to private affairs to supreme headquarters, and then back to an army unit.

Aragon's Design

The opening of *Les Communistes* recounts the attempts to get wounded members of the defeated Spanish loyalists across the border past hostile French guards, and is a first indication of Aragon's courageous wager: to make the novel do more than its form permits— simultaneity of action, designed to impress on the reader the interrelationship of cause and effect among events at all levels. He aims to demonstrate that France's failure to side with the Spanish loyalists strengthened fascism everywhere, that private lives and public events are closely linked, and that decisions and actions at one level affect all other levels.[5]

This is Aragon's great design, but unfortunately the novel (and the reader's ability to absorb its contents) can only be stretched so far. The author's overambitious extension of the form results in psychedelic writing. Scenes flicker past the reader's eyes with the speed and effect of a revolving light dome casting ever-changing colors, lights, and shadows on a dance floor filled with marijuana-smoking couples. Although, in a discotheque, the ears are deafened by the unmerciful beating of the amplified sound, and the eyes blinded by the unnatural flickering of constantly changing images, at least the body can still mechanically continue to move. But when the mind of the reader is pounded by a similar experience, it goes numb. The question remains whether, in *Les Communistes,* Aragon was a failure or a forerunner. If he had jumbled the chronology of the action, his novel might have been a precursor of the *nouveau roman.* Perhaps a new genre in the future will retrospectively honor Aragon as a great innovator.[6]

The Ideal Couple

The foregoing is not to say that *Les Communistes* does not have a structure or principal characters. Throughout the many interruptions, the reader follows a love story, and a most unusual one at that. Cécile d'Aigrefeuille, the daughter of an important banker, is married to Fred Wisner, the nephew of the famous auto manufacturer whom we have encountered in *Le Monde réel.* On the surface, theirs seems an ideal marriage: both are beautiful and rich; they have nice children; they move in the finest circles, and, in fact, one of Cécile's best friends is Georgette Leurtillois, the wife of our old acquaintance Aurélien. But Cécile gradually realizes that her husband is an anti-Semite (she has some Jewish blood in her) and that he and his friends are heartless, unfeeling people.

One day her good-for-nothing brother, Nicolas, arrives with a friend, Jean de Moncey, who resembles Armand Barbentane in many ways: rather timid and undecided, he vacillates in the choice of his profession. At first attracted to the priesthood, he eventually decides to study medicine. Jean and Cécile, who are both seeking their place in the world, fall in love, have some misunderstandings, and are completely separated when Jean joins an ambulance unit at the outbreak of World War II. Meanwhile Cécile matures through the experience of talking to an invalid soldier, her maid's brother, and by the example of Yvonne, Jean's sister, who is imprisoned for her communist activities. Cécile takes care of Yvonne's children, and the couple is united when Jean finds her again upon returning home after the French defeat.

Their love is as intense as that of Aurélien and Bérénice in Aragon's earlier novel; in fact, it is more authentic in the author's view, because the two are united not only in their personal, but also in their political, passion. Nevertheless, Jean does not have the interesting personality of

Aurélien, nor Cécile the mysteriousness of Bérénice. Of course, war-time does not provide them with the luxury of leisure, and they also have to share the spotlight not only with long war episodes but also with those whom Aragon no doubt intended to be the real heroes of the novel.

The Communist Heroes

Strange heroes and heroines they are, these Communists. None of them is memorable in the manner of the great Wisner, Joseph Quesnel, Pierre Mercadier, Edmond Barbentane, or Aurélien Leurtillois. Only Armand Barbentane and Jean de Moncey emerge from the crowd of nearly anonymous, antlike cell members. Sincere, honest, warm-hearted, they lick stamps, distribute pamphlets, read *L'Humanité* for their daily enlightenment; and, when the newspaper is prohibited, they type stencils and run ditto machines. Courageous, they are prepared to go to prison; patriotic, they make model soldiers. Among them we find people of all sorts: intellectuals (Armand Barbentane), teachers (Cormeilles), simple workers (Blanchard), as well as sympathizers (Watrin, the lawyer).

The Communist Religion

It seems no accident that both Armand Barbentane and Jean de Moncey flirted with the priesthood, for communism is a religion that one can turn to after losing one's faith without having to change habits too much. Stalin is God; Soviet Russia is paradise; Maurice Thorez, the leader of the French Communist party, represents Jesus Christ; the party stands for the Church; and *L'Humanité* is the Communists' Bible. They even have their martyrs; the French Communist deputies who have been imprisoned after the party was dissolved and who may be condemned to death. Aragon underlines this religious aspect of communism when he says of Watrin, who is busy with his private happiness while the Communist deputies are being tried, "He knows very well, at this moment of Good Friday, this new Pontius Pilate, that this time nobody can wash his hands of it." [Il sait bien, à cette minute du Vendredi-Saint, ce nouveau Ponce Pilate, que cette fois, personne, personne ne pourra s'en laver les mains. (*Les Communistes,* 4:121)]

Not unlike God, Stalin has strange and unfathomable ways of acting. How can one explain the pact he made with Nazi Germany to divide up Poland? When Robert Gaillard, Yvonne's husband, asks advice on how to reply to the criticism from all sides, Professor Cormeilles says, "The terrible thing is how to answer without *L'Huma* the questions people ask." [Le professeur Cormeilles disait, le terrible c'est que sans *L'Huma* comment répondre aux questions que les gens se posent? (*Les Communistes,* 1:182)]

The contrast is striking between these idealistic Communists and the brutal Fascists and their allies, the police. Fred Wisner, Cécile's husband, is nearly killed by Gaëtan Le Bozec, a Fascist goon with whom he had been involved in violent rightist activities in his younger days and who now demands to be employed in the Wisner factory.

Another contrast, this one between himself and Maurice Barrès, is indicated by Aragon when he compares the respective attitudes of Armand Barbentane and a doctor who is a member of the Action Française.

The difference between him [Armand] and the other is that the other does not believe in the existence of the French people. When he speaks of the "real country," he means the country with its traditions, that is to say, the traditions that appeal to him, with their dead, and the earth on the dead, which keeps them down; and all the while you can make them speak the way you want to, but all that without the living, without the people who make the traditions. Armand's optimism rests on the very existence of the French people.

[La différence entre lui [Armand] et l'autre, c'est que l'autre, il ne croit pas à l'existence du peuple français. Quand il parle du *pays réel,* c'est le pays avec ses traditions, c'est-à-dire les traditions qui lui chantent, avec ses morts, et la terre sur les morts, qui pèse, alors on les fait parler comme on veut, mais sans les vivants, sans le peuple qui fait les traditions. L'optimisme d'Armand tient dans l'existence même du peuple français (*Les Communistes,* 2:59).]

Aragon's Theses

As a novel, *Les Communistes* is a letdown from *Le Monde réel.* The characters as individuals are less interesting, the plot line gets blurred, even the style has lost some of its sharpness. But ideology compensates for these defects. In his earlier work Aragon exposed the thesis that the capitalists had wanted war and had been responsible for World War I, but this thesis was overshadowed by the ambitions, loves, successes, or failures of the main characters.

In *Les Communistes,* two theses come through very clearly. The more immediate one claims that the French government did not make war on

Nazi Germany, but on the French Communists, and consequently on the workers. This argument appears over and over again, and it matters little for our purposes whether it can stand up under historical scrutiny.[7] Spied on, provoked, always under suspicion, the Communists in the French Army, some of whom are officers, have to be constantly on their guard. It is like a war within the war, and it lends additional dramatic tension to the war episodes.

The second thesis states that France was defeated not because of German superiority but because the capitalist and republican system produced statesmen and military chiefs who were incompetent, quarreled among themselves, or followed their personal interests rather than those of the country.

By contrast, we see what sort of person communism produces. No matter what their ordeals may be, these men and women remain faithful to their ideal and will sacrifice everything to achieve the final victory. Quartered in a magnificent mansion, where now soldiers trample on well-kept lawns,

Pierre Cormeilles, professor of history and geography at the Lycée Janson de Sailly, kept looking at this eighteenth-century scenery, a perfect setting for Choderlos de Laclos. . . . Who might be the proprietors? Merchants? Aristocrats? "It would make," he thought, "a wonderful rest home." . . . Since his trip through the Crimea, he automatically had this reaction when looking at historic mansions.

[Pierre Cormeilles, professeur d'histoire et géographie à Janson de Sailly, s'attachait à ce décor du XVIIIe siècle, à ce cadre pour Choderlos de Laclos. . . . A qui cela pouvait-il bien être? Quels marchands ou aristocrates? "On en ferait, pensait-il, une merveilleuse maison de repos." . . . Depuis son voyage en Crimée, ça devenait un tic pour lui que de penser ça devant les demeures historiques. (*Les Communistes*, 5:34)]

Obviously, Aragon too had traveled to the Soviet Union since writing *Le Monde réel*. Although exquisitely cultured in literature, painting, and music,[8] and with good will, Aragon's call for rest homes recalls Goering's infamous attack on culture.[9] When observing this evolution, we can retrospectively sympathize with the dilemma of Stendhal, torn between a liberal heart and a cultured mind.

Despite these shortcomings, Aragon adds his milestone to the road the French novel has traveled since Stendhal wrote *Le Rouge et le noir* (1830). By viewing the differences in ambitions we can understand the changes that had taken place in social attitudes during some one hundred years.

Stendhal's Julien Sorel is concerned with social inequities, but only insofar as they concern him as an individual. All he asks for is that there should be more room at the top, so that the most capable can rise. Despite his reading of Danton, it is only romantic Mathilde de La Mole who sees in him a revolutionary. Give him a military commission and a place among the elite, and his social agitation will stop at once.

In Marcel Proust's *A la recherche du temps perdu,* the wealthy and cultured bourgeois want to have their assets recognized in the form of noble titles, and the social classes eventually mingle as Mme Verdurin marries the duc de Guermantes. In *Le Monde réel,* too, there is mingling, not so much of social castes as of ambitious young men and established wealth.

But in *Les Communistes,* the final stage of the process is achieved. The Communist militants are not satisfied with individual promotions of whatever sort; they want to overthrow the existing social and economic order, so that an entire class may rise and destroy or bring down to its own level the classes above it, a longtime process for which Julien Sorel would not have had enough patience.

It is worthy of note that both Jean de Moncey and Cécile d'Aigrefeuille are nobles, even though not of high rank. But whereas Julien Sorel wanted to rise from peasant to aristocrat, these modern nobles want to descend from the level of aristocrats to that of proletarians. Like their liberal ancestors on the night of 4 August 1789, these two lovers cast away whatever privileges they may still happen to possess to join the new revolution. Only this will be the last time such a gesture will be made. Jean and Cécile are not stepping down just one flight to join the third estate—they are taking the elevator down to the basement. After that there will be no more estates or social classes to join, because the classless society will have come about.

The Dangers of Relevance

The classless society is the ultimate symbol of hope that underlies Aragon's ten volumes of novels. The hope still existed, but Stalin, his god, was not immortal. *Les Communistes* was to cover the period from February 1939 to January 1945, and the publication of the next volume (June 1940–January 1943) was scheduled for the year 1952. But this volume never appeared. In that year Stalin passed on to whatever thereafter had been reserved for him. And shortly after, Nikita Khrushchev revealed terrible things about the dead god—who may not have been a god after all.

If *Les Communistes* can teach us anything about the durability of political literature, it is that the writer takes a great risk when he ties himself too closely to figures who still have to appear before the court of history, because if history condemns them, the writer's work will suffer the fate of an accomplice.

Chapter Seven

The Greek Connection

Occupation and Resistance, 1940–44

When speaking of this tragic period, one must continually bear in mind the conditions in France at the time. In June 1940, the French Army was defeated; the roads were crowded with people transporting themselves and their most precious and necessary belongings by any means, ranging from automobiles to pushcarts; and the French in general were bewildered and humiliated, still unable to comprehend the disaster that had befallen them. By contrast, the victorious Germans were occupying the country with the same efficiency they had demonstrated during the short campaign, when they had demolished the French forces and made a mockery of French illusions of invulnerability.

On 14 June 1940, the government moved to Bordeaux, where Reynaud was pressured to sign an armistice. On 16 June he resigned, suggesting to President Lebrun that Marshall Pétain be appointed to head the government. On 22 June the armistice was signed, under the terms of which France was divided into occupied and unoccupied zones. The former contained the Atlantic and Channel coasts and the most important areas of northern, eastern, and western France, including Paris. The government set up quarters at the health resort of Vichy.

On 10 July the members of the National Assembly present voted full powers to Pétain, and, shortly after, new constitutional laws were adopted under which Pétain assumed a personal regime as Chef de l'Etat français, a title which avoided the word République. Technically, the Vichy regime remained an interim government, and, in this sense only, the Third Republic continued to exist, albeit in a state of abeyance. But for all practical purposes it was dead, killed by war the way it had been born, but ready to be resuscitated by a miracle, or for lack of a better system in better times to come.

It is easy to condemn Pétain and Laval, his vice-premier, and they were certainly far from angelic, but those who level accusations must also be prepared to answer some obvious questions: What other solution was there in these circumstances? And who else could have assumed these functions?

As Creon, of Anouilh's *Antigone,* will state in a little while, somebody had to assume the burden of government, somebody had to say yes, and Pétain obviously was that man. Perhaps he said yes more eagerly than Creon and probably for different reasons, but it should be remembered that there was no line of candidates, that he had been legally appointed by President Lebrun on Paul Reynaud's advice, and that former government officials, including Daladier, were then attempting to reach North Africa, a luxury very few French had at their disposal.

If there had not been a Pétain in place at the time the armistice was signed, the Nazis could easily have appointed a German *Gauleiter,* or they could have chosen out-and-out collaborationists, such as the ex-Communist Doriot or the ex-Socialist Déat. In either case, France would have lost any semblance of identity and been turned into a large German province and an ally in the war.

The trouble with governments is that they not only tell their people that they are invincible but actually believe it themselves. Consequently, there are no handbooks on how to run an occupied country. Considering that in a war one side is likely to lose and that France had been occupied twice before (in 1814 and in 1870), such a manual was long overdue.[1]

The situation of the Vichy government was such that, no matter how it acted, it was bound to be blamed by one side or another. If it refused to cooperate with German demands, its members would be ousted and replaced by fervent collaborationists; in that case, the French people would have had every right to condemn Pétain. If it acceded to German demands, no matter to what degree, it would be condemned by those who insisted that an occupation government could and should carry out a policy of constant resistance.

As if this were not enough trouble, the Vichy government was far from harmonious. Laval wanted Pétain to be a ceremonial president in the tradition of the Third Republic. He plotted to take power and was dismissed in December 1941, but returned in April 1942. Then there were the enthusiastic collaborators, Fascists such as Déat and Doriot, who, disillusioned with the delaying tactics of Vichy, went to Paris and attacked the government from there. Finally, there were the technocrats, who ran the actual government operations and survived its fall.

Regardless of postmortem claims, there is no doubt that the majority of the French in France supported the Vichy regime, at least to the extent to which the French ever support any government. Pétain and Laval adopted a policy best described by the popular expression that if you can't beat them, join them. Marshall Pétain was not much of a political thinker, although he obviously believed in order and discipline, and he took on his function the way he would have accepted the appointment of supreme commander. If he was to be put on trial after the end of the war, it should have been for his role in determining French military policy prior to World War II rather than for his actions in the Vichy government. Laval bet more consciously, it seems, on the odds that Nazi Germany and fascism were the wave of the future, and as a trained politician, he acted in politics the way George Sand had in literature when she said, "Monsters are in fashion; let us make monsters." [Les monstres sont à la mode, faisons des monstres.]

The Vichy regime faced so many problems that it had to operate on a day-to-day basis: settling refugees, helping demobilized soldiers return to civilian life, and trying to keep France going while Germany took a large part of its raw materials, machinery, and manpower. Close to seven hundred thousand French workers were conscripted for work in Germany, and an incredible occupation cost, rising to five hundred million francs per day, had to be paid.

We still do not know whether Laval was sincere in his collaboration or played a double game, officially carrying out German demands but actually delivering as little as possible. Where human lives were threatened, he opted for the lesser number. He set up a special police that turned over to the Germans captured Resistance fighters rather than risk the lives of large numbers of hostages, and he sacrificed foreign-born Jews in return for a promise that French Jews would be spared. The important politicians of the Third Republic were interned and some of them, including Daladier and Blum, tried at Riom in 1942. But the defendants were able to raise so many embarrassing questions about the causes for the collapse of France that the trial was abandoned.

Obviously, acts of atrocity were committed or abetted by the Vichy government, even if done under duress, and responsibility must be assigned for them. But the agonizing questions of who else was prepared and acceptable to head an occupation government, and what else could have been done, still remain to be answered.

In this respect those who had managed to leave France and set up a resistance group in London found themselves in a much more comfortable position. Their goals were clearly defined and their consciences were clear. General Charles de Gaulle, at forty-nine the youngest general in the French Army, had warned against the limitations of the Maginot line and proposed a modern style of warfare. He escaped to London, where he formed a loose government-in-exile. His famous call for resistance, on 18 June 1940, met with little response at first. The French in France had another priority at the time: survival.

The German invasion of Russia in June 1941 gave a new impetus to resistance in France. After the Russo-German pact, the Communist party had tacitly aligned with Nazi Germany. It had opposed the defense of Poland and de Gaulle's call to resistance, and had been hostile to Great Britain. But now, as the group most experienced in militant action, the Communists eagerly joined the Resistance movement. Admiral Darlan, who had replaced Laval in Vichy, also changed sides in November 1942, when he happened to be in Algiers during the American campaign in North Africa. He was assassinated soon thereafter, but the orders to scuttle the French navy, which he had prepared in 1940, were carried out in 1942 at Toulon before the Germans could get there.

It is difficult to estimate the effectiveness of the Resistance in France. Its numbers were swelled by workers who wanted to escape compulsory service in Germany. De Gaulle dispatched Jean Moulin, who succeeded in coordinating the various Resistance groups in 1943. He was arrested and killed, and Georges Bidault took his place. Operating from North Africa, Resistance fighters liberated Corsica in September 1943; acts of sabotage kept large numbers of German troops tied down in France; and when the Allies invaded France in June 1944, calls went out to the French Resistance, which rose up, sometimes too early, and diverted German defense efforts. About twenty-four thousand of them were killed in battle.

Nevertheless, the Allies never took the French Resistance very seriously. Both Churchill and Roosevelt had little liking for de Gaulle, and he was informed of the Allied invasion only at the last moment. Still, it was he and the Free French forces who triumphantly entered Paris at its liberation on 25 August 1944, when he was enthusiastically greeted by the population and now recognized by all as the leader of liberated France.

World War II ended in Europe in May 1945. It had been the most costly and, at the same time, the most unnecessary war of all times. It had not started because Germany was overcrowded or threatened by attack, but had been conceived in the Wagnerian delirium of a murderous, shouting and stomping madman. Perhaps the British and French statesmen of the time thought that was the way German is spoken; at any rate, it had been easily within their power to call the repeated bluffs of Nazi Germany.

Now Europe was in ruins, millions had died or been maimed for life. The war had solved no problems; it had only created new ones. Nazi Germany was destroyed, but the new threat to freedom came from a strengthened Soviet Union, which was gobbling up its neighbors. France had to undertake the task of rebuilding its destroyed areas, of setting up a new government, and of dealing with its disintegrating colonial empire. But first, after four years of occupation, a cry for revenge arose. It was a time of reckoning.

Chronology

1940: French government moves to Vichy; Pétain obtains full powers; ministry of Laval; Hitler-Pétain interview at Montoire; Laval dismissed.

1941: Darlan takes Laval's place; Communists join Resistance after German invasion of Russia; dismissal of General Weygand.

1942: Riom trial of former politicians (Daladier, Blum); Laval returns to power; Allied invasion of North Africa; Germans move into unoccupied France; assassination of Darlan.

1943: Committee of National Liberation formed at Algiers under de Gaulle and Giraud; Resistance forces liberate Corsica; Sartre: *Les Mouches.*

1944: Paris collaborationists enter Vichy government; Anouilh: *Antigone;* Allies land in Normandy; de Gaulle enters Paris; Ho Chi Minh proclaims independence of Vietnam.

Jean-Paul Sartre

A *Nativity Play for Prisoners of War:* Bariona

Life did not stop in France during the German occupation. Parisian theaters, encouraged by the German authorities, reopened and did a thriving business. Of course, plays had to be submitted to censorship, like all other media of communication and entertainment. Just the same, the Germans were taking a considerable chance in their policy of turning Paris into a recreation center for their troops. If they had studied French literary history, they would have learned that the French traditionally have been very successful in conveying defiant messages in plays right under the nose (and eyes) of censors. We need only recall a number of Voltaire's plays or Beaumarchais's *Le Mariage de Figaro,* described in volume 1 of this study.

Tradition was not to be denied and, as the Germans began to suffer reverses and French resistance grew stronger, opposition literature appeared. Two playwrights produced works that can be considered classic models of plays that send out secret codes to those who can look beyond the literal text and read between the lines. Although Jean-Paul Sartre's *Les Mouches (The Flies)* and Jean Anouilh's *Antigone* are quite different plays, both are based on classical Greek sources. The obvious advantages of this choice of material are that censors are awed by Greek authors and that the modern playwright can claim that any objectionable passage was already contained in the Greek original, or that all he was doing was adapting the material to modern taste and demands.

Sartre had tried his hand at this kind of writing while he was a prisoner in stalag 12 at Trier. In 1940 he wrote *Bariona; ou, Le Fils du tonnerre,* which was performed by French prisoners on Christmas of that year. A supposed Nativity play, it was actually addressed to his fellow prisoners to give them hope and to demonstrate the change the hero undergoes from refusal to act to total commitment.

The play takes place during the occupation of Palestine by the Romans, and Bariona, the young leader of a Jewish village, has agreed to pay new taxes but has decided to resist any further imposition. The news that the Messiah has been born makes the villagers hope for a new age; only Bariona does not believe in the angel's message. Afraid that his people will be lulled into inactivity by a peaceful Messiah, Bariona decides to go to Bethlehem and kill the child. Seeing the child and Joseph, who is in the same state of uncertainty as he, Bariona abandons his project. A talk with King Balthazar convinces him that the Messiah is the incarnation of human freedom. Thus encouraged, he leads his men in a fight against Herod's troops who have been dispatched to kill the Messiah. He now welcomes the child his own wife is carrying, as a symbol of hope regained. The play ends with an appeal by Bariona to the imprisoned spectators not to be discouraged by their present situation but to have hopes for a better future.

Sartre himself supplies all the clues we need (if, indeed, they are still needed) in writings and interviews.

When I was a prisoner is Germany in 1940, I wrote, staged, and acted in a Christmas play that, while pulling the wool over the eyes of the German censors by means of simple symbols, was addressed to my fellow prisoners.[2]

Finding out that I had written a mystery play, some people have gone so far as to suppose I was going through a spiritual crisis. Not at all! I was linked with the priests who were prisoners in the camp by a common rejection of Nazism. The Nativity seemed to be a subject more likely to appeal to both Christians and unbelievers. And it was agreed that I should say what I liked.

What was important to me in this experiment was that as a prisoner I was going to be able to address my fellow prisoners and raise problems we all shared. The script was full of allusions to circumstances of the moment, which were perfectly clear to each of us. The envoy from Rome to Jerusalem was in our minds the German. Our guards saw him as the Englishman in his colonies![3]

Sartre judged *Bariona* to be a bad play and would not permit future performances of it, but the experiment, as well as the experience gained from it, revealed two important facts to him: 1) that plays adapted from unattackable sources (the Bible, Greek mythology) gave the modern author a great deal of latitude; and 2) that the German censors could be more easily fooled than one would have suspected.

These realizations helped him no doubt when he undertook a far more extensive and courageous enterprise: to put on the stage, right in Paris, a play that would speak not just to fellow prisoners in a restricted camp but to the entire French people during the German occupation.

A Model Existentialist: Les Mouches

Sartre's play *Les Mouches* was first performed on 3 June 1943 at the Théâtre de la Cité[4] under the direction of Charles Dullin. On the surface the text respects all the basic elements of the Orestes subject. The only important character Sartre added is Jupiter, with whom Orestes has several discussions.

The son of Agamemnon and Clytemnestra, Orestes is exiled after the slaying of his father by his mother and her lover Aegisthus. He returns to the city of Argos, and urged on by his sister Electra, he kills the royal couple. While Electra is overcome by regret, Orestes feels no remorse and is pursued by the Furies in the shape of flies, who follow him as he leaves the city.

Underneath the pretext of merely modernizing a classical Greek play, Sartre reveals what he wants to convey to "trained eyes," to use Voltaire's term. He not only deals with the evolution of an authentic existentialist hero; he also sends a message to the Resistance fighters and to the French people.

The existentialist hero has been extensively treated in the voluminous literature about Sartre and existentialism and will therefore be only briefly summarized. Reduced to its simplest terms, Sartre's view states that we are thrown into a world which, in and of itself, has no meaning or purpose. In such a world without God or any guiding or innate principles, we are condemned to be totally free and we must define ourselves by the choices we make. To choose means to act, for we are in the world and in a particular situation. Being totally free, we are also totally responsible, because we are not alone in the world, and by our acts we not only define ourselves but determine what kind of a world we want to live in. Once we realize all this, we are gripped by anguish, and many are tempted to escape into bad faith by using all kinds of excuses for failing to act or for acting badly. But the authentic hero accepts total freedom and responsibility and defines himself by an act that will favor or enlarge freedom.

Les Mouches is a model play for illustrating the evolution of a hero from indifference to total and authentic commitment. At first Orestes feels unconcerned about the situation in Argos. Aegisthus and Clytemnestra have made their guilt collective by having it shared by the whole population, but Orestes refuses to pronounce judgment. "I don't care; I don't live here." [Je m'en moque; je ne suis pas d'ici (*Les Mouches,* 29)].[5] As a result of the teachings of his tutor, he is now "wise like an old man, free of all servitude and belief, without family, without country, without religion, without a profession, free for all commitments and knowing that one should never commit oneself." [. . . avisé comme un vieillard, affranchi de toutes les servitudes et de toutes les croyances, sans famille, sans patrie, sans religion, sans métier, libre pour tous les engagements et sachant qu'il ne faut jamais s'engager (*Les Mouches,* 26).] In short, Orestes is free to go in any direction yet tied to none, *disponible,* an ideal André Gide had proposed in such works as his novel *L'Immoraliste.*

Orestes realizes that he can define himself by an act, even if it were a crime. But before he can act, he must first liberate himself from the gods, so that even a miraculous sign produced by Jupiter no longer detains him from his act.[6] Having acted authentically by freeing the people of Argos from the oppression of guilt imposed on them by the royal couple and Jupiter, Orestes feels no remorse. By contrast, Electra, who had passionately urged him to slay the royal couple, cannot withstand the attacks of the Furies, and she repents. Although the population of Argos reacts in a hostile manner, Orestes will take the Furies with him and thus free the people of their guilt.

Sartre's Intentions

Those who attended the performances of *Les Mouches* during the German occupation were probably less struck by its illustration of the model existentialist hero than by the plot's implications for their historical situation. To a French mind at the time these parallels must have appeared:

Aegisthus (Nazi Germany) has married Clytemnestra (the Vichy government) after they have assassinated Agamemnon (France prior to the occupation). Orestes (the Resistance) has come to free Argos (occupied France) from the oppression and guilt imposed on it by the royal couple, supported by religious authority (Jupiter), which has traditionally cooperated with oppressive governments. Finally, Electra represents those French who are sympathetic to the Resistance but do not have the strength of character to commit themselves without remorse.[7]

Concerning his intentions, Sartre has supplied us with abundant information. During a discussion on 1 February 1948, when *Les Mouches* was performed at the Hebbel Theater in Berlin, the author freely answered questions.

The play must be accounted for by the circumstances of the time. From 1941 to 1943 many people were extremely anxious for the French to plunge into repentance. The Nazis primarily, and Pétain too, and likewise his press. The French had to be convinced, and had to convince themselves, that we had been madmen, that we had sunk to the lowest depths of degradation, that the Popular Front had lost us the war, that our leaders had been derelict in their duty, and so on and so forth. . . . The aim was to plunge us into such a state of repentance, of shame, that we would be incapable of putting up any resistance. We were to find satisfaction in our repentance, even pleasure in it. . . .

By writing my play I was trying by my own unaided effort, feeble though it might be, to do what I could to root out this sickness of repentance, the complacence in repentance and shame. What was needed at the time was to revive the French people, to restore their courage. The people who were revolted by the Vichy government, who regarded it as an abject thing, all those in France who wished totally to reject domination by the Nazis, understood the play remarkably well. . . .

The second reason is a more personal one. At that time there was the problem of attacks against the Nazis, and not only the Nazis but all members of the Wehrmacht. Those who took part in these attacks obviously did so without losing their peace of mind about it. They certainly never dreamed of making it a matter of conscience. In their view, they were at war, and throwing a grenade at the enemy was an act of war. But a further problem became attached to it—and it was a moral problem—that of the hostages. The Wehrmacht had started executing them at that time. Six or eight hostages were shot for every three Germans; and that had very important moral implications. Not only were these hostages innocent, but, it should especially be borne in mind, they had done nothing against the Wehrmacht, and most of them were not even members of the Resistance. . . . The problem of these attacks was, therefore, of prime importance. Anyone who committed an attack like that had to know that, unless he gave himself up, fellow Frenchmen would be shot at random. So he was liable to a second form of repentance: he had to resist the temptation to give himself up. This is how the allegory in my play is to be understood.

That is why people did not consider the play pessimistic at the time it was performed, but quite the reverse—optimistic. In it I was saying to my fellow Frenchmen: You do not have to repent, even those of you who have in a sense become murderers; you must assume your own responsibility for your acts, even if they have caused the deaths of innocent persons.[8]

Sartre's explanations are very helpful, because they reveal that, at least in his view, Les Mouches is not only a play about resistance and revenge but also (perhaps primarily) about repentance, guilt, and shame. Liberating the people of Argos consists not only in the slaying of their oppressors; Orestes also has to take away with him the traditional feelings of repentance and guilt, which the royal couple had imposed and which are represented by the Flies. It should also be noted parenthetically that Les Mouches is a play against collective guilt, a view perfectly in accordance with existentialist principles but one not always accepted by many of Sartre's political allies.

At another point in the discussion, Sartre deals with the thorny question of how the play ends. Having committed his authentic act, Orestes, instead of staying on in Argos to assume the throne and assure freedom for the people, leaves the city haughtily, almost disdainfully.

Besides, his gesture of assuming the guilt of the people inevitably leads to comparisons with the life of Jesus Christ. To these questions Sartre replied:

> Orestes finally decides in favor of freedom; he wants to liberate himself by liberating his people, If we do not quite understaand that, it is perhaps because we do not think enough about the situation in Argos. But in the theater, on the stage as well as in life, this free choice amounts always to a true liberation. It is the expression of a freedom that affirms its own existence. . . .
>
> I had not thought of comparing Orestes and Christ. In my mind, Orestes is at no time a hero. I do not even know whether he is exceptionally gifted. But he is the one who does not want to be cut off from his people. He is the first to take the road of liberation, at the very moment when the masses can and should become conscious of themselves; he is the one who, by his act, first shows them the way. Once he has succeeded in this, he can return in peace to his anonymous state and rest in the midst of his people.[9]

Critical Reactions

Despite its popularity in the post–World War II years, *Les Mouches* was anything but a success when first staged. Sartre himself informs us that it was played in a half-empty theater, and it had only some fifty performances.[10] Without Dullin's stubborn faith in the play, it would not have had even that many. One reason for the apathy of the public may have been the original reviews, which criticized just about everything: the direction, the scenery, and the play itself. "Giraudoux's *Electre* reworked by a belated dadaist or surrealist, not to say by a neurotic" (André Castelot, *La Gerbe,* 17 June 1943); "a heavy and long play, . . . a spectacle that puts us back into an unlikely cubist and dadaist bric-a-brac" (Alain Laubreaux, *Le Petit Parisien,* 5 June 1943); "Sartre seems to be a writer of essays rather than a playwright" (Jacques Berland, *Paris-Soir,* 15 June 1943). Only the clandestine *Les Lettres Françaises,* no. 12, which praised the political message of the play in an unsigned article by Michel Leiris, and Maurice Rostand, in *Paris-Midi* of 7 June, 1943, had favorable things to say about the play.

A good deal of the criticism is justified. *Les Mouches* is not a great play. It is verbose, long for what it has to say, and contains too may philosophico-psychological speeches and too little dramatic action. Its subsequent popularity was due primarily to the interest in existentialism that developed during the postwar years. Once existentialism was no longer "in," *Les Mouches* faded along with the philosophy.

What is most surprising is that only the clandestine *Les Lettres Fran-çaises* and the critic of the *Pariser Zeitung* detected any political meaning in the play, and the latter took care to gloss this over by favorable comments on other aspects of the play. "Most critics pretended to have seized not a single allusion," Simone de Beauvoir recalls. "They gave the play a good beating, but using as their weapon purely literary pretexts."[11] Perhaps there existed even among the literary critics of the collaborationist press some sense of patriotism, which resulted in a tacit conspiracy of silence, so as not to reveal to the German censors what should have struck them as obvious. After all, not every literary critic writing in the Vichy press was necessarily a collaborationist at heart, and even the most subservient French Nazi sympathizer would be tempted to turn his nose up at the German masters from time to time, especially when it came to dealing with French language and literature.

How the Play Got By the Censors

How, indeed, was it possible that *Les Mouches* received the green light from the German censors, who should have at once realized Sartre's intentions as he expressed them in *Carrefour* of 9 September 1944. "Why would I make the Greeks declaim . . . if it were not for the purpose of disguising one's real thoughts under a fascist regime?"

Some interesting information on this intriguing question is contained in the memoirs of Gerhard Heller, who held the rank of lieutenant in the German army and who was assigned as *Sonderführer* to the *Propaganda-Staffel,* located at 52, avenue des Champs-Elysées in Paris, and later to the Germany embassy. He occupied these functions from November 1940 until August 1944. Steeped in French literature, Heller seems to have made a courageous effort to protect French authors from the onslaught of German censorship and possible arrest. Although personal accounts of that period should be viewed with extreme skepticism, testimony from writers such as François Mauriac lends considerable credibility to his accounts.

Concerning Sartre, Heller remarks that he often saw the existentialist author at the Café de Flore but preferred not to approach him because it might have been dangerous for both of them. He then continues:

I nonetheless facilitated, without his knowledge, the acceptance of his play *Les Mouches* by the German authorities. At that time I was already attached to the embassy. Somebody from the Propaganda Section who was in charge of theater asked me: "Could you come with me to a rehearsal of *Les Mouches?* Many French say that it is a Resistance play. I would like to have your opinion." I went with him to the rehearsal at the Théâtre de la Cité (Sarah Bernhardt) and we wrote the following joint review: "The play has nothing to do with the Resistance. The subject is drawn from classical antiquity. It is a great play that does honor to universal literature." And despite the hostility of the collaborationist press, *Les Mouches* received permission to be performed. Sartre was courageous: I had very clearly understood that the words and actions of Electra and Orestes were aimed not only at Aegisthus and Clytemnestra.[12]

In the long run the circumstances surrounding the performance of Sartre's play may be as interesting as the play itself. But *Les Mouches* remains a daring act by a writer who believed that words can move men and who always had the courage to write and to speak them.

Jean Anouilh

An Offer You Can Refuse: Antigone

In contrast to Sartre's *Les Mouches,* Jean Anouilh's *Antigone* was an immediate and lasting success. First performed at the Théâtre de l'Atelier on 4 February 1944 and directed by André Barsacq, it had 475 performances during 1944 and 1945.

Anouilh adheres very closely to the Greek play by Sophocles. Oedipus, once he has discovered that he killed his father and married his own mother, blinds himself, is chased out of the city of Thebes while his two sons, Eteocles and Polynices, do nothing to help him, and, accompanied by his daughter Antigone, dies mysteriously near Colonus. Returning to Thebes, Antigone finds her brothers engaged in a struggle over who is to assume the throne. In their combat the two brothers kill each other. Creon, Antigone's uncle, now becomes the ruler of Thebes. In order to set an example, he orders that Eteocles be buried with all the honors. But the corpse of Polynices, who had called on help from outside forces and had thus been a traitor to his city, is to lie unburied. Antigone refuses to obey this order and, despite Creon's efforts to have her change her mind, continues to throw earth over her dead brother's body, so that Creon is forced to condemn her to be buried alive. Haemon, Creon's son and fiancé of Antigone, rushes to her prison and kills himself when he finds that she has hung herself.

Eurydice, Creon's wife, cuts her throat upon learning of her son's death. In the end Creon remains all alone.

All these elements can be found in Sophocles' play. What has changed is the emphasis and the decor. For one thing, the performers wear modern dress: the principal personages in dress suits and elegant robes, and the guards in smoking jackets that have been colored black. Anouilh not only emphasizes the immaturity of Antigone but indicates that she does not want to give up her ideal of the purity of childhood. And, in contrast with Sophocles, Creon is not a cruel dictator but a sensitive man, who has assumed the burden of ruling over Thebes from a sense of duty because somebody has to do the job. Again in contrast with Sophocles, the people are on his side. Finally, the guards are depicted in greater detail: they are men who will serve whoever is in power, insensitive, materialistic, concerned only with supporting their families, eating and drinking well, and petty advancement.

For Anouilh, the dramatic issue is not between an excessive authoritarianism and religious belief in burial, but between an obsession with order and discipline on the one hand and a sense of ethics on the other. This is why the roles of Creon and Antigone are carefully balanced; one might even suggest that the author does his best to give Creon advantages over Antigone. To begin with, Creon is more mature. He has reached adulthood by giving up his childhood dreams of purity and by looking at life in a practical way. He reluctantly has agreed to take on his responsibilities, because somebody had to say yes. He would have preferred not to be obliged to leave Polynices unburied. He sincerely wants to avoid having to order Antigone's death; in fact, he wants her to be happy in her future marriage to his son Haemon, raise a family, and live a normal life.

Dark-skinned, skinny, nowhere as pretty as her sister Ismene, Antigone strikes us as fanatic, childish, unreasonable, someone who says no, who refuses the happiness offered to her. And for what? Creon reveals to her that he is not sure of the identity of the two corpses he has found. He decided that the one better preserved would be designated as Eteocles. Besides, Antigone learns from him that her brothers were vicious rascals, and that Polynices was a drunkard, who hit his father in an argument. Momentarily she is so overcome by these revelations that she agrees to give up her quest to bury her brother. But when Creon proposes his conception of a sort of bourgeois happiness, she returns to her original position.

The high point of the play is the dramatic confrontation between

Creon, the compromiser, the practical and paternal ruler; and Antigone, the uncompromising seeker of the absolute, of the purity of childhood. It is, apparently, the argument between the yes-sayer and the no-sayer; and even though Creon claims to have the bad role, in reality he has the good one. [13]

ANTIGONE: Why do you do it at all?

CREON: My dear, I woke up one morning and found myself King of Thebes. God knows, there were other things I loved in life more than power.

ANTIGONE: Then you should have said no.

CREON: Yes, I could have done that. Only, I felt that it would have been cowardly. I should have been like a workman who turns down a job that has to be done. So I said yes.

ANTIGONE: So much the worse for you, then. I didn't say yes. I can say no to anything I think vile, and I don't have to count the cost. Because you said yes, all that you can do, for all your crown and your trappings, and your guards—all that you can do is to have me killed. . . .

CREON: But God in heaven! Won't you try to understand me! . . . There had to be one man who said yes. Somebody had to agree to captain the ship. She had sprung a hundred leaks; she was loaded to the water line with crime, ignorance, poverty. . . .

ANTIGONE: I am not here to understand. That's all very well for you. I am here to say no to you, and die.

CREON: It is easy to say no.

ANTIGONE: Not always.

CREON: It is easy to say no. To say yes, you have to sweat and roll up your sleeves and plunge both hands into life up to the elbows. It is easy to say no, even if saying no means death. All you have to do is to sit still and wait. [14]

[ANTIGONE. Pourqoi le faites-vous?

CREON. Un matin je me suis réveillé roi de Thèbes. Et Dieu sait si j'aimais autre chose dans la vie que d'être puissant. . . .

ANTIGONE. Il fallait dire non, alors.

CREON. Je le pouvais. Seulement, je me suis senti tout d'un coup comme un ouvrier qui refusait un ouvrage. Cela ne m'a pas paru honnête. J'ai dit oui.

ANTIGONE. Eh bien, tant pis pour vous. Moi, je n'ai pas dit "oui"! Qu'est-ce que vous voulez que cela me fasse, à moi, votre politique, votre nécessité, vos pauvres histoires? Moi, je peux dire "non" encore à tout ce que je n'aime pas et je suis le seul juge. Et vous, avec votre couronne, avec vos gardes, avec votre attirail, vous pouvez seulement me faire mourir, parce que vous avez dit "oui." . . .

CREON. Mais, bon Dieu! Essaie de comprendre une minute, toi aussi, petite idiote! . . . Il faut pourtant qu'il y en ait qui disent oui. Il faut pourtant qu'il y en ait qui mènent la barque. Cela prend l'eau de toutes parts, c'est pleine de crime, de bêtise, de misère. . .

ANTIGONE. Je ne veux pas comprendre. C'est bon pour vous. Moi, je suis là pour autre chose que pour comprendre. Je suis là pour vous dire non et pour mourir.

CREON. C'est facile de dire non!

ANTIGONE. Pas toujours.

CREON. Pour dire oui, il faut suer et retrousser ses manches, empoigner la vie à pleines mains et s'en mettre jusqu'aux coudes. C'est facile de dire non, même si on doit mourir. Il n'y a qu'à ne pas bouger et attendre.][15]

Critical Reactions

The critics have had a field day with *Antigone*. Gabriel Marcel criticizes the absence of the religious aspect that inspires the heroine's action in Sophocles. Jean Sauvenay and Hubert Gignoux insist that Anouilh's play lacks the tragic element and that the author turned Sophocles' work upside down and merely re-created two of his former characters: Thérèse in *La Sauvage* (1934), and Eurydice (1941). In a very perceptive article, William Calin underlines the childlike nature of Antigone and suggests that "Antigone incarnates the virtues of wild nature, Créon those of domestic society." Although most commentators praise Anouilh for maintaining a balance between the two antagonists, Pol Gaillard accuses the author of having created in Creon a dictator for his fascist play. As further evidence, critics offer the fact that the play was passed by the German censors and praised by the collaborationist paper *Je suis partout;* this criticism is condemned by Gabriel Marcel, however, as an expression of contemptible bad faith.[16]

The Great Confrontation

Before we enter into the crucial conflict of the play, a few points have to be made. To begin with, who is really responsible for the tragic situation? At the end of the play, the Chorus expresses a definite opinion.

And there we are. It is quite true that if it had not been for Antigone they would all have been at peace. But that is over now. And they are all at peace. All those who were meant to die have died: those who believed one thing, those who believed the contrary thing, and even those who believed nothing at all, yet were caught up in the web without knowing why. All dead: stiff, useless, rotting. And those who have survived will now begin quietly to forget the dead: they won't remember who was who or which was which. It is all over. Antigone is calm tonight, and we shall never know the name of the fever that consumed her. She has played her part.

A great melancholy wave of peace now settles down upon Thebes, upon the empty palace, upon Creon, who can how begin to wait for his own death. (*Antigone*, 53)

[Et voilà. Sans la petite Antigone, c'est vrai, ils auraient tous été bien tranquilles. Mais maintenant, c'est fini. Ils sont tout de même tranquilles. Tous ceux qui avaient à mourir sont morts. Ceux qui croyaient une chose, et puis ceux qui croyaient le contraire—même ceux qui ne croyaient rien et qui se sont trouvés pris dans l'histoire sans y rien comprendre. Morts pareils, tous, bien raides, bien inutiles, bien pourris. Et ceux qui vivent encore vont commencer tout doucement à les oublier et à confondre leurs noms. C'est fini. Antigone est calmée maintenant, nous ne saurons jamais de quelle fièvre. Son devoir lui est remis.

Un grand apaisement tombe sur Thèbes et sur le Palais vide où Créon va commencer à attendre la mort. (*Antigone*, 206–7)]

Dramatically speaking, the Chorus is right. Antigone has been the troublemaker who refused to obey the king's orders, thus causing chaos; and now that she is dead, life in Thebes will return to normal, whatever that may be in that place at that time. But if we view the cause of the trouble from a realistic point of view, then the picture changes. Dramatically, it is only fair to accept Creon's decision to leave Polynices unburied as a given, as inevitable. But practically, it is not an inevitable decision at all—it is, in fact, a terribly bad decision.

Creon has assumed the throne after an internal struggle in which both antagonists died, and instead of preaching harmony, unity, and peace, his first concern is to set an example for those who might be tempted to imitate Polynice's treason. And what an example! Of all the possible measures at his disposal, this one is certainly the most outlandish and counterproductive. Creon himself has to suffer from the stench of it! And like any poor statesman who is unsure of himself, he stubbornly sticks to his bad decision, which he covers up with seemingly reasonable arguments, just as the French government did during the Dreyfus affair or the American government during the Watergate scandal.

So while Creon uses reason to justify his bad decision, he is not reasonable, for a reasonable king would have managed to get Polynices buried, and save face and Antigone's life at the same time. Who, indeed, is reasonable? Creon, who says, "There may be people in Thebes who are tempted to revolt and betray; those I rule over are brutes, so I have ordered Polynices left unburied and I shall not change that order"? Or Antigone, who says: "I don't care what your reasons are. You simply do not leave human beings unburied, and I shall do whatever I can to cover Polynices with earth"?

In the conflict, Antigone's position is so strong that she actually does not have to say anything—she stands before Creon like Jesus stands before Dostoevski's Grand Inquisitor. But she is not Jesus. She is young, she is immature, and so she speaks, she wavers; in fact, Anouilh underlines her weaknesses. She is not beautiful, she has a bad character, she is stubborn and does not listen to Creon's arguments. Yet even these bad traits are not sufficient to tip the scale in Creon's favor.

The Human Borderline

Antigone's act is not political, it is ethical. She does not want to overthrow Creon or liberate the people, and she has no objections to the way Thebes is governed—all she wants is to bury a dead human being. That, and nothing else, is the point of the play. In the final analysis it does not matter whether Antigone is beautiful or not, whether she is mature or childish, whether she is likable or despicable, whether she longs for life or for death, whether anything else she does or thinks is right or wrong—in this act she is right. And it does not even matter whether the particular body left unburied is that of her brother or of a stranger, whether he was nice or a good-for-nothing. Her intital reaction may well have been caused by blood relationship, but these personal feelings diminish in importance as she learns more about the real character of Polynices, while at the same time the ethical imperative gets stronger. [17]

To the question why she has committed her act, Antigone replies: "For nobody. For myself." If this is selfishness, it is beneficial selfishness. A partisan of freedom of speech, for example, is first of all concerned with his own right to speak freely. What he eventually realizes is that he has to extend this right to everybody, including those with whom he disagrees. But that occurs at a later stage.

The feelings we have about dead people and burial go far deeper. It is so elementary a reaction that it needs no explanation, and in fact, Antigone cannot and does not bother to give an explanation. [18] Obviously, we do not want to be treated like Polynices. Beyond that, it creates in us an atavistic bond with the rest of humanity in defense of what it means to be human. We find Creon's command not only ethically and aesthetically repulsive but also a serious threat to the line that separates humans from animals. That line has been obscured more and more. We know that human beings can be reduced to the state of animals, that they can be used for experiments in place of guinea pigs, that human skin can be used to make lamp shades. But not until the Nazi period did modern man realize that this possibility (which had to be admitted on logical grounds) could be turned into a reality by which all mankind is imperiled, because it threatens the laborious, immemorial efforts man has made to rise above the animal state.

It is in this light that we must interpret the repeated references to animals in the play. When Creon tries to convince Antigone to adopt his yes-saying attitude by using the example of animals who do not say no to their instincts of hunt and propagation, she replies: "Animals, eh, Creon! What a king you could be if only men were animals!" (*Antigone,* 37). [Quel rêve, hein, pour un roi, des bêtes! Ce serait si simple! (*Antigone,* 180).]

True enough, Antigone loves her dog, perhaps even too much. She implores her nurse to speak to the dog after her death, to treat the dog like a human being. She has no objection to seeing animals rise to the state of humans; she even wants them to be treated as such—but she will not tolerate seeing human beings reduced to the state of animals. And in the face of a retreat from a fixed borderline between the two species, she draws a firm limit: burial. And thereby she strikes a profound note in all of us.

We are awed by the dead. People we paid no attention to during their lives become transfigured on their deathbeds, and their last words, sometimes pronounced in a weakened mental state, take on meanings they would never have been accorded under normal circumstances. We uncover our heads when a funeral procession passes by, even though we would probably not have noticed the person inside the coffin when alive. Even in war we bury our dead enemies, who, only a short while before, were shooting at us. This reaction is not tied to religion. It goes far deeper.

It is incorrect to say that Antigone refuses life and seeks death. Anouilh takes pains to show that she loves life intensely; she wants to embrace all of it, exhaust it, to be Haemon's wife and have children, but she refuses a certain kind of life and a certain conception of happiness. She wants no part of a dog's life and a dog's happiness. "I spit on your happiness! I spit on your idea of life—that life must go on, come what may. You are all like dogs that lick everything they smell!" (*Antigone,* 42). [Vous me dégoûtez tous avec votre bonheur! Avec votre vie qu'il faut aimer coûte que coûte. On dirait des chiens qui lèchent tout ce qu'ils trouvent (*Antigone,* 188).]

No, Antigone does not seek death, but neither does she want to live in a world in which human beings are left to rot unburied. In her apparently childlike and instinctive way she is a more profound existentialist than Sartre's Orestes, because her stand concerns the whole world, and not just a city.

Political Implications

Antigone's act does have political implications, not because of her intentions, but because of the situation she finds herself in. Creon happens to be a king. That is not her fault. If he were a tyrannical head of a large family and she were a servant washing dishes, she would act in the same way. Her act has even more important political implications because of the situation in France at the time the play was first performed. That may be the author's fault, or "la faute de la fatalité," but not Antigone's. She knows little about Greek politics and obviously even less about Nazi Germany and occupied France.

Political fact gave to the legend a grim relevance. The clash between the morality of protest and the morality of order had so direct a bearing on the condition of the audience in occupied France that Anouilh could preserve intact the meaning of the Sophoclean play. His translation of Greek values was literal in the sense of being a translation into present anguish. Moreover, Anouilh had to produce the work in the face of the enemy; he presented an

Antigone in the court of Creon. . . . Had he chosen a contemporary episode, the play could not have been performed. [19]

Most critics have paid little attention to the relevance of *Antigone* to the situation in France at the time; some have even denied any political intentions on the part of the author. We have observed in earlier instances that opposition literature created under censorship operates by indirection and extension. While protesting only against a particular case of inhumanity, Antigone condemns implicitly all inhuman acts. It is true that the problem in France during the German occupation was not unburied bodies left to rot in the streets of Paris. But how could a French spectator in February of 1944 see this play and not immediately establish a connection with all the inhuman acts that everybody had witnessed or heard about? The execution of innocent hostages, the torturing of French Resistance fighters, the rounding up of entire Jewish families, including women, children and the aged; and the rumor, if not the direct knowledge, of concentration camps where inmates were reduced to the state of animals, of gas chambers, of mass graves, of unburied bones! How, finally, could a spectator at the time have failed to make the analogy between Creon and Pétain? Just like Creon, the aged Marshall Pétain had said yes when he was called upon to head the occupation government; and, in contrast to Sophocles, Anouilh portrayed a well-intentioned ruler who nonetheless had to give orders to have inhuman acts carried out.

Why did the public understand this play so well, and why have the critics generally preferred to make pedantic comparisons with Sophocles' play, to do psychological and artistic studies rather than deal with the heart of the matter? Clearly, they feel uncomfortable with the play. They are looking for a model, for a character such as Sartre's Orestes, who is an unequivocal liberator and who tells us so, just in case we might have missed the point. Antigone is nothing of the sort. She is anything but a model character, she has not studied existentialism; in fact, in philosophical arguments Creon not only beats her on points— he knocks her out!

Still, the spectators, so maligned by Gabriel Marcel, [20] sensed or understood that, so far as they were concerned, *Antigone* was not only a far better play than *Les Mouches* but also contained a more poignant message than Sartre's play. For, after all, how many Orestes are there in a country? How many people are capable of assassinating anybody, let alone their mother and her lover, a royal couple? It is as absurd to claim that anybody can become an Orestes as it is to insist that anybody can become president of the United States. But what comes through very clearly in Anouilh's play is that anybody can become an Antigone.

Lacking in beauty, in maturity, in philosophy, she nonetheless does what she feels she has to do. Anybody can throw earth on an unburied body. It requires no special education or special tools. Just a child's shovel and, failing that, one's fingernails.

"What good will it do?" Creon asks. "You know that there are other men standing guard over Polynices. And even if you did cover him over with earth again, the earth would again be removed."

"I know all that," Antigone replies. "But that much, at least, I can do. And what a person can do, a person ought to do." (*Antigone,* 32)

[CREON. Que peux-tu donc, sinon t'ensanglanter encore les ongles et te faire prendre?

ANTIGONE. Rien d'autre que cela, je le sais. Mais cela, du moins, je le peux. Et il faut faire ce que l'on peut. (*Antigone,* 172–73)]

"Il faut faire ce que l'on peut." The humbler the means, the more powerful the message. Sartre's Orestes appeals to the exceptional person; Anouilh's Antigone supplies an answer to the question asked by millions of average French people who opposed the German occupation: What can I do? The answer is simple: You must do what you can. Even if you only have a child's shovel or your fingernails.

The message seems unmistakably clear, and yet, among others, two persons close to Anouilh have denied that he had any political intentions. One of these is Jean Davy, who played the role of Creon in the original cast. After a performance of *Antigone* at Stanford University, M. Davy, upon being questioned by me, stated that Anouilh had made no remarks to that effect nor given any special instructions to the actors. He added that the author had begun working on the play much earlier and, using the type of heroine he had depicted in previous works, had simply completed it at that particular time.

Likewise, the analogy between the black uniforms of the guards and that of the German SS or the Gestapo is played down by none other than André Barsacq, the director of the original performance. "In reality, there was no premeditation in this modernization. We had simply mulled over what clothing could best serve as a sort of uniform for our interpreters, and we hit on the idea of formal evening dress. The king and all the members of the royal family wore tails, Antigone and her sister, Ismene, long gowns, black and white, and the guards smoking jackets on which a coat of black had been applied."[21]

Perhaps Davy and Barsacq are right. Perhaps Anouilh simply wrote just another play, because the heroine fitted his artistic needs. But if he did so at that particular time, then that must have been one of the strangest coincidences in all of literature, and Anouilh must have spent the German occupation in a taxi with blinds drawn as he drove from an ivory tower to rehearsals and back. Considering that he was to produce two pointedly political plays, which will constitute the subject of our next chapter, it seems even more difficult to imagine that his intentions in *Antigone* were purely artistic and dramatic.

Whereas Sartre provides us with overabundant comments on his work, Anouilh refused to give interviews and rarely said or wrote anything about his plays. Nevertheless, in 1944 he did at least give a slight indication that he may have had an inkling of the effect the play would produce. Again our witness is Gerhard Heller, the German officer who revealed how Sartre's *Les Mouches* had been passed by the German censors.

I had seen Jean Anouilh's *Antigone* at the Théâtre de l'Atelier in 1944. . . . I had sensed in the character of Antigone a representative of the eternal resistance of humanity against the oppression of unjust laws, and I very much wanted to meet the author. . . . I met Anouilh for a lunch with just the two of us in a restaurant at the esplanade of the Invalides. . . . He admitted that this play could have seemed to the Germans as directed against them. Little Antigone standing up all alone against the government made one inevitably think of the Resistance fighters at the time, and the interpretation underlined this audacious aspect even more, because the actors playing the soldiers appeared on stage in boots and black trench coats, bringing to mind the inspectors of the French police or of the Gestapo.[22]

No one can claim to know what went on in Anouilh's mind when he wrote *Antigone*. But even if he did not intend to make any references to the situation in France during the German occupation, a literary work escapes its author once it is printed or performed. And there cannot be the slightest doubt what was going on in the minds of the French spectators when they saw the play in February of 1944.

Chapter Eight
The Headhunters

Provisional Government and the Fourth Republic,
1944–58

After his return to France in August 1944, Charles de Gaulle became the head of a provisional government. In the confusing and difficult situation in France, he managed to keep control by indirect chess moves. The greatest political power block was the Communists, who had regained much of their lost prestige by their active participation in the Resistance. Outwardly de Gaulle seemed to be playing into their hands by authorizing the return of Communist leader Maurice Thorez from Moscow, even though he had deserted the French Army in 1939, and by signing a twenty-year alliance with the Soviet Union. Yet these acts deprived the Communists of issues on which to attack him, while he staunchly refused to give them cabinet posts.

After the Third Republic had been voted out of existence in October 1945, a Constituent Assembly was elected, in which the parties of the Left (Communists: 25%; Socialists: 23%) had a near majority, but which also included a surprisingly large representation from a newly formed Catholic party, the MRP (Mouvement Républicain Populaire), headed by Georges Bidault. Since it seemed impossible to establish a government with a strong executive, de Gaulle resigned in January 1946.

The first proposed constitution, which contained a provision for a single legislative chamber, was rejected by the voters. The second draft, which provided for a second chamber, barely passed. It tried to make it more difficult for small groups to change governments, but in practice this turned out to be as prevalent under the Fourth Republic as it had been under its predecessor. Thus, between January 1947 and June 1954, fifteen ministries succeeded each other, with an average duration of seven months.

In 1947 a Gaullist party, the RPF (Rassemblement du Peuple Français), was founded, which won a considerable number of seats in the Assembly. But since de Gaulle was not prepared to lead the Fourth

Republic, and the Communists opposed the badly needed economic aid offered by the Marshall Plan, a Third Force was formed by the Radicals, the MRP, and the Socialists. Although divided on the question of Catholic education and other issues, the Third Force governed during the remaining years of the Fourth Republic by managing to keep both the Gaullists and the Communists out of power.

The swing to the Right was accompanied by a return of confidence in the business community, and economic conditions took a remarkable upturn. But those left out of the general prosperity (small shopkeepers, small farmers) found a voice in Pierre Poujade, who led a tax rebellion and managed to win fifty seats in the 1956 elections.

Buoyed by economic and social progress, the Fourth Republic might have hobbled on for many years, if it had not been for the problem of the French colonies. Syria and Lebanon had been granted their independence, and reforms in the relationship between France and its remaining colonies had been instituted, but these were formal rather than practical.

The first serious challenge came from Indochina, where Ho Chi Minh had proclaimed independence as early as 1945. The war in that area proved to be both unpopular and burdensome. With the fall of Dien Bien Phu in 1954, all hopes for an eventual victory came to an end. Mendès-France, who had opposed the war, was elected premier and negotiated a settlement at Geneva that was overwhelmingly approved, even though it meant the loss of France's colonies in the Far East. In 1956 the independence of Morocco and Tunisia also was voted.

But matters were different when it came to Algeria, where over one million colonials, also called *pieds noirs,* had settled, many of whom had been born there. To combat Algerian rebel forces, some 350,000 soldiers were sent to that country. The war itself was a brutal affair with atrocities being committed on both sides. Fearing that they would be let down once again by the politicians at home, army extremists, joined by hysterical *pieds noirs,* took control of government offices in Algiers and proclaimed a revolutionary government under a Committee of Public Safety on 13 May 1958.

Faced with the danger of a revolt that might threaten France itself, President René Coty asked the recently named premier, Pierre Pflimlin, to resign, so that he could call on de Gaulle to take charge. On 1 June 1958 the Assembly approved de Gaulle as premier. As conditions of his acceptance he demanded that he have decree powers for six months and that a new constitution be submitted to the voters.

Chronology

1944:   De Gaulle accepted as head of provisional government.

1945:   Trials of collaborators, Brasillach executed; end of World War II; referendum ends Third Republic; election of Constituent Assembly.

1946:   (January): de Gaulle resigns; (May): voters reject proposed constitution; (June): election of new Constituent Assembly; (October): referendum accepts second constitution, initiating Fourth Republic.

1947:   Vincent Auriol elected president; revolt in Madagascar; formation of Gaullist party RPF; Ramadier dismisses Communist ministers; strikes by Communist-dominated unions.

1948:   Formation of Third Force; strikes.

1949:   Signature of North Atlantic Treaty.

1951:   Coal and steel agreement with Germany, Italy, and Benelux countries.

1953:   Formation of Poujadist League; René Coty elected president.

1954:   Fall of Dien Bien Phu; government of Mendès-France; acceptance of Indochina settlement; rejection of European Defense Community; Algerian revolt.

1956:   Front Républicain government of Guy Mollet; independence of Morocco and Tunisia; failure of Suez Canal intervention; Anouilh: *Pauvre Bitos;* return of Saar territory to Germany.

1957:   Treaties of European Common Market ratified; resignation of Mollet government; partial devaluation of the franc.

1958:   Army revolt in Algeria; de Gaulle accepted as premier.

Purging: The Case of Brasillach

As the Allied armies advanced in France, the Vichy government collapsed, leaving the country in a state of near anarchy until de Gaulle was able to assume authority. During that relatively brief period, many accounts were settled by the Resistance forces. We still remember the photos and films where women who had either collaborated or who had had a German lover were stripped naked and their hair shaved off. Matters did not stop there, of course. The number of people summarily executed is officially given as three to four thousand, but those figures may have to be multiplied by perhaps as much as ten.

Once an administration was set up, courts were created to try collaborators. In the heat of hatred a number of hasty sentences were imposed after trials that made a mockery of judicial procedures—trials that still make the French very uneasy. One of the most famous cases in point was the trial of Laval, who was "silenced and sentenced, allowed to poison himself in the night, and ignominiously resuscitated for the sake of being hauled out at dawn and shot."[1]

As a result of this purging policy *(épuration),* almost forty thousand persons were imprisoned for collaboration with the Germans; they were successively released until, by 1964, none of them remained in prison. Of 2,071 death sentences imposed, de Gaulle commuted 1,303 and maintained 768.[2]

The *épuration* included writers who had collaborated and especially those who had done so enthusiastically. Drieu la Rochelle escaped judgment by committing suicide, but Robert Brasillach chose to stand trial.

Contrary to the rather open-minded Drieu la Rochelle, Brasillach was an out-and-out Fascist. Born in 1904, he found his first inspiration in the *Action Française.* A visit to Nazi Germany in 1937 left him elated at the ceremonies he saw in Nuremberg. He wrote voluminously, authoring novels, poems, and plays, as well as works of history that extolled Franco's Spain. During the occupation Brasillach assumed the editorship of the openly collaborationist and violently anti-Semitic newspaper *Je suis partout.* His manner of writing is demonstrated by his ironic offer to make peace with his enemies "by pumping lead into their vital organs and through the definitive and peaceful conciliation of the coffin," and by his desire to have P. Cot and Léon Blum shot.[3]

The question to be decided by the court that tried Brasillach was whether a stroke of the pen can be as deadly as a thrust of the sword. Regardless of the claims made by authors such as Victor Hugo or Jean-Paul Sartre that the word is an act, jurisprudence does not necessarily share their view. In this case, however, Brasillach's demand that Jews be shot or imprisoned was made at a time when the Vichy government was trying to protect French Jews; and an article protesting the influence of resisters, Jews, and Anglophiles in certain publications in the southern zone of France amounted to denunciation and posed a threat to their lives.[4]

Brasillach's trial took place on 19 January, and a verdict condemning him to death was pronounced after five hours of deliberation. Thereupon fifty-nine French intellectuals signed a petition of reprieve for Brasillach. The signers included François Mauriac, Paul Valéry, Paul Claudel, Georges Duhamel, Jean Paulhan, Jacques Copeau, Maurice de Vlaminck, André Derain, Arthur Honegger, Albert Camus, and Jean Anouilh. The last named had knocked on doors and obtained eight of the signatures.

In prison Brasillach wrote poems, modeling himself consciously on André Chénier. His demeanor during and after the trial was dignified, and impressed even his enemies. Apparently he appealed for clemency only to please his mother. Just why de Gaulle rejected this appeal is not entirely clear. Brasillach's lawyer believes that the file may have been tampered with or that de Gaulle confused a photo of someone else in Nazi uniform with Brasillach, who was executed by a firing squad on 6 February 1945, exactly eleven years after the Paris riots, which Brasillach, Drieu la Rochelle, and other rightists considered to be the best occasion for fascism to seize power.

Jean Anouilh

Pauvre Bitos

Directly involved in efforts to save Brasillach from execution, Jean Anouilh was strongly opposed to the *épuration* practiced after the liberation of France. He incorporated his attacks on that policy in two plays, *Pauvre Bitos* (1956) and *La Foire d'empoigne* (1962), both set in times when similar situations had existed in French history.

The subtitle of *Pauvre Bitos* is *Le Dîner de têtes,* which takes on a double meaning, because the dinner hosted by the aristocrat Maxime not only requires that the guests make up their heads to resemble characters from the French Revolution—it also implies that revolutionary leaders, such as Robespierre and Saint-Just, were eager for heads to roll.

Maxime has asked his noble and wealthy friends to come disguised as Danton, Mirabeau, Tallien, Louis XVI, Marie-Antoinette, Camille

Desmoulins and his wife, Lucile. He has chosen the role of Saint-Just for himself. But the star of the dinner is Bitos, a poor former schoolmate of theirs, who used to win prizes for excellence, then acquired degrees in several subjects, and has now been appointed assistant prosecutor in the area. He has been particularly zealous in bringing to justice former collaborators, going so far as to obtain a verdict of death in the case of a former friend of his, who had joined the German militia but had been practically forgotten in his prison cell. Naturally, Bitos comes as Robespierre and, ignorant of the custom, he is wearing not only the makeup of the character but his costume as well, while everybody else is in evening attire.

The first act is a brilliant tour de force in the style of Pirandello, where the present and the past, reality and illusion, alternate or mingle, so that the persons onstage both act the parts of their personages and comment on them. Maxime's intention is to humiliate their former schoolmate, in order to take revenge not only for his constant academic superiority at school but especially for his overzealous efforts to purge collaborators. In their disguises Maxime and his friends can express freely what they might not otherwise dare say to so powerful a person as the assistant prosecutor. The act ends with the sudden arrival of a young man whom Bitos prosecuted some time ago. This guest comes disguised as Constable Merda, who had fired at Robespierre in 1794 and wounded him in the jaw. A shot is heard, the lights go out, and Bitos is clutching his jaw.

Act 2 is a dream sequence, as Bitos lies in a faint, watched by two indifferent guards. It shows Robespierre in various stages: as a boy, being punished by a Jesuit schoolmaster for his pride; as a young deputy from Arras, earning the contempt of Mirabeau; as the most powerful man during the Reign of Terror, in conversation with Saint-Just; dining at Tallien's home in the company of Danton and Desmoulins, both of whom he intends to liquidate.

The last scene of the act shows Robespierre dictating to Saint-Just the *loi de prairial* which will be voted the next day. Its purpose is "less to punish than to annihilate" the enemies of the people and so speed up that process. The punishment will be death. If proof of guilt is considered sufficient by the Tribunal, then no witnesses will be called. Juries will consist of revolutionary patriots. Saint-Just summarizes: "To take effect retrospectively. Prejudiced juries. No defense. It's a model of its kind."[5] [Effet rétroactif. Jurés partisans. Pas de défense. C'est un modèle du genre.][6]

This is, of course, the key scene in Anouilh's attack against the *épuration* after World War II. The direct comparison between the Reign of Terror and the vengeance inflicted on collaborators may seem harsh, and the author certainly does not intend to equate General de Gaulle with Robespierre. Yet the *loi de prairial* was uncomfortably close to the practices followed in a number of collaborationist trials.[7]

The last act simply ties up the loose ends. We learn that Bitos has actually not been hurt but has fainted of fear. The guests persuade the angry assistant prosecutor to stay, and a few glasses of whiskey establish an almost cordial atmosphere. Maxime's intention is to take Bitos to an unsavory establishment while he is drunk, but Victoire, whose father had rudely refused Bitos's request to marry her, warns him of the plot and he leaves unreconciled with everybody.

Pauvre Bitos was first performed on 11 October 1956. It was a moment of tension, due to the Hungarian uprising, the Suez crisis, and the Algerian revolt. Twelve years had gone by since the liberation of Paris, but wounds had not been healed and memories were still fresh. As happens so often, people had idealized their past. After the end of the occupation everybody claimed to have participated in the Resistance movement. By 1956 even those who had not done so believed, more or less sincerely, that they had.

And here comes that killjoy Anouilh, who revives uncomfortable memories of less than proper postwar trials and reminds his countrymen that during the Revolution everybody likewise claimed to have been present at the taking of the Bastille. Charles, the servant who plays one of the guards watching the unconscious Robespierre, admits that he was not there.

Mind you, everybody couldn't be there. I mean, you couldn't have moved! But I know some that got themselves fake certificates to say they were there. At one time there were no jobs going except for Bastille men. (*Poor Bitos*, 44)

[Remarque que tout le monde ne pouvait pas y être. Ça aurait plutôt gêné. Mais j'en connais qui se sont fait faire de faux certificats comme quoi, ils y étaient. Et à eux les bonnes places. Il y a eu un temps où il n'y en avait que pour les bastillards. (*Pauvre Bitos*, 430)][8]

In his play, Anouilh took on more than his share: the sacrosanct Revolution (even though only its most somber period), the equally sacrosanct Liberation (again, only its least charitable actions), and the self-congratulations of his countrymen. But those for whom he reserved his harshest words are those who claim to be purer than anybody else, who send people to the guillotine "for their own good," and who shout from the rooftops that they are, or that they represent, the people; in short, the fanatics of the extreme Left or Right, regardless of whether they are sincere or mere opportunists.

Vulturne-Mirabeau draws a comparison between the actions of those who protest that they are defending the cause of humanity, and the atrocities committed by kings.

I've observed that those who talk too often of mankind have a curious propensity for decimating men. . . .
Kings have massacred since the dawn of the world too. But they at least had the courage to say it was for the advancement of their affairs or for their own good pleasure. . . . You and your like, while doing the same sort of work, lay your hands on your hearts. That's what I find repugnant in you. (*Poor Bitos*, 31)

And Anouilh cleverly chooses Deschamps, who shares many of Bitos's political ideas, to clarify what is meant by "the people."

Neither André Bitos, nor the ringleaders of M. Brassac's factories, nor, incidentally, those figures of the Revolution we tried to bring to life this evening, are the people. All those men are more like yourselves than you can possibly imagine. The people, the real people, have the distinction and the elegance to belong to the race that does nothing else but give. (*Poor Bitos*, 77)

[J'ai remarqué que ceux qui parlent trop souvent de l'humanité ont une curieuse tendance à décimer les hommes. . . .
Les rois ont massacré, eux aussi, depuis l'aube du monde et autant que vous, c'est vrai. Ils avaient du moins le courage de dire que c'était pour le bien de leurs affaires, ou pour leur bon plaisir. . . . Vous et vos pareils, en faisant la même besogne, vous y avez posé la main sur le coeur. C'est en cela que je vous trouve répugnants. . . .
Ni André Bitos, ni les meneurs des usines de Monsieur Brassac, ni d'ailleurs, les figures de la Révolution, que nous avons essayé d'évoquer ce soir, ne sont le peuple. Tous ces gens-là vous ressemblent plus que vous ne pouvez l'imaginer. Le peuple, le vrai peuple a seul l'honneur et l'élégance d'appartenir à la race qui ne fait que donner. (*Pauvre Bitos*, 412, 413, 477]

And just to make his attitude unmistakably clear, Anouilh fires a parting shot by establishing the comparison between the uncompromis-

ing Robespierre, who had the poet Chénier executed, and the vengeful
Liberation judges, who voted to execute the writer Robert Brasillach,
who had also written poems in prison. When Robespierre complains
that they need poets who would exalt the Revolution, Saint-Just mentions Chénier, whereupon Robespierre replies: "Chenier is not a poet.
He is a counterrevolutionary! . . . Thank you for reminding me of
him! I'll send Fouquier a note. . . . What are they waiting for to do
away with him?" Saint-Just concurs: "You are right. One less poet, that
always puts you ahead when you want to set the world in order."[9] [—
Chénier n'est pas un poète. C'est un contre-révolutionnaire! . . . Tu as
bien fait de m'y faire repenser, à celui-là! Je vais envoyer un mot à
Fouquier. . . . Qu'est-ce qu'on attend pour le supprimer? — Tu as
raison. Un poète de moins c'est toujours ça de gagné quand on veut
mettre le monde en ordre (*Pauvre Bitos,* 472).]

Critical Reactions.   The critics were nearly unanimous in tearing
Pauvre Bitos to pieces. While some found fault with its conception and
its philosophy, and judged its sociological and political views confused,
most of the critics accused Anouilh of distorting French history and
blamed him for attacking the Republic, the Resistance, the Liberation,
French justice, and the country in general. The public was not in the
least influenced by the bad reviews. *Pauvre Bitos* had 308 performances
in France and 245 abroad, making it one of Anouilh's most successful
plays.

Both critics and public were partially right. *Pauvre Bitos,* however
successful at the box office, is not among Anouilh's best plays. The
three acts are uneven: the first is brilliant, the second drags a bit, and
the third does little more than tie up loose ends. But that is not the
greatest defect of the play, for the author remains as skillful as ever in
keeping our interest. It is rather Anouilh's personal involvement that
detracts from the effectiveness of the play. *Antigone* is a masterpiece to a
great extent because the author resisted the temptation to load the dice
and gave equal weight to the positions of the two adversaries. In *Pauvre
Bitos* that precious balance is absent. Not only is Bitos depicted as an
ambitious and self-seeking nonentity, but historical scenes are intentionally falsified, and Robespierre is made to say things he would never
have said. Strange as it may seem, the censorship of the German
occupation had a more beneficial effect on Anouilh's theater than the
freedom he enjoyed under the Fourth Republic.

The Point of the Play.   Still, the spectators who flocked in great
numbers to see the play displayed better judgment than the critics.

Anouilh had once again raised a burning issue. The fanaticism of the ultrapure that kept the guillotine busy during the Reign of Terror had again led to excesses (fortunately less numerous than in 1793–94) during the period of *épuration,* and the brutal suppression of the 1956 Hungarian uprising had shown that this spirit was far from dead.

Those critics who accused Anouilh of insulting France obviously missed the point of the play. Anouilh was pleading for a better France, one that would admit its mistakes, for a better judicial system, and for an end to purist fanaticism. In that wish he joined hands across the centuries with Voltaire, who had devoted all his energy to combating fanaticism during his time.

Musical Chairs: La Foire d'empoigne

In *La Foire d'empoigne* (1962),[10] Jean Anouilh returned to the themes he had previously treated: purging, fanaticism, and the dirty business (*la cuisine*) of politics. And he dared to criticize the two most popular heroes of France, Napoleon and de Gaulle, and defend one of the most unpopular kings of France, Louis XVIII. But he chose a period and characters that enabled him to turn a critical searchlight on contemporary affairs.

The historical background of the play is laid in the famous Hundred Days during which Napoleon returned to France from exile in 1815. As Louis XVIII and Napoleon take turns as master of the Tuileries, it is difficult to tell who is loyal and who is a collaborator, but each of them is beseeched by a "purist" to purge those who rallied to the other's government: Louis XVIII by an émigré noble, the duc de Blacas, and Napoleon by a young fanatic, d'Anouville. While Louis XVIII, who pursues a policy of reconciliation, rejects the idea, Napoleon eagerly accepts it; the term obviously delights him. "Purification! There's a word I should never have thought of. . . . Up till now one always spoke of repression. It was too crude. . . . 'Purification.' It has a little hygienic feel to it. . . . It's a brain wave."[11] [Epurer! Voilà un mot auquel je n'aurais pas pensé. . . . Jusqu'ici on avait toujours parlé de répression. C'était trop franc. . . . "L'épuration." Cela vous a un petit air hygiénique. . . . C'est une trouvaille. (*Foire,* 321).][12] But Napoleon does not want to go as far as young d'Anouville; he prefers a selective purge to bring about what he calls "unity in appeased fright" [l'union dans la frousse apaisée] with those he has decided to spare.

The plot is thin and at best pseudohistorical. Anouilh contrasts a

paternal Louis XVIII and a dictatorial and histrionic Napoleon.[13] Both
agree that politics is *la cuisine* (dirty) and *la foire d'empoigne* (ruthless),
but Louis XVIII, whose legitimacy needs no proving, can play the
game for the common good, while Napoleon is only concerned with his
personal glory and the image he will leave behind. Like a bad actor (the
commediante described in Alfred de Vigny's *Servitude et grandeur mili-
taires*), Napoleon is much concerned with entries and exits. And the
motive for his desperate return to France is to make a better exit than
the last time. He is disappointed once again when there is no crowd to
watch his final exit on the boat bound for Saint Helena.[14]

The only other characters of any importance in the play are Fouché,
who serves whoever happens to be in power with equal devotion born of
self-interest, and a guard who, like the guards in *Antigone,* will obey
orders from the most powerful and shout "Vive le Roi" or "Vive
l'Empereur" as the situation demands.

Napoleon and de Gaulle   Even though Anouilh denies that his
characters resemble real historical personages or that he intended to
make allusions of any sort, and calls his play a farce,[15] it is not difficult
to discover certain parallels between Napoleon and de Gaulle. Both
were "great men" and de Gaulle returned to France with a feeling of
hatred for those who had collaborated with the Germans. It is true that
he eventually pardoned most of them, but Anouilh felt strongly that he
had taken too much time to do so and that he should have dissociated
himself from those who called for a purge.

Like Louis XVIII, de Gaulle was subjected to pressure to purge
collaborators and to reward those who had shared his exile. One can
detect at least an oblique reference to de Gaulle's position after the
Liberation in Louis XVIII's refusal to give in to the demands of Blacas.

But I cannot be King of the little handful of men who stayed faithful—to me
or to their hatred. . . . I am not the King of the few folk over in London. I am
King of millions of men, who willy-nilly stayed where they were and who had
to adapt themselves, as best they could, to what befell them. Exile was a
luxury, after all. It has become a badge of glory. I've no objection. But if
nobody at all had remained in France, it would have been pretty awkward,
you'll admit. (*Catch,* 260–61)

[Mais je ne puis être le roi de la petite poignée d'hommes qui m'a été fi-
dèle. . . . Je ne suis pas le roi des gens de Londres. Je suis le roi des millions
d'hommes qui, bon gré mal gré, sont demeurés et qui ont dû composer,
comme ils ont pu, avec ce qui leur tombait dessus. L'émigration, c'était tout

de même un luxe. On s'en est fait un titre de gloire. Je veux bien. Mais s'il
n'était resté personne en France, avouez que cela aurait été bien embêtant.
(*Foire,* 342)]

The allusions become more direct in the contrast between the spirits
with which Napoleon and Louis XVIII return to France. While Napoleon comes back from exile with a desire to punish those who served the
Restoration, Louis XVIII recalls the example of Henri IV, who began
his reign by embracing his former enemies. "To return to France with
hatred on my lips would be quite simply the sign of an unintelligent
man. And a third-rate politician. (*Catch,* 258). [Rentrer en France en
parlant de haine, serait tout simplement le fait d'un homme inintelli-
gent. Et d'un médiocre politique (*Foire,* 337).]

The Lesson of Louis XVIII. Anouilh's comparison of Napoleon
and Louis XVIII raises some fascinating and slightly embarrassing
questions. Who was better for France? Napoleon, whose useless campaigns cost the life and limbs of well over a million soldiers, who left
France defeated, occupied, and reduced to its borders of 1792? Or Louis
XVIII, who inherited the mess left behind by Napoleon, who returned
to France with a Charte that, however imperfect and imperfectly en-
forced, offered reconciliation and elections, who managed to terminate
the occupation of France by foreign troops, who sent but very few
soldiers to their death, and who asked no more of the French than what
they could reasonably be expected to do?

The trouble with history is that it is written primarily by university
professors who are accustomed to granting partial credit for examination answers that are partly wrong, and who give a B+ grade for work
that starts out with good intentions, even uses the right method, but
fails in its application and thus ends up with the wrong result.

History grants no partial credit for good intentions—only the final
result counts! And it does not know the grade B+. History only knows
two grades, success or failure, and that holds true especially for statesmen who live by the sword. The question of pathetic or grandiose
failure is largely academic, except that grandiose failures result in
proportionally larger suffering and payment of reparations by those on
the losing side, provided they have survived the slaughter.

If historians paid a little more attention to the people and a little less
to strutting warlords, a great number of presently famous names would
disappear from the honor roll of history and join those suffering souls in
Dante's *Inferno.*

Tweedledee and Tweedledum.   *La Foire d'empoigne* displays
the same strengths and weaknesses as *Pauvre Bitos*. The choice of the
historical situation is another stroke of genius, and the text is full of
interesting, witty, and often profound lines, but Anouilh again fails to
maintain not so much dramatic balance as a sense of fairness. Napoleon
has been turned into a caricature, while Louis XVIII is depicted too
favorably. The long and sentimental speech by Fouché, which reveals to
d'Anouville that he is his father, is simply embarrassing, and the
criticism in the play does not neatly apply to de Gaulle.

Obviously Anouilh was less concerned with writing a perfect play
than with making a point. And that point is made very clearly. In a
way, *La Foire d'empoigne* is the continuation and conclusion of *Pauvre
Bitos*. It does not merely condemn the *épuration* but shows how a
statesman returning to France from exile should act.

One may be tempted to say that these two plays resemble those of
Voltaire's which dealt with contemporary issues and hence were destined for oblivion, but this comparison falls short of the mark. The
unjust dismissal of a general or the execution of an admiral (to encour-
age the others, as Voltaire would say) excites people for a while and
then fades away. What distinguishes Anouilh's plays from Voltaire's is
that, beyond the momentary appeal that fills the theater, he raises
questions of concern to all humanity.

Pauvre Bitos and *La Foire d'empoigne* not only deal with the execution
of Brasillach and other excessive punishments of collaborators; they
raise fundamental questions about what we may reasonably expect of
human beings. Is everybody expected to behave like Corneille's Horace,
who unhesitatingly kills Curiace, his brother-in-law and the fiancé of
his sister, for the sake of the state?

Anouilh's point is that it is inhuman to expect of normal humans what
only superhumans can do. Normal human beings muddle through as
best they can, while conditions and governments keep changing. Was
every French citizen expected to join the Resistance at the risk of life?
Were all French women expected to suppress their femininity until
France would be liberated at some unknown time in the future, if ever?
Instead of cutting off the hair of French women who had slept with
German soldiers (which neither caused nor prolonged the war), the angry
Resistance fighters might have been well advised to adopt the concilia-
tory attitude of Louis XVIII and use their vengeful shears on those who
were responsible for bringing on the defeat of France in the first place:
those who failed to act at the critical moment in 1936 and who waved a

peace document in 1938 that was worth less than toilet paper. But the politicians in power at the time not only kept all their hair but were honored as patriots, while the members of the French General Staff who devised the Maginot line strategy and the French generals who failed their people so miserably were collecting their retirement pay.

Anouilh's disturbing plays demonstrate what happens when revolutionary justice is practiced: it knows neither procedure nor discrimination. No wonder he has been given all sorts of political labels. Anouilh is neither a rightist nor a leftist nor a monarchist. He is a humanist. For him, the choice between two sides in politics is basically between Tweedledee and Tweedledum, and the dumb ones are those who are willing to die for either. Tweedledee may be preferable to Tweedledum, not because he is necessarily more intelligent or more qualified, but because he will do less harm and cause fewer people to be killed.

Going beyond the particular situation of postwar France, Anouilh has something to say about government in general, expressing a view very close to the one Stendhal espoused, namely, that those who rule should govern not for their own glory or for the retention of power, but strictly for the good of the people. Although not a royalist, Anouilh chose the example of Louis XVIII out of dramatic necessity. Stendhal would have chosen a liberal statesman—if he could have found one.

Chapter Nine
The Children's Crusade

The Fifth Republic, 1958–71

The proposed constitution, worked out under the direction of Michel Debré, was accepted by a majority of 80 percent of the voters in September 1958 and gave birth to the Fifth Republic, which weighted power heavily in favor of a strong executive. A new Gaullist party, the UNR (Union pour la Nouvelle République) won some two hundred seats in the Assembly.

As sibylline as the oracle at Delphi, de Gaulle was all things to all people. At times he satisfied their demands by phrases rather than by acts. Visiting troubled Algeria, he told the French settlers, "I have understood you" [Je vous ai compris], which they took to mean that he was supporting their position, when in reality he was preparing measures to make Algeria independent. The rebellious army officers had confidence in the general, but when they staged a second revolt in January 1960, he resisted them, and their uprising turned into a terrorist campaign by the OAS (Organisation armée secrète), which he ruthlessly crushed. The French at home were assured that "France must be France" [Il faut que la France soit la France], which could mean whatever one wished to read into it. And, when visiting Canada at a moment of tensions due to French-Canadian dissatisfactions, he exclaimed, "Long live free Quebec" [Vive le Québec libre], which cost him little except that it did not add to his reputation as a gracious guest. And he maintained a skeptical distance from the United States, eventually even withdrawing from the Western defense alliance of NATO.[1]

But de Gaulle did more than just talk. He completed the reconciliation with Germany and collaborated in the European Economic Union, even though he often prevented agreement, especially on agricultural products. Although France continued to suffer from inflation, his introduction of the new franc (100 old francs = 1 new franc) did create a psychological climate that led to greater stability—all of which, however, did not prevent most French from continuing to count in old francs in the same way in which Parisians continue to call the Place du Général de Gaulle by the old name of l'Etoile. Finally, to give France status among the big powers, de Gaulle placed emphasis on an independent nuclear striking force, the *force de frappe.*

In its inimitable way, France completed its reconstruction long after the rest of Europe and caught up with the twentieth century at its own pace, the way it had skeptically lagged behind during the Industrial Revolution. On the positive side, France avoided the economic ups and downs of the other countries and most French enjoyed prosperous economic conditions during the 1960s.

Nevertheless, in the presidential elections of 1965, de Gaulle was forced into a second ballot to defeat a strong challenge from the Socialist candidate, François Mitterrand. His failure to obtain a clear majority on the first ballot should have been taken as a warning sign that the French people were becoming restive under paternal rule, but de Gaulle would not (and probably could not) change his style. In the 1967 legislative elections the Gaullists lost some forty seats, retaining only a bare majority.

Elected president of the Republic in 1958 for a seven-year term, de Gaulle surrounded himself with capable ministers; nevertheless, his administration had two close calls. The first was caused by the brutal assassination of Moroccan opposition leader Ben Barka in October 1965 just outside Paris. The murder itself was the work of the Moroccan minister of the interior, but it turned out that French police (several kinds of police, in fact) had collaborated with the Moroccan officials and that underworld figures were involved in the affair. The case had all the makings of a French Watergate affair, but the judge in charge of the investigation received no cooperation from the government, and questions were limited to the narrow scope of the assassination itself in a manner reminiscent of the Zola trial in 1898. It must be added that the French tend to take a more tolerant view of governmental indiscretions than the Americans.[2]

It was neither elections nor financial problems nor scandals that led to de Gaulle's downfall, but students. Although the government had made efforts to improve the situation of the French universities, the heavy demand made on them by the large postwar baby boom led to serious overcrowding; moreover, the selective admission policy and the rigid requirement system had changed but little since the nineteenth century and aroused the ire of frustrated students. Unrest began at the Nanterre branch of the University of Paris in March 1968, and open confrontation between students and police broke out on 3 May, when students set up barricades and burnt cars in the Latin Quarter.

The rebellion spread to universities in the provinces, and workers seized on the indecisiveness of the government to strike and occupy factories, until more than seven million workers were striking. De Gaulle went on television promising a referendum, but that strategy had lost its appeal by then. Premier Pompidou set up talks with industrialists and union leaders that resulted in an attractive offer to workers, but the union members turned it down. Was it to be 1830 or 1848 all over again, or was this perhaps even a revival of the Commune uprising?

De Gaulle had been ineffective, and his resignation was expected when, on 29 May, he cancelled a cabinet meeting and disappeared for destinations unknown. But the old fox proved to be more clever than his adversaries. He returned the next day and made a powerful radio address, giving the French a choice between his government or chaos. His followers now came out of hiding and thousands of them paraded through Paris in his support. The strikes ended, the workers received generous salary increases, and the student revolt came to an end after promises of university reforms. In the June elections the Gaullist party scored a landslide victory.

Despite these triumphs, de Gaulle's prestige (and, even more, his pride) had suffered. He replaced Pompidou, who had become too important during the May events, by the more discreet Couve de Murville. In April 1969 he went again before the voters with proposed constitutional amendments. They provided for greater autonomy for the provinces and for changes in the Senate to make it representative of all social and economic groups. On both of these proposals a single yes or no answer was to be given. This time the general lost both the battle and the war. Fifty-three percent of the voters turned down the proposed changes. Thereupon de Gaulle resigned. He died in November 1970.

There can be no denying that Charles de Gaulle was the greatest French leader of the twentieth century. He not only maintained hope and faith in a French recovery after the disastrous defeat in 1940 and during the German occupation, but he gave to the French a sense of self-respect after a long period of humiliation. His character and professional formation, along with his unique prestige during a chaotic period, could have inclined him to assume dictatorial powers, but his profound understanding of the desires of his people led him to adhere to republican principles; and the constitution of the Fifth Republic will leave his deep imprint on the future of France.

Georges Pompidou won the 1969 presidential election and followed a more flexible domestic and foreign policy. He died while in office in 1974 and was succeeded by Giscard d'Estaing.

Chronology

1958: Referendum accepts constitution of Fifth Republic; de Gaulle elected president for seven-year term; devaluation of the franc.

1959: Debré appointed premier; de Gaulle proposes autodetermination for Algeria.

1960: Introduction of new franc; first French nuclear bomb exploded; André Stil: *Le Foudroyage.*

1961: Referendum on future of Algeria approved; army revolt in Algeria collapses.

1962: Franco-Algerian agreement at Evian; resignation of Debré, succeded by Pompidou; independence of Algeria proclaimed; Anouilh: *La Foire d'empoigne.*

1964: France recognizes Communist China.

1965: Presidential election campaign; Ben Barka affair; de Gaulle reelected on second ballot.

1966: French withdrawal from NATO.

1967: Legislative elections, Gaullist party loses seats; de Gaulle in Montreal: "Vive le Québec libre!"

1968: Student riots, Sorbonne closed; students occupy Sorbonne and Odéon Theater; workers take over workshops; de Gaulle in Rumania; strikes spread; de Gaulle announces referendum; Pompidou negotiates with industrial and labor leaders; de Gaulle leaves Paris for destination unknown; de Gaulle returns and dissolves Assembly; radio address, march in his support; workers end strikes, Sorbonne evacuated; Gaullist party wins absolute majority in legislative elections; Pompidou dismissed, succeeded by Couve de Murville.

1969:   Constitutional referendum rejected; de Gaulle resigns;
         Pompidou elected president.

1970:   Death of de Gaulle; James Jones: *The Merry Month of
         May*.

1971:   Mitterrand merges small leftist group with Socialist
         party; Merle: *Derrière la vitre*.

Colonial Wars

André Stil: Torture in Algeria

The war in Indochina lasted from 1946 to 1954, but it was largely a
guerilla war in a faraway place that annoyed the French but did not
become a burning issue until military reversals in its final stages required important reinforcements. No important literary work came out
of this war. There was simply no new Malraux in France to depict
exotic revolutionary heroism; besides, the mood of the times was quite
different from that of 1933.

The Algerian war, which began in November 1954 and lasted until
1962, was quite a different matter. It involved large forces and severely
divided the country. While most of the French sympathized with their
countrymen in Algeria, liberals denounced the war as colonialist and
brutal. A book by the Algerian journalist Henri Alleg entitled *La
Question*[3] (The Torture) aroused French public opinion by revelations of
the torturing by French forces of Algerian prisoners and led to protests
from liberals, among them Sartre, who wrote a preface to Alleg's
documentary work.

The Algerian war inspired a great number of books, most of which
are primarily personal accounts of the war experience.[4] The most notable work of opposition to the war was produced by André Stil, then the
editor of the Communist newspaper *L'Humanité*. Stil devoted three
novels to the Algerian war: *Nous nous aimerons demain* (1957), *Le
Foudroyage* (1960), and *Le Dernier Quart d'heure* (1962).[5] The first two
are of particular interest to us.

Nous nous aimerons demain.   In *Nous nous aimerons demain* the
action takes place between June 1955 and May 1956. Raymond, a
worker known in his town as the goalkeeper of the local soccer team,
has to leave to perform his military service in Algeria. When he re-

turns, he is a changed man. Melancholy, suffering from insomnia, uncommunicative, he drives his fiancée, Annie, to despair. Little by little, as his experiences in Algeria come back to him in involuntary flashbacks, we discover the causes of his guilt and humiliation.

Three episodes stand out: (1) when he refused to paint "Algérie Française" on walls, an officer ordered him to dig a grave and step into it; (2) when he saw an Algerian woman carrying her dead child; (3) when he killed an Algerian rebel who was about to shoot one of his comrades. He will never again be the carefree, popular, and loving fiancé of Annie's.

Le Foudroyage   Stil's *Le Foudroyage* opposes two brothers: Albert, the older, works in the dark mine, while Bernard has decided to enlist and fight in sunny Algeria. Contrary to appearances, the one in the dark sees clearly, and the other is blinded by the sun. Bernard's fatal moment arrives when his unit is caught in an ambush and several of his comrades are killed. He believes that his friend Doffenies is among the dead (it later turns out that he was only wounded and recovered). In a rage Bernard volunteers to execute an old Algerian accused of having aided the rebels.

From then on his comrades no longer talk to him. Eventually he gets caught up in the torturing of Algerian prisoners. When he comes home on leave, his brother has learned of his actions from Doffenies, and Bernard is again shunned; in fact, before he leaves, the two brothers get into a fight. Once back in Algeria, he mends his ways and regains the friendship of Doffenies. He dies heroically while continuing to drive a truck through an ambush, even though wounded, thereby saving the lives of those in the rear of the truck. A few days later his family hears his voice in a radio broadcast of recorded messages from soldiers.

Opposition to the Algerian war is expressed by indirection, almost insidiously. The novels illustrate what happens to nice, ordinary young men who are exposed to the war. Stil very cleverly sidestepped the question of whether the war was justified, for emotions were running so high that he would have lost quite a few readers; instead, he attacked the manner in which it was fought. His special target is the French officers, who are depicted as brutal and sadistic, torturing prisoners not only for information but for the enjoyment of it. No reference is ever made to the possibility that the Algerian rebels may be committing atrocities, too. In fact, in one case it turns out that what appeared to be an atrocity perpetrated on French soldiers had been staged by French officers in order to motivate their men! When Bernard, once again changed into a nice person, denies in a letter that he is a hero, he adds: "Besides, you would look in vain for heroes in a war like this one! If there are any, you'll find them perhaps on the other side." [D'ailleurs, des héros tu peux toujours les chercher dans une guerre pareille! Si, de l'autre côté, peut-être (*Trois Pas*, 297).]

André Stil does not limit his attack to the bad colonialists[6] and to the French Army in Algeria or the CRS at home, who seem to engage in brutalities and torture, rounding up and killing Algerians for no apparent reason. He takes aim at the entire French capitalist system, which is the real culprit. Both brothers are in reality victims of that system. Bernard is forced to commit inhuman and humiliating acts by the French army; and Albert, the miner, is forced to perform inhuman and humiliating work by the exploitative capitalist system. Both have to risk their lives. Bernard, who made the error of enlisting in the army, dies partly because of his own fault; while Albert, who resisted that temptation, saves himself by changing his type of work.

Revolt on the Left Bank

Was May 1968 a revolution, a revolt, or a happening? A revolution it was certainly not. For that, its base was not broad enough and its political philosophy too thin. A revolt? Certainly, but a revolt too limited to carry with it the entire nation. Can you imagine a country overthrowing its government for a reform of university education or for coeducational dormitories? It would have been just another student riot, if it had not found an echo at that time in a general sense of dissatisfaction which, like the student revolt, cannot easily be pinpointed. There had been no tampering with the right to vote, no hateful new taxes had been imposed, economic conditions were relatively favorable or, at least, in no way bad enough to cause an uprising. But both the students and many other French citizens shared a common resentment against paternal authority: against the administration and professors in the case of the students, against de Gaulle in the case of many people. And the World War II generation, which had spent its youth in war, occupation, prison camps, or the Resistance, could not resist conjuring up the imaginary youth they had missed and joining their sons and daughters in a political *monôme*, a parade in which students let off steam after examinations, turning over the lecterns of professors and mussing up the hair of their self-assured and dignified presidents.

Even though the usual causes of a revolt were not present in May 1968, was this all there was to it? Obviously not. Underneath the street fighting, the burning cars, and the interminable speeches at the Odéon Theater, lay far deeper causes that were coming to the fore. For some, the time of resolving the class struggle seemed to have arrived (even though the French Communist party remained aloof); others joined because they were protesting against the brazen materialism of the period. Still others saw in the May events a unique moment of true companionship, a chance to break out of the isolation of modern life by joining fraternally with all other French people, regardless of social class. And forever present, especially in France, are the bourgeoisie's self-hatred and guilt, which make them militate against their obvious self-interest, ever ready to recreate another 4 August 1789, when young nobles joyfully signed away the privileges they felt they did not deserve.

Perhaps the causes of this outbreak of discontent are best expressed by Martine, the realistic French mistress of the narrator in James Jones's novel *The Merry Month of May*.

Also, they are tired, the people. They love de Gaulle, he is their great hero, but they are tired of him now. They are bored with him. You must remember, they get bored easy, the French people. They are bored with this kind of sacrifice *pour la Patrie* which asks the people and workers to sacrifice while the Patronat sacrifices by buying more old chateaux and changing their grounds into beautiful private parks for themselves and relatives. . . .

Too, you must remember we are a race of anarchists. Maybe the last left. Periodically for no reason we want to change. It is some kind of mass hysterical. Do not forget that we still keep the *louis d'or* in the mattress. And we do not complain of the bruises caused by this, or the lack of good sleep.

And now the people are tired, of all this, and they are what you say? pissed off, and they are going to just sit down. They will refuse to work or do anything, just like the students are.[7]

Literary Productions

Fiction concerning the May 1968 events illustrates the diminishing ability of French writers to take political sides. Most of the novels dealing with that short but exciting period attempt to be objective, showing all the points of view from a more or less sympathetic perspective. The result is, at best, fictionalized documentaries, but it is not the stuff that literary opposition is made of.

One gets the impression that those who write about the May riots seem embarrassed, and they may well be. As intellectuals, most sympathized with the protesting students, but as professionals (some of them are university professors) they realized that their livelihood was threatened; as property owners (most of them owned at least two homes, one of them in the country) they stood only to lose; and as adults they must have sensed, however dimly, that this outburst of leaderless emotion would lead nowhere.

That may be the reason none of the few readable works in this group deals head-on with the entire period of the riots. Robert Merle's *Derrière la vitre* (1970) is limited to a single day, 22 March 1968, when the students at Nanterre staged their first successful occupation of university property; Maurice Clavel's *La Perte et le fracas* (1971) takes place during the summer vacation after it was all over.

Perhaps the real literature of May '68 was written in graffiti on the walls of universities. There the "philosophy" of the movement was bared for all to see. "Society is a carnivorous flower." "I take my desires for reality, because I believe in the reality of my desire." "One pleasure has the bourgeoisie, that of degrading all pleasures." "Be a realist; demand the impossible." "Those who make a revolution by halves, dig their own graves." "A Philistine's tears are the nectar of the gods." "Acid is yellow." "Imagination power." "Sex power." "Cunt power." "Commodities are the opium of the people."[8]

Compared to the vitality of opposition literature inspired by the 1830 and 1848 revolutions (Stendhal's novels, Hugo's *Les Châtiments*), the mediocre quality of the fifty-plus fictional works concerned with the May '68 uprising renders only too apparent the decline in this type of literature in recent years. Patrick Combes reluctantly cites seven novels as having at least some merit,[9] and even these are at best only readable.

A Crowd on the Top: Robert Merle's Derrière la vitre

Of the French novelists dealing with the May '68 events, only Robert Merle, in *Derrière la vitre* (1970), captures the atmosphere of the period, without taking sides.

Reading through the rather shabby love affairs Merle describes, one gains the impression of part-time revolutionaries who do not quite know what they want, but who can turn very ugly when in large groups. As the title implies, these young bourgeois intellectuals are cut off from the realities of life, which they view through the windows of their protected existence, and they play out their psychodramas in an enclosed area, capturing, on 22 March 1968, not the city of Paris, but the conference room at the top of the administration building at Nanterre.

Divided into numerous splinter groups, their only visible opponent is Beaujeu, a Latin professor who substitutes on that day for the absent dean. In their confrontation, the old, courageous professor comes out by far the better when compared with the immature student leaders and the hate-filled, bitter, and violent females. The only one among them of any stature is Daniel Cohn-Bendit, yet he too is typical of the spokespeople of the movement, none of whom wants to be a real leader. This is not so much a sign of their attempt to avoid the cult of personality, as they pretend, as their fear of assuming responsibility, a phenomenon not too surprising in young people still suffering from the ills of adolescence considered as a permanent state.

James Jones

Three's Company: *The Merry Month of May.* With French writers unable to make up their minds, it was left to a foreign observer to pen the best work to come out of a period that should have been a fertile inspiration for masterworks of opposition literature. James Jones's novel *The Merry Month of May* (1970) towers above the ambivalent French half-attempts on the subject, the way his professional screenwriter, Harry Gallagher, stands above the amateurish work of the revolutionary student Cinema Committee.

James not only faithfully chronicles the events of May and early June of 1968; he exhibits a large panorama, displays various shades of attitudes, and, above all, establishes fascinating ties between the near-revolution and the demons it releases in his characters. Having experienced the student rebellion at Berkeley a few years before, the developing rift among generations, and the effect of the Vietnam War in America, Jones was in a position to view the May events in France in the larger perspective of tensions created by the baby boom on the one hand and foolish government policies on the other.

Jack Hartley, the narrator and friend of the Gallaghers, at whose swank apartment on the Ile Saint-Louis in Paris a group of Americans gathers, has not only digested his adolescent experiences but has gotten them out of his system; in fact, he is growing into an old, doting godfather of Gallagher's little daughter, McKenna. But he gradually reveals some unexpected depths: he has gone through student rebellions, political liberalism, and even Zen. The editor of a Parisian review in English, he is also well read.

Harry Gallagher and his Bostonian wife, Louisa, for their part have never quite digested their adolescent liberal life, but have compromised with wealth and commercial success. Harry left the United States when he was about to be blacklisted by the McCarthy Committee on Un-American Activities, and established himself in Paris as a successful screenwriter. Both Harry and Louisa fully approve of their son, Hill, who has joined the student rebellion as a member of the Cinema Committee, which is to make a film of the May events.

David Weintraub, a lonely man who makes his living as a harp player, finds the companionship he needs in his association with the revolutionary students. Unwilling to admit that he has passed the age of forty-five, this pathetic figure plays a key role by introducing Samantha Everton, a nineteen-year-old black American girl, into the group.

Young Hill represents the rebellious baby boomers to the point of caricature. Equally fluent in English and French, he has been studying cinema at the Sorbonne; he swallows everything—from rebellion against the capitalist establishment to rebellion against his parents to Zen and to dope—and ends up meditating in a cave in Spain in the company of hippies who live off his money.

Just about everybody in the American group supports the cause of the students more or less actively. Weintraub throws himself into the fray by hiding in his place the film shot by the Cinema Committee; Hartley, the narrator, works hard to have articles about the movement published in his review; Gallagher agrees to write the screenplay for their film and direct the project free of charge, and Louisa is one hundred percent behind them.

The only dissident voice comes from somewhat unexpected quarters, from Samatha Everton, world-wise and street-wise. Having studied in Paris and in Swiss private schools but possessing a realism and experience gained from participation in leftist student organizations, she does not think much of student activism. "Students are all assholes and jerks. If I could ever find one person who didn't have a personal ambition mixed in with his altruism. If I could find one. Students give me a royal pain in the ass" (*Merry Month,* 132). And she will make no exception for those who got themselves killed down South in the

United States. "So what about them? They knew what they were getting into. Or should have. They knew the chance they were taking. They went down there. Those two white Jewish boys were white Northern assholes. They were fools. They didn't believe those crazy rednecks would ever kill them. And the nigger, James Chaney, knew the chance he was taking in his home country. They all wanted to be there" (*Merry Month*, 132).

She thinks even less of the current student uprising.

These kids are out there in the streets having the time of their lives. They're having *their* "war." They're playing games. They're getting their kicks. All getting their rocks off. . . . Your students'll get their reforms. Or watered down half-assed versions of them. And so what? Meanwhile they're all out there running and yelling and having themselves a vacation, playing cops and robbers. They're enjoying it, you're enjoying it, the police're enjoying it, and the French're enjoying it. It's a bore. I'd rather talk about dancing. (*Merry Month*, 132, 133)

In fact, Samantha, the black girl who calls blacks niggers, thinks that revolutions are outdated. "Revolutions can't happen in the kind of highly organized societies we live in today. And I'm not so sure they should happen. Look at what their Revolution cost the Russians. Anyway, today everybody's got to have his electricity and his water and his gas and his automobile. But Revolution? That's all horseshit. The TV wouldn't work" (*Merry Month*, 131–132).

If the realists in Jones's novel are right, then the May protests turned into an uprising because there was no rain (Hartley), the whole thing is sexual and will end when the people are deprived of comfort or can get gas to go on vacation (Samantha), and the most important thing is to keep on hand a good supply of food and gasoline (Martine).

While the realists keep away from the student revolt or, as Hartley, step only gingerly into it, the others pursue in it their adolescent dreams: Weintraub, that of companionship, the Gallaghers, that of liberal activism. Meanwhile, as the clashes between students and police continue, the meeting rooms, and later the captured Odéon Theater, resound with unending motions, discussions, and "democratic" votes, and sexual promiscuity becomes as casual as the eating of a heated can of soup.

But gradually sobering realizations, and tiredness with the whole business, set in among the French people. Traffic jams, gasoline lines, garbage piled up on the sidewalks—revolution is no fun after a while. But, more seriously still, the students are losing control over their movement as violent outside groups become involved, some for the sake of fighting and some called in by the students themselves. And it is the students' incompetence that turns off the adult participants.

Jones illustrates these factors in a series of antithetical scenes: the savagery with which an ugly-looking mob tears out paving stones at the Square Monge to set up a barricade (*Merry Month,* 216–217) as compared to the exquisite art with which Italian specialists re-lay the paving stones ripped up by the rioters at the Place Maubert (p. 144), and finally the senseless destruction of old and beautiful trees along the boulevard Saint-Michel (p. 222). The artistic paving stones torn out will eventually be replaced by ugly asphalt, but the trees will not grow back for years to come.

By now Hartley, the aesthetically minded realist, has given up. " 'I do not think you can win,' I said bluntly. 'De Gaulle is tough. And the people will get tired of the discomfort and the misery. The workers will take what they can get from the Patronat and give up and go back to work. And they will be worse off than before, even with their pay raises. Because what your Revolution is doing to those trees along the Boulevard, it is also doing to the national economy of France' " (*Merry Month,* 233).

Harry Gallagher gives up for another reason, the students' incompetence, sloppiness, and self-indulgence. Their films, showing anonymous crowds surging forward, are under- or overexposed, and they are streaked because the students failed to clean the lenses of their hand-held cameras. Yet the entire committee applauds wildly when their amateurish efforts are projected on the screen. He lectures them. "There's no point in showing all of this over. I don't even know if I could stand to see it all through another time. You ought to be ashamed of yourselves. And you ought to be doubly ashamed of yourselves for liking it. . . . Jesus Christ! I didn't think I'd ever be in the position where I'd have to tell advanced cinema students of the University of the Sorbonne that they should keep their God damned lenses clean. Don't any of you know how to use a God damned light meter properly?" (*Merry Month,* 283).

And, as the disorders drag on, the man in the street joins in. "How do they think they can run a government when they can't even wipe their own asses?" (*Merry Month,* 266). [10]

Jones sees farther and deeper than his French colleagues. This was not only a revolt against the establishment; it was also the flaming up of the fires fanned by those who preached the generation gap. Harry Gallagher is particularly hurt by the fact that the rebellious youths look contemptuously on his liberal record, accusing him and his kind of having compromised with the establishment, of having made a mess of things, and of being unable to understand them.

Hartley, a childless divorcé, is much less impressed by the young people. "I suppose that we are a generation of drunks, as Hill's younger generation are all the time so loudly proclaiming. I have talked with them about it, and about the cowardice, wastage, and lack of responsibility in it. But I fail to see much difference between that and the pot-smoking and the LSD-taking of their generation; and the slush-brained pot-heads, acid-heads, dropouts and even junkies that they produce." (*Merry Month,* 116).

Hartley may be fairly clear-sighted about what is going on in France, but he is blind when it comes to judging what is going on in the Gallagher family. To him they are the perfect, happy American family, even though living abroad. Yet he should know better, since Louisa threatened to leave her philandering husband back in 1959, and their full rupture was averted only by Harry's oath of faithfulness and repaired by the embrace out of which McKenna was to be born.

Perhaps they would have lived on that way, with a rebellious son, a heavily drinking husband, and a perfect hostess-wife—in short, like any perfectly normal American family—if two things had not happend: (1) a change in atmosphere, caused by the May events, replacing normal, orderly, stable conditions with a mood of anarchism, of vacation from work and responsibility, a mood in which anything was possible and everybody, like the students, could turn his nose up at rules, morality, and discipline and make a reality of his fantasies—in short, one of those brief moments during which people can let their hang-ups hang out; and 2) the realization, in the person of Samantha Everton, of Harry's obsessive fantasy, right before his eyes in his own home.

One night, after a stressful session with film producers and in a half-drunken state, Harry Gallagher reveals to his friend Hartley the most delirious sexual experience of his life, one he cannot get out of his mind. It seems that for Harry to be totally happy, it takes "three to tango": two women going passionately at each other, and Harry in the middle or some other place.

And now there is Samantha, all sex. Weintraub has related in detail how she brought a girlfriend along and what transpired. Samantha is openly propositioning Harry, and even more urgently Louisa, his blushing wife. But, of course, you do not do such things with your own wife. What Samantha is really after is the money that will enable her to join her sabra girlfriend in Tel Aviv. It matters little to Harry that Samantha is sleeping with Weintraub or with revolutionary students, or even with his own son. If you love to have two women, it makes little sense to be jealous of men. What matters is that the wheels of fantasy have begun to turn in Harry's mind.

Of course, Harry forgets all about his oath of faithfulness, and when he goes to the Cannes Film Festival to strike against his own film in support of the May movement, he has a liaison with Samantha and the other girl. On his return to Paris, he installs Samantha in a small hotel on the Ile Saint-Louis (of all places)!

When Samantha leaves for Rome and from there to Tel Aviv to join her beloved girlfriend, he follows her—despite Louisa's hovering between life and death—until he catches up with her. Was he really so incensed by the view of Louisa and Samantha embracing passionately? Does he really see it? In *nouveau roman* fashion, we cannot be sure of what really transpired, for Louisa denies everything. Of course, Louisa proposes to have an affair with Hartley, and, of course, Hartley refuses. So Louisa takes a heavy overdose of pills and will probably suffer serious brain damage, perhaps turn into a vegetable.

The Unchaining of the Demons. It gradually dawns on us what James Jones is really saying: May '68 was a short spell of what in the nineteenth century was called "Bovarysm" and is now called an alternate state of consciousness.[11] Both terms denote a state in which a person thinks himself to be something other than he really is, and/or a state in which he temporarily acts and perceives in a qualitatively different way from his usual state. Just as Madame Bovary, a country doctor's wife, believed herself to be an exquisite and superior lady, and Homais, an energetic mediocrity, saw himself as a great *philosophe,* so the staid French bourgeoisie assumed temporarily the role of liberal reformers, the inexperienced students imagined they were revolutionaries and statesmen, and people who had nothing to say imagined they were great orators.

But for others May '68 had the opposite effect: it revealed to them what they really were and what they really wanted. That is the case for Harry Gallagher, who, very much like Aragon's Pierre Mercadier, takes the plunge into complete and hedonistic freedom. Gallagher is no more meant to be a nice husband and father than Mercadier. He realizes that he has stayed with Louisa out of a sense of duty, and Hill certainly gives him no reason to sacrifice himself as a parent. Of course, there is little McKenna, but what does she weigh against a ménage à trois Gallagher-style? Perhaps even Louisa discovers her lesbian tendencies during these days, but we shall never know.

May '68, as analyzed by Jones, was one of those periods of social and mental disorder when only the useless traffic lights and the ominous black police wagons recalled orderly routine, the kind of period during which hidden or unavowed demons in us are released that make us behave in ways such that, once we have sobered up, we do not recognize ourselves as the same person. It was a period in which the double in us, the sort of double of which Aragon speaks, Freud's id, separates from the other self, the superego, to become independent and go on a rampage, a phenomenon so brilliantly described by Heimito von Doderer as occurring during medieval witch hunts, in his novel *Die Dämonen (The Demons)*.

The Merry Month of May contains a political point of view, but rather than opposition literature, it should perhaps be called position literature, because Jones heaps equal criticism on the French government and the amateurish student rioters.

None of the habitués at the Gallagher gatherings has much good to say about the government. Louisa is the most violently opposed to it. But even the more moderate Hartley resorts to Voltairean irony when describing the government's misjudgment of the May uprising and the "pattern of dissimulation, false promises, and downright lies to gain their ends" (*Merry Month,* 65). He relates the government's reaction when, on 17 May 1968, workers struck all over the country and factories were occupied. "That same day General de Gaulle, with his usual caution and good sense, said, in effect, that he'd be damned if he would cut short his state visit to Romania for such silly tomfooleries. And on Saturday, 18 May, the major railroads, the post offices, and the airports began to go" (*Merry Month,* 172).

When all sides are behaving foolishly and most of the nation joins in, somebody has to pay the bill. Financially, it was, of course, the taxpayers—and the bill was high, around six billion dollars. The cost in human misery cannot be stated in exact figures, but it was considerable. Who paid the horrendous price? Not the students, who got some bumps on the head and some apparent concessions and then went on vacation, receiving slightly increased scholarships. Not the politicians, who played a bit of musical chairs to give the impression of change.

No, the price was paid by the foolish and the innocent: poor, dear, darling, foolish Louisa, punished far, far more than she could possibly have deserved; and little, innocent McKenna, who will be an orphan for all practical purposes.

Politically, Jones's *The Merry Month of May* achieves the demystification of May '68, a short period that has been celebrated and commemorated annually (especially in 1978) as if it had been an event on the same level of importance as the 1830 or 1848 revolutions or the Hungarian uprising in 1956. To that, Jones categorically says "nuts." There was little, if any bloodshed; it was not a struggle between oppressors and oppressed; people were not exiled and there were no boat people; and its failure did not mean the end of freedom. If anything, it was a comic-opera revolution, and proved only once again that the French, who can be fooled only until they run out of gas, are unwilling to trade in their Republic for any other type of government.

A Modern Candide   On the literary level, Jones has written a novel that ties in with French traditions. On the one hand, he has created a mock-epic that compares May '68 with the seventeenth-century civil war known as the Fronde, the slingshot war or *La guerre en dentelle,* the lace war. Both were characterized by tacitly accepted rituals. Just as during the earlier strife the French would call across the lines, inviting the English to fire first ["Tirez les premiers, Messieurs les Anglais"], so in May '68 the two sides seemed to observe certain rules.

The police did not really try to capture the students, and the students did not really try to stay and fight hand-to-hand on their barricades. The volleys of paving stones by the students seemed to reach a definite peak and subside, after which the police would prepare to make their charge. It was like a ritual dance almost. There was always a 20 to 40 yard no-man's land between the two, with the students on the defensive and retreating slowly, while the police took the offensive charging, but slowly enough to let the defenders retreat. Their strategy obviously was to take over more and more blocks of streets, while herding the students back away from the Sorbonne until they dispersed. The tactic of the police was to keep close enough and charging, so as not to give the students time to pull up paving stones and erect new serious barricades. (*Merry Month,* 103)

But there the similarities between the Fronde and the May uprising end. In 1968 there was no elegance, no panache, and the ladies did not join their cavaliers at the front in the manner of the Grande Mademoiselle or Roxane in Rostand's *Cyrano de Bergerac*. Nor was there any clever and precious love-bantering. The 1968 ladies fought in the front lines, lay down in dingy rooms, and used vulgar language.

On the other hand, Jones's novel is set in a framework that parodies Voltaire's *Candide* in a curious and cruel way. Harry Gallagher appears as a sexually obsessed Baron, while his wife, Louisa, assumes the role of Pangloss, maintaining stoutly that their son is right to "do his own thing" and that she is backing him one hundred percent, even though it is evident that he would be better advised to learn to keep his camera lens clean and know how to use a light meter before aspiring to change the world. But while Pangloss miraculously recovers from his grave wounds, Louisa pays for her blindness with her health.

Samantha carries a double function: that of Cunégonde, the sex object desired by all men (but most deeply by Hill), and that of Martin, the realist who maintains that people will always be the same.

Finally, Hill is the Candide of the novel, the young man who lives by what has been put into his poor head by his mother and the student leaders. But, contrary to Candide, he learns nothing from his experiences, and instead of ending up in a garden, the symbol of hope for progress and future happiness, he ends up in a cave, the symbol of darkness and regression.

And so we have come full circle, from Voltaire's Candide, who goes through hell and ends up in a kind of paradise, to Jones's Hill, who starts out in paradise and ends up in hell; from an eighteenth-century Candide, who, however slowly, learns from experience and announces the French Revolution that will find its terrestrial garden in the founding of the Third Republic, to a twentieth-century Hill, who renounces experience in favor of psychedelic phrases, ending up contemplating emptiness in a shelter that an atomic bomb would destroy as if it were made of the empty speeches shouted at the occupied Odéon Theater, during the May '68 uprising.

Conclusion

Qu'est-ce que cela prouve?

After attending a performance of a Racine play, a mathematician is reported to have remarked, "Qu'est-ce que cela prouve?"[1] Ever since, that poor mathematician has been the spittoon of literary critics, and he has been held up as the ultimate example of incomprehension. How can one be so stupid as to demand that literature should prove anything?[2] Yet these same critics, or at least many of them, would agree with the demand that literature should be moral and useful; in short, that it should teach us something. If that is so, then why should literature be exempt from proof?

Instead of blowing indignation through their pipes, our estimable critics might have taught that impertinent mathematician a thing or two. For example, that some literary works are primarily aesthetic or imaginative and prove no more than a musical composition, while others prove a great deal, to wit *Iphigénie* and *Phèdre,* both of which have a great deal to teach us.

Iphigénie proves, or at least posits, this eternal lesson: "Don't play golf with the gods—you'll lose every time"; that it is impossible to explain why the gods do what they do, that a father who blindly follows their orders may lose his daugher and a daughter who blindly obeys her father may lose her life, that matters may indeed turn out well in the end but one had better not count on that happening every time.

Phèdre proves, among other things, that if a woman wants to fool around with her stepson, she had better make sure that he feels the same way she does and that her husband is dead and buried; that, if one has a secret, it is best to keep it to oneself; that it is fine to be a gentleman and not to accuse a woman, but the consequences may be monstrous; that a father should not condemn his son until he has carefully gathered and examined all the evidence; and that it is very difficult, perhaps even impossible, to escape one's heredity.

In fact, our critics could even have singled out *Phèdre* as a play that proves ideas based on a system of determinism, because the people in it are endowed with a certain heredity and character traits, and once the forces in their limited universe are set in motion, everything happens in a predetermined way. So that one may go so far as to suggest that *Phèdre* is a problem in mathematics in which factors in an equation have been replaced by the relative forces of heredity, character, circumstances, and passions.

Now, that ought to give that ignorant mathematician something to chew on for a while and prevent him from annoying literary critics with any more embarrassing questions.

For our part, we would like to restore the maligned mathematician to his rightful place of honor in literary history by attempting to prove that opposition literature in France did more than just entertain, amuse, or interest its readers (which is already quite an achievement), that it contributed substantially to bring about changes in attitudes, changes in governments, and even revolutionary movements during the past 250 years by proving that injustices are unjust, that stupidities are stupid, and that official pretenses "ain't necessarily so."

To understand the influence of literary people, we must remember the high esteem in which they are held in France. The death of a great writer or poet is mourned in France like the passing of a president in America. The great writers of the classical age repose in the Panthéon in Paris, and Victor Hugo's coffin was followed by thousands in a national funeral procession. Montesquieu, Voltaire, Rousseau, and Diderot formed modern political theories; Béranger did as much as anybody else to overthrow the Restoration government and usher in Louis Philippe; Balzac and Alfred de Vigny unsuccessfully sought political office; Lamartine was president of the provisional government formed after the 1848 Revolution; Victor Hugo and Maurice Barrès were members of the French legislature; Léon Blum, who wrote an excellent book on Stendhal, was president of the Third Republic during the Popular Front government. And the list goes on, with men like Anatole France, Charles Péguy, Albert Camus, and Jean-Paul Sartre.

So much for the political activities of literary artists.[3] What influence did their fictional works or poetry have? It is true that opposition literature is unlikely to change the views of those who have firm convictions, although it may humanize them, as Irving Howe remarks very aptly,[4] but it can strongly influence the enormous majority of uncommitted or undecided citizens of a country.

There exist, indeed, several levels of relationship between literature and social and political attitudes. Micheline Tison-Braun characterizes one of them.

Literature is like the consciousness of a society. It spontaneously expresses the states of mind of a period at the same time as it judges and analyzes them. Like a seismograph, literature registers by amplification the shocks that perturb the social body: general opinions, moods, confused aspirations, dissatisfaction, hopes—all these are expressed in literary works, and even those which by the nature of their subject matter seem to be insulated against the problems of the moment are no less profoundly affected by them.[5]

The good or bad effects of literature on society gave rise to studies long before our times. In 1857, Eugène Poitou devoted a long book to this subject, anticipating Tison-Braun's view. He suggests that literature can exert a direct influence by the moral principles it expresses, and an indirect influence by the way it presents characters, actions, or objects as either beautiful or ugly, worthy of admiration or of contempt. "It evokes in us, by a law of sympathy, sentiments in accord with the sentiments it expresses: the human soul is like an instrument that vibrates and comes to life through contact with the vibrations of an instrument close to it."

Examining the effects of works by Montesquieu, Voltaire, Rousseau, Balzac, Stendhal, George Sand, Dumas père, and others, Poitou concludes that their literature has stood morality on its head. "It has exalted what humanity had until then condemned; it has proclaimed as beautiful and great what good sense had always held to be petty and ugly. . . . In a word, it has introduced anarchy in moral ideas and, along with that anarchy, doubts and gloom."[6]

To illustrate his point, Poitou cites statistics that, although interesting, cannot be ascribed to the supposed bad influence of literature alone: suicides in France increased from 1739 during the period 1826–30 to 3415 in 1853, while suits for separation of husband and wife rose from 743 in 1840 to 1191 in 1851.

Statistically, most of the opposition literature in France has been produced by writers from the left of the political spectrum. The reason for this is, of course, explained by the predominance of conservative or middle-of-the-road governments. But when liberal adminstrations got their turn in power, especially after the Dreyfus affair and in the 1930s, they met with violent opposition from writers of the Right.

Although pursuing the same goal of attacking those in power, the manner and methods employed by the two groups tend to be quite different.

The liberal writers of the eighteenth century chose wit and satire as their favorite weapons, and in this they showed excellent judgment, for theirs was an audience capable of appreciating that sort of communication. In the nineteenth century the tone grew more serious, although Stendhal still drew on wit within that atmosphere. In the twentieth century, under the influence of two murderous world wars, the mood became even more somber, as if the modern authors were unable to put much distance between themselves and the events they were dealing with.

Regardless of tone, one can discern a common thread that runs throughout almost all liberal opposition literature: the intention to inspire in those attacked a feeling of guilt, or at least of moral malaise. Moral accusation is the weapon of the weak, but it is effective only if those in authority have a moral sense. Experience has shown that dictators, such as Stalin or Hitler, are not in the least disturbed by moral blame.

During the eighteenth century the philosophes succeeded in pumping so much guilt into the hearts and minds of young and liberal aristocrats that those who would have been expected to defend their privileges were turned into enthusiastic collaborators who joyfully signed away their privileges.

Since the Revolution, the bourgeoisie has filled the void left by the demise of the aristocracy, and in its turn, the new ruling class has been the target of unceasing attacks, beginning with the romantic writers and continuing in the novels or plays by Balzac, Flaubert, Zola, Aragon, and Sartre, to mention only the most prominent. Although, contrary to the eighteenth-century aristocracy, the bourgeoisie has not lost its function, and even though in recent times literary attacks launched against that class have not exactly been brilliant, the long sledgehammering of the French middle class is showing its effect. The general sympathy shown for the miscarried May 1968 uprising and the election of a leftist government, including Communists, in 1981 constitute signs that the French bourgoisie is in the process of turning against itself.

Opposition literature from the Right tends to be serious in tone. Instead of satire and/or exotic backgrounds, conservative writers usually prefer to place their stories in a contemporary and semidocumentary framework. For their yardsticks, they are less likely to resort to rational arguments, preferring instead to appeal to traditional values or even irrational sentiments (for example, ancestor worship, a belief in a "True" France). And their *raisonneurs* are not the moderate mediators of

Molière but powerful dogmatists who create disciples. While liberal writers look to a future France as they feel it ought to be, the conservative ones set up an idealized model of France at some time in the past. But whether pointing to the future or to the past, this much the two sides have in common: they do not like the France they live in.

Generally speaking, those who attack authority enjoy considerable advantages. They appeal, particularly in France, to a deep-seated instinct for rebellion against those in power. They can poke fun at those grave people burdened down with responsibilities, who find it nearly impossible to mount a counterattack because the accusers have usually not been in a position to do anything that would expose them to criticism. On the other hand, those who govern are obliged to defend themselves, which is always awkward because it implies a tacit admission of guilt or error. Besides, important people are constantly under pressure and have less time to devote to their defense than their opponents to attacking them.

But those in power are not powerless against attacks, especially where totalitarian governments are concerned. Their most common weapon is censorship and laws punishing writers who offend them.[7] We have seen that some writers, such as Crébillon fils, Diderot, and Béranger, had to pay for their audacity with heavy fines or imprisonment. They can also be tried for immorality, as Baudelaire and Flaubert learned only too well in the middle of the nineteenth century.

One would think, therefore, that the best opposition literature should have been written at times when France enjoyed the free speech guaranteed by republican rule. But the facts do not bear out this assumption. Montesquieu, Crébillon fils, Voltaire, Beaumarchais, Stendhal, Sartre, and Anouilh all wrote during times of severe censorship, and theirs are masterworks of opposition literature. It would indeed appear that constraints and limitations have done for this type of literature what the much-maligned rules did for the masters of the French classical period.

Under censorship and threat of imprisonment, the opposition writer had to call on all his faculties, his wit, and his wiles to communicate and to survive. As we have observed, satire, wit, clever irony, apparent good humor, and detachment have been the ingredients for success. Unable to portray actual historical conditions, these writers had to use their powerful imaginations to invent fairy tales and adventure stories in exotic countries, or to transform established and well-known subjects in subtle ways. Or when an author did use a contemporary setting, for example, Stendhal, he had to pretend he was dissociating himself from his young and inexperienced hero.

In a free society, the opposition writer can indulge in the luxuries of indignation, anger, name-calling, and nearly undisguised autobiographical narration. But whatever the merits (and they are many) of modern writers such as Aragon, Barrès, or Drieu la Rochelle may be, they have had neither the impact nor the universal appreciation achieved by their politically less fortunate predecessors. While these more recent works often contain valuable historical dramatizations (Barrès on the Boulanger affair and the Panama scandal, Aragon on the underground activities of the French Communist party during 1939–40, Drieu la Rochelle on small political groups and the rise of fascism during the interwar years), the "pistol shots" of politics in their works are too loud to be dampened even by the talents of their authors.

During the past twenty-five years or so, opposition literature has noticeably declined. After the fever of post–World War II, a reaction of tiredness set in, interrupted only by the May 1968 uprising, which may be viewed as a sort of aftershock. The advent of the *nouveau roman* in the 1950s signaled the arrival on the scene of a new generation of writers more concerned with form than with content. And although authors of the *nouveau roman* and directors of the *nouvelle vague* cinema were profoundly interested in politics, with few exceptions (Jean-Luc Godard, for example) they did not choose to turn their pens into swords or their cameras into machine guns.

The enormous impact of the modern media that continually bombard the public with images and indiscriminate (and frequently banal) information has resulted in picture-oriented generations, few of whose members are likely to make the effort necessary to "glimpse some subtle truth that escapes ordinary people" beneath the veil of the story, as Voltaire invited his readers to do.

To be sure, the expression of opposition has not disappeared in France, but, given these radically changed conditions, the media have also been undergoing changes: documentaries on screen and television, "happenings" in which the spectators are invited to participate, and films dealing with opposition themes have provided new expressions for dissenting artists. In fact, the importance of television in political life has grown to such an extent that candidates for high office have had to learn the art of presenting a favorable image of themselves.

In all likelihood future historians will look back on the second half of the twentieth century as a period of prolonged peace for France. The colonial wars in which France was engaged can in no way be compared to the cataclysm of the earlier world wars. In addition, the country has enjoyed a large amount of freedom and many years of prosperity. In a way, the decline of opposition literature in France may be a good sign. It seems to indicate that conditions have become more tolerable in recent decades and that the deep divisions of class and of interests, which made stable governments a near impossibility during most of the Third Republic, have become blurred, so that a Socialist president can cohabit with a conservative premier. These are not conditions that normally engender great opposition literature. So much the worse for opposition literature, so much the better for France.

All this is not to say that there has been a lack of subject matter for satire or political opposition in literary works, but, as we have noted, the colonial wars of the 1950s and the May 1968 uprising did not provoke any major creations. The Ben Barka affair in 1965–66, for example, would have been an ideal subject for either satiric or serious literature, but the writers who would have been capable of producing such works chose instead to express their views in newspaper articles, in televised debates, or in political meetings.

Still, there is no reason to pronounce French opposition literature dead. Declarations of that sort tend to be premature. The sumptuous harvest of novels inspired by the May 1968 events is proof that the tradition itself remains firmly rooted in France. Thus it is not quantity that is lacking, but quality. It is indeed ironic that an American author, James Jones, had to remind his French colleagues that indispensable to a successful opposition work is a fusion of story line and political conditions—underlined by a stand, a judgment, however expressed.

The illiterate mathematician may have been right after all. Even literature has to prove something, and if it happens to be opposition literature, it has to prove a great deal to be valid.

Now, let us ask the fundamental question: What was this study all about and what does it prove? At the risk of oversimplifying, I would answer this way: we have dealt with methods of bringing about change—political, social, economic change.

This can be achieved by brutal military force, but, as the Soviet experience in Eastern Europe has proven, even nearly fifty years after the end of World War II the Soviets are forced to maintain their domination by military threat or they even have to interfere directly to quell uprisings. One does not conquer minds with arms.

Another method, used by modern dictatorships, is to close off the country and hammer away at the population with a blaring propaganda that attempts to instill in it a political ideology, that appeals to nationalism and selects scapegoats for all the country's ills. But this method requires a threat from the outside and concentration camps for political opponents on the inside. Even if the dictatorial regime maintains itself for a long time, in today's world information from the outside can no longer be shut out. Thus, after some seventy years of rule, Soviet communism still has to contend with refuseniks and citizens who desperately want to leave the country.

By contrast, we have examined the method of bringing about change by changing minds, not via military threat or crude propaganda but through outstanding literature.

To succeed in this effort, several conditions are both desirable and necessary:

1. It works best in a country with a high standard of education and sophistication, where an ambitious social class wants to be recognized and change the existing situation.

2. It requires authors who are both excellent literary creators and political thinkers.

3. It needs to advocate a cause that is just and universally admitted to be so; for example, the ideal of a society in which advancement is based on merit rather than on birth or party membership.

4. The writers advocating change must be on the side of history; that is, the forces of history must be moving in the direction of their ideal. Montesquieu, Crébillon fils, Voltaire, Beaumarchais, Béranger, Stendhal, and Victor Hugo were riding the large crest of history in foreseeing a more open, democratic society. Barrès, Drieu la Rochelle, and Aragon were betting on the shorter range of history in supporting dictatorships of one sort or another; while Zola, Sartre, and Anouilh supported the eternal cause of justice, humanity, and freedom from oppression.[8]

When we look at the past 250 years of French history through the subjective eyes of opposition literature, a synthetic pattern develops that offers a unique perspective on that changing and dramatic period.

During the ancien régime, opposition writers did not call for a revolution that would replace royal rule by a popular government, but for social and economic changes that would abolish the unjustified privileges of the nobility and recognize the merits of the rising bourgeoisie.

From the time of the Revolution until the establishment of the Third Republic, the opposition struggled to turn the frustrated ideals of the Revolution into a reality. In this effort the greatest obstacle was no doubt Napoleon, who not only reestablished an empire more absolute than the ancien régime but suffered a military defeat that led to the Restoration of the Bourbon kings and subsequent royal governments.

Since 1871 the opposition has largely come from groups that wanted to overthrow the Republic (rightists, Fascists, Communists, and other revolutionaries).

Events have shown that the French prefer a republlic, even if it is imperfect, to all other forms of government. So let us conclude with an affectionate salute to the spirit of the French people, who, throughout their challenges and trials, have stubbornly held high their banner of freedom.

Notes and References

Preface

1. Edmond Scherer, *Etudes sur la littérature contemporaine* (Paris: Calmann Levy, 1894), 7:72–73.

2. Morris Edmund Speare, in *The Political Novel: Its Development in England and in America* (New York: Oxford University Press, 1924), 336, laments the lack of political novels set in Washington, D.C.. "So far as the political significance of the city is concerned, there seems, astonishingly enough and in spite of all these years, but one serious reflection of it. Henry Adams still stands a lone figure." And Michael Millgate, in *American Social Fiction: James to Cozzens* (Edinburgh and London: Oliver and Boyd, 1964), 199, ascribes the failure of American social novelists to the influence of realism and of naturalism. "Most American social novelists have lacked a sense of proportion in their treatment of society. . . . The most persistent tendency in American realism is for the realist to become obsessed with his material. He not only fails to shape it, he allows the novel to be shaped by it: the material takes charge."

3. John Newman, *Vietnam War Literature: An Annotated Bibliography of Imaginative Works about Americans Fighting in Vietnam* (Metuchen, New Jersey and London: Scarecrow Press, 1982), 7.

4. Peter Leonard Stromberg, "The Long War's Writing: American Novels about the Fighting in Vietnam While Americans Fought,"*Dissertation Abstracts International* 35 (1975): 4562–A (Cornell University).

Chapter One

1. This account of the birth of the French Third Republic might give a historian from the planet Pluto the mistaken impression that Bismarck was the founder of the Third Republic. Nothing could be further from the truth, since Bismarck is not known to have held any particular love for the French or for republics. But then, there are no other candidates, no George Washingtons to point to. Malicious tongues might even suggest that Bismarck did more to bring about the realization of the Revolution's dreams than the Revolution itself, since he did to the obstacle of a republic (to wit, the Second Empire) what the Revolution had done to the ancien régime; they might further suggest that the Prussian victory, in fact, brought about a republic far more quickly and effectively than the Revolution, without having to cut off any imperial heads.

These rather paradoxical views of French history lead to a question about French revolutions in general. If, indeed, it is agreed that their purpose was to create a republican government, they were all failures. The Revolution of 1789 resulted in the Terror, the First Empire, and the Restoration; that of 1830 merely changed royal families (from Bourbon to Orléans); and the much vaunted revolution of 1848 soon ended up with the Second Empire. Perhaps only the May 1968 uprising can be considered a success, and then only because it had no recognizable purpose other than university reform, which was achieved, at least in some manner.

What may we legitimately conclude from all this? Perhaps that the French have been more successful in overthrowing governments they did not like than in setting up those they wanted. One of the many ironic twists of history is that the first workable parliament was bestowed on France by, ironically, the Bourbon Restoration, which also came about as the result of military defeat.

One may, of course, argue that these revolutions paved the way for the belated arrival of the Third Republic. But that proposition can be twisted in many ways, for by the same token one could claim that Napoleon's final defeats prepared the French for defeat in the War of 1870.

While, in practical terms, these are rather idle considerations, they do nevertheless suggest that if history runs on rails, they must have been designed by a strange engineer, since the end result of actions often turns out to be not only different from but contrary to their original aim.

2. Quoted in Frederic H. Seager, *The Boulanger Affair: Political Crossroad of France, 1886–1889* (Ithaca, N.Y.: Cornell University Press, 1969), 33.

3. This version is denied by Frederic H. Seager, *The Boulanger Affair,* 204–5. Barrès, who was an eyewitness, does not report these exact words, but when Boulanger wants to leave the Restaurant Durand, where the leaders of the movement have gathered, through the front door, someone shouts: "What folly! The excited crowd will carry you to the Elysée." [Quelle folie! cria-t-on, la foule emballée vous porterait à l'Elysée (Maurice Barrés, *L'Apppel au soldat,* Paris: Charpentier, 1900, 212).]

4. We think of such characters as Rastignac in Balzac's *Le Père Goriot,* Lucien de Rubempré in his *Illusions perdues,* or Julien Sorel in Stendhal's *Le Rouge et le noir.*

5. The name Bouteiller may by symbolic. A *bouteiller* fills empty glasses with wine. Bouteiller fills the empty minds of his students with bad ideas, according to Barrès's judgment.

6. In reality, it was not Barrès but Charles Maurras who had received this visit from Taine. A Hegelian and a conservative thinker, Taine was ideally suited to be opposed to the dry Kantian and republican philosophy of Bouteiller. But in many other ways Taine's views were far different from those of Barrès. He had criticized not only the Revolution but also Napoleon, he had personally suffered from the Catholic-dominated educational councils while at

the Ecole normale, and his concepts of the French character had little in common with the exalted image of it projected by Barrès. See Leo Weinstein, *Hippolyte Taine* (New York: Twayne, 1972), on these subjects.

7. Page numbers refer to Maurice Barrès, *Les Déracinés* (Paris: Charpentier, 1898).

8. Napoleon's tomb would probably have been the last place suggested by Taine for such a meeting. He had roundly criticized Napoleon for having imprisoned France in "philosophical barracks," and attacked the emperor for his egoism.

9. Barrès had that revelation in church during the requiem mass after the death of his parents.

10. Page numbers refer to Maurice Barrès, *L'Appel au soldat.*

11. Barrès's trilogy is another example of the phenomenon of accusing scapegoats, so brilliantly analyzed by René Girard, in *Le Bouc émissaire* (Paris: Grasset, 1982), especially chap. 2.

12. It is noteworthy that *Leurs Figures* is dedicated to the anti-Semite Drumont.

13. Barrès had written an earlier trilogy, *Le Culte du moi,* published from 1888 to 1891 and comprising *Sous l'oeil des Barbares, Un Homme libre,* and *Le Jardin de Bérénice.*

14. Page numbers refer to Maurice Barrès, *Leurs Figures* (Paris: Charpentier, 1917).

15. Paul Bourget had written a novel, *Le Disciple* (1889), in which he criticized his master, Taine.

16. Alfred Jarry's play *Ubu-Roi* had been performed in 1896, only a year before *Les Déracinés* was published.

17. Sturel's own friends call it a "fever" (Saint-Phlin, in Barrès, *L'Appel au soldat,* 283) or a "skirmish" (Roemerspacher, ibid., 403).

18. Seager, *The Boulanger Affair,* 26.

19. It is remarkable that two French generals have made an important contribution to the preservation of the republican system: Boulanger in 1888 and Charles de Gaulle in 1958. Circumstances in both cases were such that they could probably have seized power by military *coups* and ruled as the heads of military dictatorships. It is to the credit not only of the two men but also of the French Army that they chose to respect the republican institutions. Boulanger may also deserve some credit for the honorable behavior of French officers during the Dreyfus affair (see chap. 2) because of the reforms he introduced in the army while he was war minister.

20. After relating Boulanger's hesitations to take power by force, Barrès comments: "He remembers that his father recited Victor Hugo's invectives against the Man of 2 December. He fears the judgments of historical writers. Completely ignorant of the literary craft, he shudders at the noise of the pen." [Il se rappelle que son père récitait les invectives de Victor Hugo contre

l'Homme du Deux-Décembre. Il redoute le jugement des rédacteurs de l'histoire. Tout à fait ignorant du métier littéraire, il s'épouvante d'un bruit de plumes (*L'Appel au soldat,* 210).]

21. Alceste recites this popular song to illustrate the difference between true and affected sentiments. It goes like this:

> If the king had offered me
> Paris, his big city,
> And I'd have to part
> From the love of my sweetheart,
> I would say to King Henri:
> "You can keep your big Paris,
> I prefer my love, I do,
> I prefer my love."
>
> [Si le roi m'avait donné
> Paris, sa grand'ville,
> Et qu'il me fallût quitter
> L'amour de ma mie,
> Je dirais au roi Henri:
> Reprenez votre Paris,
> J'aime mieux ma mie, au gué,
> J'aime mieux ma mie.]
> (Molière, *Le Misanthrope,* 1.2)

Chapter Two

1. The Dreyfus case confirms the saying that truth is stranger than fiction. After observing how inconsistently many of the people involved behaved, one wonders whether consistency is a valid literary criterion, and we are more ready to accept the behavior of characters in Victor Hugo's play *Hernani* (1830), for example, where, out of a sense of honor, everybody seems to protect his own enemies from arrest.

2. Jean Denis Bredin, *L'Affaire* (Paris: Julliard, 1983), 448.

3. Ibid., 428.

4. For example: Anatole France, *L'Ile des pingouins* (1908); Roger Martin du Gard, *Jean Barois* (1913); or references to the Dreyfus affair in Marcel Proust's *A la recherche du temps perdu* (1913–1922). On this subject see Cécile Delhorbe, *L'Affaire Dreyfus et les écrivains français* (Paris: Attinger, 1932).

5. Anatole France, *L'Anneau d'améthyste* (Paris: Calman-Lévy, 1905). Page numbers refer to this edition. Maurice Bouchor, the poet mentioned in the quotation, is today best remembered for his lyrics to Ernest Chausson's *Poème de l'amour et de la mer,* op. 19, for voice and orchestra, which ends on the well-known melody "Le Temps des lilas."

6. Émile Zola, *Vérité,* in *Oeuvres complètes,* vol. 8 (Paris: Cercle du Livre

Précieux, 1968). Page numbers refer to this edition. Publication of the novel began on 10 September 1902 in the newspaper *L'Aurore*. Zola died on 28 September 1902, and the novel appeared in book form in 1903.

7. These two novels form parts 3 and 4, respectively, of Anatole France's *Histoire contemporaine*, and are preceded by *L'Orme du mail* and *Le Mannequin d'osier*.

8. Page numbers refer to Anatole France, *Monsieur Bergeret à Paris* (Paris: Calman-Lévy, 1906).

9. *L'Anneau d'améthyste*, 389–94.

10. During the nineteenth century, religious schools had regained a good part of the territory lost during the Revolution. In 1893 there were 68,000 public elementary schools compared to 15,000 religious ones, and 84,000 public lycées compared to 52,000 religious ones.

11. Anatole France, *Monsieur Bergeret à Paris*, 248–259, is more specific in describing his dream of a future France established on socialist principles.

Chapter Three

1. *Les Cloches de Bâle* (Paris: Denoël, 1934); *Les Beaux Quartiers* (Paris: Denoël, 1936), for which Aragon received the Prix Renaudot; *Les Voyageurs de l'impériale* (Paris: Gallimard, 1947) first published in 1942 in the United States; and *Aurélien* (Paris: Gallimard, 1944). All page numbers refer to these editions. Typical criticism can be found in David Coute, *Le Communisme et les intellectuels français, 1914–1966* (Paris: Gallimard, 1962). Coute sees in *Le Monde réel* merely one of the many novels "written by members of the middle class for the middle class against the middle class" (p. 396). As for *Les Communistes*, the author considers this work "not really a novel but a gigantic tract that gives the impression of a collection of newspaper articles placed end to end on a role of Chinese parchment, it is an unreadable birthday gift offered to those already converted" (p. 403).

2. This is particularly noticeable in his six-volume novel *Les Communistes* (1949–51).

3. Aragon left no doubt about what he meant by the "real world" in an address to the International Convention of Writers for the Defense of Culture. "I call for a return to reality. I say, who is opposed to it except those in whose interest it is to cover up, to keep it from being seen? At a time when the bourgeoisie abandons everything that was enlightened in its early program, when, to maintain its bloody domination, it throws off the mask of liberalism and burns its parliaments, . . . it can no longer stand the spotlight of realism, the consideration of reality. . . . We, allies of the revolutionary proletariat, its brothers in combat, have the duty to unveil this sham, we have everything to hope for from the denunciation made by reality. We have nothing to hide, and that is why we welcome as words of joy the precepts of Soviet literature, the

socialist realism." Remarks quoted in Jean Bessière, *Les Ecrivains engagés,* Collection Idéologies et Sociétés (Paris: Larousse, 1977), 88.

    4. *La Nouvelle Critique* 8 (July–August 1949): 82. Quoted in Roger Garaudy, *L'Itinéraire d'Aragon,* Collection Vocations, no. 10 (Paris: Gallimard, 1961), 297.

    5. It must be recalled that the novel was written at the time of the Spanish civil war, in which Aragon took an active part. The diatribe against individualism is directed at those intellectuals who practiced nonintervention and divorced their private lives from politics.

    6. *Les Cloches de Bâle* takes place from 1904 to 1912; *Les Beaux Quartiers* covers the period 1912–13; *Les Voyageurs de l'impériale* begins in 1889 and ends in 1914.

    7. To leftist critics who saw in *Aurélien* decadent literature detached from history, Aragon replied: "I accept the criticism that *Aurélien* is bourgeois literature. . . . I am fond of love stories and say frankly: Too bad for those who consider them some sort of amusement, of cowardice at a time of war and revolutions." Quoted in Garaudy, *L'Itinéraire d'Aragon,* 376.

    8. Aragon revealed that Aurélien was not a portrait of himself, but that he had in mind Drieu la Rochelle, a notorious ladies' man. See *Oeuvres romanesques croisées d'Elsa Triolet et Louis Aragon* (Paris: Laffont, c.1964), 19:12.

    9. A similar view of the divided man who can find his unity only by a political solution (implied: the Communist party) is presented by Paul Nizan, in *Antoine Bloyé* (Paris: Grasset, 1933), 261. "Every being is divided into the one who is awake and later the one who falls asleep, and the two rarely form a good couple. . . . Which is the man who can overcome his division? He will not overcome it all by himself, for the causes of his divided state are not within him. . . . As long as men will not be complete and free, steady on their legs and on the ground which supports them, they will dream at night." [Tout être est divisé, il est celui qui veille, plus tard celui qui s'endort et le dormeur et le veilleur font rarement bon ménage. . . . Quel homme sait triompher de sa division? Il n'en triomphera point tout seul car les causes de sa division ne sont pas en lui. . . . Aussi longtemps que les hommes ne seront pas complets et libres, assurés sur leurs jambes et la terre qui les porte, ils rêveront la nuit.]

Chapter Four

    1. Pierre Drieu la Rochelle, *The Comedy of Charleroi and Other Stories,* tran. with introduction by Douglas Gallagher (Cambridge: Rivers Press, 1973), 44–45.

    2. Pierre Drieu la Rochelle, *La Comédie de Charleroi* (Paris: Gallimard, 1934), 57–58.

    3. Henri Barbusse, *Le Feu: Journal d'une escouade* (Paris: Flammarion, 1917), 330. Paradis does not quote the woman correctly; she had called attacks "superb" (p. 300). All page numbers refer to this edition.

Chapter Five

1. This blindness to obvious and imminent danger is brilliantly satirized in the 1953 play *Die Brandstifter (The Firebugs)* by Max Frisch, where a landlord rents an apartment to people carrying gasoline cans at a time when arson rages all over the town.

2. The same holds true for certain keys that have been suggested: The group Révolte seems to have been inspired by the political role of the dadaist and surrealist groups; Caël, by André Breton; Cyrille Galant, by Louis Aragon; and Clérences, either by Drieu's political friend Gaston Berger or by Jouvenel.

3. In the preface to an earlier short story, "La Valise vide," Drieu claims: "I flagellated pitilessly my epoch in myself, that epoch when society was rapidly aging." The story is part of a collection, *Plainte contre inconnu* (Paris: Gallimard, 1924).

4. "What did he know about his race?" [Que savait-il de sa race? (p. 145).] All page numbers refer to Pierre Drieu la Rochelle, *Gilles,* Edition Folio (Paris: Gallimard, 1939). When *Gilles* was published in 1939, some passages had been censored. The full text appeared only in 1942.

5. Dora judges Gilles a failure. "Gilles was nothing and never would be anything. . . . He seemed to live in a strangely mixed-up world, in which politics became a legend, a disconcerting mythology." And his own reflections confirm what she thinks of him. "All those guys hold it against me that women find me pleasing. I please them, but they don't love me. Dora has made me see that. What am I aside from that, which is also a failure?" [Gilles n'était rien du tout et ne serait jamais rien. . . . Il semblait vivre dans un monde étrangement mêlé où la politique devenait une légende, une mythologie déconcertante. . . . "Tous ces garçons m'en veulent parce que je plais aux femmes. Je leur plais, mais elles ne m'aiment pas. Dora me l'a fait comprendre. Que suis-je en dehors de cela, cela même qui est raté?" (*Gilles,* 321, 322, 486).]

6. The term "reactionary" is used here in the descriptive sense, i.e., an attitude that advocates return to an earlier state. Such an attitude, in itself, is not necessarily good or bad; it must be judged in a given context. It is regrettable that this and similar terms, such as "modern" or "innovative", which simply indicate a chronological relationship, have been tainted with judgmental connotations. If one important aim of our schools is to turn out independent thinkers, they will first have to teach students the meaning and value of words.

7. The romantics were no doubt attracted to the Middle Ages because of the atmosphere and mysterious aspects of that period, but there were also practical reasons for this preference: it was an effective way of showing that classicism and rationalism were not the only literature and philosophy in the world.

8. Hippolyte-Adolphe Taine, *Les Origines de la France contemporaine* (Paris: Hachette, 1947), 9:60.

9. In the only scene in which Gilles is shown making overtures to a woman, he simply uses the hardly original line, "You are beautiful" (*Gilles,* 505), and the matter is settled.

10. There are, of course, other types of people who are attracted to totalitarian movements. Some are completely devoid of idealism and simply enjoy the brutal gang fighting; others may drift into such a movement for material reasons, as illustrated in Louis Malle's excellent film *Lacombe, Lucien* (1974).

11. Gaëton Picon, *Panorama de la nouvelle littérature française* (Paris: Gallimard, 1949), 72. In the revised edition of 1960, Picon calls *Gilles* "one of the important novels of the century" (p. 88).

Chapter Six

1. This was one of the many foolish actions taken by the French government. By dissolving the Communist party at a time when the party was facing total discredit and severe interior divisions, the government decree let the Communists off the hook. Instead of having to answer extremely embarrassing questions, they now were able to take on the role of martyrs, and that is how Aragon presents them.

More recent governments have apparently not learned the basic lesson of letting opponents stew in their own juice. An example is the American decision to boycott the 1980 Olympic Games in the Soviet Union to protest the Soviet aggression against Afghanistan. This moral gesturing, unaccompanied by effective action, did not remove a single Soviet soldier from Afghanistan, and the United States lost thereby the unique opportunity of having hundreds of American reporters in Moscow asking highly embarrassing questions. It would have been far more intelligent to continue exporting wheat to the Soviet Union and to use the money paid for it to aid the Afghan freedom fighters. But would the United States Congress have agreed to anything so immoral but immensely useful? Moreover, could such a policy have been publicly proclaimed, as our legislators often demand?

From these experiences, one may arrive at the unpleasant conclusion that moral indignation is not always the best guide in foreign policy.

2. Louis Aragon, *Les Communistes,* 6 vols. (Paris: La Bibliothèque Française): vol. 1, *Février—Septembre 1939* (1949); vol. 2, *Septembre–Novembre 1939* (1949); vol. 3, *Novembre 1939–Mars 1940* (1950); vol. 4, *Mars–Mai 1940* (1950); vol. 5, *Mai 1940* (1951); vol. 6, *Mai–Juin 1940* (1951). All page numbers refer to this edition.

3. Aragon's description of the wounded and the maimed is more dramatic than that of Barbusse. For example, an important character, who leads the heroine to communism, is a simple soldier, the brother of her maid. He is so grievously wounded that, armless and legless, he can speak only through the prism of his bandaged face.

4. Careful selecting and editing of those portions of *Les Communistes* that deal strictly with the French World War II experience could turn Aragon's novel into a classic, but it is doubtful whether the author would have approved of such an attempt.

5. Sartre, in his unfinished series of novels, bearing the collective title *Les Chemins de la liberté,* pursued a similar aim: to show that we are totally free but also toally responsible. The first volume, *L'Age de raison,* likewise takes place with the background of the Spanish civil war haunting the uneasy conscience of the principal character, but Sartre does not attempt to concentrate simultaneity of action nearly as much as Aragon.

6. It is perhaps not quite correct to say that the novel cannot portray the simultaneity of two or more actions. In theory, the page could be divided into the desired number of vertical columns, each dealing with one of the actions. Unfortunately, the human eye is not adapted to that kind of reading experience. The sparing use of the split screen in the cinema seems to confirm the point. Perhaps, in the future, novels will be accompanied by, and coordinated with, video cassettes. An arrangement of that sort would make *Less Communistes* a very exciting experience.

7. An example of this argument can be found in *Les Communistes,* 5:180.

8. In *Les Beaux Quartiers,* Aragon uses painters, such as Sisley or Claude le Lorrain, to characterize the Parc Monceau (p. 477); he decorates Quesnel's study with a Chardin (p. 482); and he mocks a provincial beauty, who can sing airs from *Madame Butterfly* but is baffled by the melodies of Henri Duparc and Ernest Chausson (p. 39).

9. Goering said: "When I hear the word 'culture,' I reach for my revolver."

Chapter Seven

1. Every responsible government ought to prepare contingency plans on what to do in case the country is defeated in war and occupied by the enemy, but apparently such a prospect is more than tenderhearted politicians can face; it is also not the sort of precaution, although of vital importance, that will bring them popularity and votes.

A recent example of the blind conviction of invincibility concerned a report, discovered by one of our many detective journalists, that the Pentagon had drawn up exactly such a plan; namely, what action to take in case the United States were defeated and occupied. The resulting uproar from indignant patriots was such that denials had to be issued by a red-faced government and the plan had to be scrapped. And yet, it was probably the most intelligent idea to come out of the Pentagon in years, and those responsible for it should have been praised and promoted as true patriots who cared profoundly about the welfare of their country.

It is evident that the United States has been a poor student of history, not only in this hypothetical matter but also in the Vietnam War, when the lessons to be learned from the French failure in Indochina were haughtily ignored.

2. Jean-Paul Sartre, "Forgers of Myth—The Young Playwrights of France," *Theatre Arts* (June 1946), 330.

3. Jean-Paul Sartre, *Sartre on Theater*, trans. Frank Jellinek (New York: Pantheon Books, 1976), 185. Documents assembled, edited, introduced, and annotated by Michel Contat and Michel Rybalka. The original French appeared in *L'Avant-Scène Théâtre* 402–403 (1 May/15 May 1968).

4. The Théâtre Sarah Bernhardt had been renamed Théâtre de la Cité during the German occupation, because the great actress was Jewish.

5. Page numbers refer to Jean-Paul Sartre, *Les Mouches* (Paris: Gallimard, 1947).

6. JUPITER. "Once freedom has exploded in the soul of a man, the gods no longer have any power over him." [Quand une fois la liberté a explosé dans une âme d'homme, les Dieux ne peuvent plus rien contre cet homme-là (*Les Mouches*, 86).]

7. A different configuration is suggested by Hazel Estella Barnes, in *The Literature of Possibility—A Study in Humanistic Existentialism (Sartre, de Beauvoir, Camus)* (Lincoln: University of Nebraska Press, 1959), 95: Zeus = the Germans, Aegisthus = the Vichy goverment. But this parallel leaves Clytemnestra without a function and fails to establish the marriage of collaboration between the Germans and the Vichy regime. It also does not take into account the anticlerical attitude of Sartre.

8. *Sartre on Theater*, 193–194. In this discussion Sartre also deals with the question of repentance, guilt, and shame of the German people after the end of the World War II.

9. Ibid., 234.

10. *Cahiers Charles Dullin* 2 (March 1966).

11. Simone de Beauvoir, *La Force de l'âge* (Paris: Gallimard, 1960), 553–54.

12. Gerhard Heller, *Un Allemand à Paris, 1940–1944* (Paris: Seuil, 1981), 159–60.

13. Pol Vandromme, in *Jean Anouilh: Un Auteur et ses personnages* (Paris: La Table Ronde, 1965), 109, judges: "Creon does not represent order; he is happiness (and the horror of living). Antigone is not truth, she is unhappiness (and the horror of dying)."

14. Jean Anouilh, *Antigone*, trans. Lewis Galantière, in *Five Plays* (New York: Hill and Wang, 1958), 1:35–37. Page numbers refer to this edition.

15. Jean Anouilh, *Antigone*, in *Nouvelles Pièces noires* (Paris: La Table Ronde, 1967), 177–80. Page numbers refer to this edition.

16. Gabriel Marcel, "Le Tragique chez J. Anouilh de Jézabel à Médée," *Revue de Paris*, June 1949; Jean Sauvenay, "L'*Antigone* de Jean Anouilh," *Hier et demain*, 9 (1944); Hubert Gignoux, *Anouilh* (Paris: Edition du Temps présent,

1946), 94–95; William Calin, "Patterns of Imagery in Anouilh's *Antigone*," *The French Review* 41, no. 1 (October 1967), 82; Pol Gaillard, "Pièces roses: L'Antigone du désespoir," *La Pensée,* October–December 1944.

17. The detachment from personal emotions is underlined by Creon's statement that he does not know which of the two brothers lies unburied, because they were unrecognizable, mashed to a pulp after their struggle. In Sophocles' play, matters are different. Eteocles is the honorable one and he receives burial. The deviations from Sophocles' play in Anouilh's version are significant.

18. Antigone does not have to explain her act any more than Joan of Arc in Anouilh's later play *L'Alouette* (1952), but, unlike Joan, she does not have to listen to any voices: her instinct speaks loud enough. If Joan's mission is to save France, Antigone's is to save humanity. There are few better roles in all of theater.

19. George Steiner, *The Death of Tragedy* (New York: Knopf, 1961), 330. One exception needs to be taken to this otherwise fine comment. As we have already discussed, a "morality of order" does not require leaving dead people unburied—quite the contrary.

20. Gabriel Marcel, in "Le tragique," judges, "The immense success of the play, at least in France, reveals a spiritual deficiency on the part of the spectators."

21. André Barsacq, "A l'Atelier près de quinze ans," *Cahiers de la Compagnie M. Renaud–J. L. Barrault,* May 1959.

22. Heller, *Un Allemand,* 138.

Chapter Eight

1. Alfred Cobban, *A History of Modern France* (Baltimore: Penguin Books, 1965), 3:201.

2. These figures are quoted in David L. Schalk, *The Spectrum of Political Engagement: Mounier, Benda, Nizan, Brasillach, Sartre* (Princeton: Princeton University Press, 1979), 86, 102.

3. Articles in *Je suis partout,* quoted by William R. Tucker, in *The Fascist Ego: A Political Biography of Robert Brasillach* (Berkeley: University of California Press, 1975), 271, 197.

4. See the testimony of Resistance writer René Tavernier in Jacques Debû-Bridel, *La Résistance intellectuelle* (Paris: Julliard, 1970), 93–94.

5. Jean Anouilh, *Poor Bitos,* transl. Lucienne Hill (New York: Coward-McCann, 1964), 71. Page numbers of the translation refer to this edition.

6. Jean Anouilh, *Pauvre Bitos,* in *Pièces grinçantes* (Paris: La Table Ronde, 1961), 470. Page numbers refer to this edition.

7. Intentionally or by accident, performances of *Pauvre Bitos* during the latter part of 1956 coincided with the uprising in Hungary, which was brutally suppressed by Soviet tanks, and in which scores of Hungarian rebels were

sentenced to death in trials reminiscent of those during the Reign of Terror. Consequently, in the 1956 performances, whenever Robespierre and Saint-Just discussed the "model law," people in the audience shouted "Budapest, Budapest" to protest a modern Reign of Terror.

8. In French the suffix *-ard* has a pejorative sound, and *bastillards* evokes an association with *bâtards* (bastards). This is not the only linguistic game Anouilh plays. The name of the "hero" (Bitos) means "hat" in French *argot*. The proper word for "hat" being *chapeau,* one may think of the expression *porter le chapeau,* which means "to take the rap." This describes the situation of Bitos in the play, because he gets a roasting from the host and the other guests, and he is made to pay not only for his own sins but for those of Robespierre as well.

9. Translation mine.

10. *Le Grand Larousse de la langue française (1972)* defines *foire d'empoigne* as a popular expression meaning "endroit où chacun cherche à voler le plus possible, ou à se procurer sans aucun scrupule le plus de choses possibles." [A place where each one tries to steal as much as possible, or to acquire without any scruples as many things as possible.] *Acheter quelque chose à la foire d'empoigne* means "to steal." Hence the proper English translation of the play's title would be *No Holds Barred,* or *Catch As Catch Can.*

11. Jean Anouilh, *Catch As Catch Can,* transl. Lucienne Hill, in *Jean Anouilh: Seven Plays* (New York: Hill and Wang, 1967), 3:247. Page numbers refer to this translation.

12. Jean Anouilh, *Pièces costumées* (Paris: La Table Ronde, 1960). Page numbers refer to this edition.

13. Louis Aragon, in his novel *La Semaine sainte* (Paris: Gallimard, 1958), treats the same subject—the return of Napoleon and the ensuing seesawing of loyalties. But Aragon prefers neither of the rulers. According to him, the French wanted neither of the two, but a republic.

14. The similarity between Anouilh's view of Napoleon and Taine's is striking. Although Taine gives credit to Napoleon as a statesman, he agrees with Anouilh on the emperor's character in his description of Napoleon as "the greatest genius of the modern world and an egoism equal to his genius." For a summary of Taine's judgment of Napoleon, see Weinstein, *Hippolyte Taine,* 140. Another similarity between Anouilh and Taine is that both dared to attack the Revolution and Napoleon—and both paid a price for it.

15. See Anouilh's program notes to *La Foire d'empoigne* in Pol Van-dromme, *Jean Anouilh,* 243–44.

Chapter Nine

1. It is not difficult to understand de Gaulle's personal and France's general, anti-Americanism during that time. De Gaulle had never enjoyed favor with the Americans during World War II. The United States had preferred General Giraud as leader of the Free French, and President Roosevelt

disliked de Gaulle, who had to exert every effort to have his troops take part in the liberation of France.

In 1954 Secretary of State John Foster Dulles failed to keep his promise to aid the French in the defense of Dien Bien Phu. In 1956 Dulles struck a moralistic pose, blaming France and Great Britain, joined by Israel, for a legitimate move to protect their lifeline and their rights in the Suez Canal, built and largely owned by them and seized by Egypt's Colonel Nasser. And during the Algerian war, the United States openly criticized the French and made no attempt to prevent shipments of arms to the Algerian rebels.

Dulles not only ignored the basic rule that one does not treat allies the same as enemies; he managed by his erratic attitude to destroy all the good will created by the enormous American contribution to the liberation of France and by the important economic aid of the Marshall Plan.

It should have come as no surprise to anyone, except Americans unaware of the rest of the world, that the French strongly criticized the United States during the Vietnam War, and that they gloated at the embarrassment, turmoil, and humiliation caused by that war.

2. The most memorable moments in the Ben Barka trial were provided by lower-level policemen and informers, whose picturesque vocabulary enriched the French language and who were made the scapegoats of the affair.

To grasp the gravity of the Ben Barka case, American readers would have to imagine that, for example, a Philippine opposition leader had been assassinated by the minister of the interior of the Marcos government in a suburb of San Francisco with the collaboration and full knowledge of local and federal police.

When one compares the Ben Barka case with the Watergate scandal in the United States, the latter seems considerably less serious. Watergate resulted in no deaths or serious physical harm. It did not even influence the results of the 1972 presidential elections: only neurotic miscalculation and myopic confidence in public opinion polls can have induced the Nixon White House staff to imagine, even in its worst nightmares, that so weak a candidate as Mr. McGovern could pose the slightest threat to an incumbent president. Of course, those guilty of the break-in at Watergate and the subsequent cover-up deserved punishment, but it should have been for stupidity before anything else.

By contrast, the Ben Barka case involved brutal murder and, at least hypothetically, may have influenced political conditions in Morocco. Yet this scandalous affair has been ignored by even such serious historians as Gordon Wright, in *France in Modern Times: From the Enlightenment to the Present,* 3rd ed. (New York, London: W. W. Norton, 1981) and Charles Morazé, in *Le Général de Gaulle et la république; ou, La République ne civilise plus* (Paris: Flammarion, 1972).

3. Henri Alleg, *La Question* (Paris: Editions Minuit, 1958).

4. Accounts of the Algerian war can be found in Georges Buis, *La Grotte*

(Paris: Julliard, 1961); Pierre Leuliette, *Saint-Michel et le dragon* (Paris: Editions Minuit, 1961); and Philippe Labro, *Les Feux mal éteints* (Paris: Gallimard, 1967). Only the last of these contains an attack against the OAS, accusing them of assassinations.

5. These three novels have been published under the collective title *Trois Pas dans une guerre* (Paris: Grasset, 1978). Page numbers refer to this edition.

6. Stil draws a stereotypical portrait of the French colonialists in Algeria: rude, egotistical, uncouth. A quite different image emerges in the very sensitive novel by Michel Droit, *Le Retour* (Paris: Julliard, 1964), which describes the plight of those who thought of Algeria as their native country and now had to accept that this was no longer so. It is the story of a lawyer, torn between his love for Algeria and his allegiance to France, who defends a man who has participated in terrorist acts by the OAS. Although in the end he gets assassinated by a fanatical supporter of the Algérie Française group, the case of those who participated in the OAS revolt (their struggle against those who opposed the Algerian war and against de Gaulle's crushing of the revolt) is eloquently expressed in the trial.

7. James Jones, *The Merry Month of May* (New York: Delacorte Press, 1970), 167–68. Page numbers refer to this edition. The novel was translated into French under the title *Le Joli Mois de mai* (Paris: Stock, 1971).

8. Quoted in Jones, *The Merry Month*, 154.

9. Patrick Combes, in *La Littérature et le mouvement de mai 68: Ecriture, mythes, critique, écrivains 1968–1981* (Paris: Seghers, 1984), 1985 cites: Pascal Lainé, *L'Irrévolution* (Paris: Gallimard, 1971): Robert Merle, *Derrière la vitre* (Paris: Gallimard, 1970); Maurice Clavel, *La Perte et le fracas* (Paris: Flammarion, 1971); Nathalie Sarraute, *Vous les entendez?* (Paris: Gallimard, 1972); Raymond Jean, *Les Deux Printemps* (Paris: Seuil, 1971); Hélène Parmelin, *La Manière noire* (Paris: C. Bourgois, 1970); and Jean-François Bizot, *Les Déclassés* (Paris: Sagittaire, 1976).

10. Among their graffiti, the anonymous authors should perhaps have included the phrase in which Harry Gallagher sums up de Gaulle's late but effective crushing of the May uprising: "Don't mess around with the pros until you're dry behind the ears and know your business" (*Merry Month*, 263).

11. For a brief summary of this phenomenon, see Leo Weinstein, "Altered States of Consciousness in Flaubert's *Madame Bovary* and Kafka's *A Country Doctor*," in Raymond J. Cormier, ed., *Voices of Consciousness: Essays on Medieval and Modern French Literature in Memory of James D. Powell and Rosemary Hodgin* (Philadelphia: Temple University Press, 1977), 215–29.

Conclusion

1. According to A. Rebière, *Mathématiques et mathématiciens: Pensées et curiosités* (Paris: Nony, 1889), 112, it was d'Alembert who made the remark after watching a performance of Racine's *Iphigénie*.

2. This critical attitude goes back at least as far as Quintilian's admonition, "Scribitur ad narrandum, non ad probandum" (*Institutio oratoria* 10, 1, 31). And it can be found as late as 1956 in Jean Cocteau's "Discours d'Oxford," in his *Poésies critiques* (Paris: Gallimard, 1960), 2:198, "Everything that can be proven is vulgar; to act without proof requires an act of faith." Even so objective a critic as Gustave Lanson heaps scorn on d'Alembert's literary judgments. In his *Histoire de la littérature française* (Paris: Hachette, 1903), 725, Lanson has this to say about the man he calls Dalembert: "A narrow-minded critic, with a mind closed to art and poetry; an intolerant philosopher, maddened with hate against religion and priests; a heavy and dull writer without tact and with a lack of sensitivity covered inadequately by bombast and faked noble sentiments." The very possiblity of being judged in this manner ought to discourage all but the most daring from writing anything that may irritate critics.

3. While literary and intellectual people have exerted considerable influence on French politics, Michel Serres has questioned their direct participation in political activities in recent times.

It seems that for some time now the political or sociopolitical activities of the intellectuals have most frequently been reduced to a publicity performance. . . . I believe that now the intellectuals have a duty to withdraw rather than become involved, to practice the philosophy of the garden. . . .

I do not think that intellectuals are made to influence others; the philosophers who were very important in their time are often people who live in their offices. The intellectual world is as unjust as the others, and if it denounces the injustices of others, it thereby casts a veil over its own injustices. This is not a paradox: when injustice denounces injustice, it renders itself less suspicious." (*Le Monde,* 15–16 April 1979, 13)

Late in his career, Jean-Paul Sartre also was assailed by doubts about the effectiveness of his militant works. At the end of *Les Mots* (Paris: Gallimard, 1964), 211, he muses: "For a long time I took my pen to be a sword; at present I realize our impotence. No matter, I am writing, I shall continue to write; it serves a purpose after all."

4. Irving Howe, *Politics and the Novel* (New York: Horizon Press: 1957; New York: Avon Books, 1970), 24.

5. Micheline Tison-Braun, *La Crise de l'humanisme: Le Conflit de l'individu et de la société dans la littérature française moderne* (Paris: Nizet, 1958), 1:11–12.

6. Eugène Poitou, *Du Roman et du théâtre contemporains et de leur influence sur les moeurs* (Paris: Durand, 1857), 109, 112.

7. On the subject of censorship, see the excellent study by Victor Hallays-Dabot, *Histoire de la censure théâtrale en France* (Paris: Dentu, 1862).

8. Obviously, there are risks involved in viewing history as moving

toward greater freedom and democracy. The modern means of communications, when used skillfully, can be employed by dictatorships to enslave minds just as they can be effective to set minds free. The final score in the struggle between a world fashioned in the manner of Orwell's *1984* and one that favors democratic regimes cannot be prognosticated with any certainty. However, the formation of an ever more united Europe, the disappearance of nearly all dictatorships in South America, and the promise of increased freedom in the Soviet Union and the Eastern European nations seem to favor a more optimistic forecast for the future.

Selected Bibliography

PRIMARY SOURCES

Anouilh, Jean. *Antigone*. In *Nouvelles Pièces noires*. Paris: La Table Ronde, 1967.
———. *Antigone*. Adapted and translated by Lewis Galantière. In *Jean Anouilh: Five Plays*, vol 1. New York: Hill and Wang. 1958.
———. *Catch As Catch Can*. Translated by Lucienne Hill. In *Jean Anouilh: Seven Plays*, vol. 3. New York: Hill and Wang, 1967.
———. *La Foire d'empoigne*. In *Pièces costumées*. Paris: La Table Ronde, 1960.
———. *Pauvre Bitos*. In *Pièces grinçantes*. Paris: La Table Ronde, 1961.
———. *Poor Bitos*, Translated by Lucienne Hill. New York: Coward-McCann, 1964.
Aragon, Louis. *Le Monde réel*. (1934–44):
    1. *Les Cloches de Bâle*. Paris: Denoël, 1934.
    2. *Les Beaux Quartiers*. Paris: Denoël, 1936.
    3. *Les Voyageurs de l'impériale*. Paris: Gallimard, 1947.
    4. *Aurélien*. Paris: Gallimard, 1944.
———. *Les Communistes*. 6 vols. Paris: La Bibliothèque Française, 1949–51.
Barbusse, Henri. *Le Feu: Journal d'une escouade*. Paris: Flammarion, 1917.
Barrès, Maurice. *Le Roman de l'énergie nationale* (1898–1917)
    1. *Les Déracinés*. Paris: Charpentier, 1898.
    2. *L'Appel au soldat*. Paris: Charpentier, 1900.
    3. *Leurs Figures*. Paris: Charpentier, 1917.
Drieu la Rochelle, Pierre. *Gilles*. Editions Folio. Paris: Gallimard, 1939.
France, Anatole. *L'Anneau d'améthyste*. Paris: Calman-Lévy, 1905.
———. *Monsieur Bergeret à Paris*. Paris: Calman-Lévy, 1906.
Jones, James. *The Merry Month of May*. New York: Delacorte Press, 1970.
Sartre, Jean-Paul. *Les Mouches*. Paris: Gallimard, 1947.
Stil, André. *Trois Pas dans une guerre*. Paris: Grasset, 1978. Reprint of the original editions:
    1. *Nous nous aimerons demain*. Paris: Editeurs français réunis, 1957.
    2. *Le Foudroyage*. Paris: Editeurs français réunis, 1960.
    3. *Le Dernier Quart d'heure*. Paris: Editeurs français réunis, 1962.
Zola, Emile. *Vérité*. In *Oeuvres complètes,* vol. 8. Paris: Cercle du Livre Précieux, 1968.

SECONDARY SOURCES

Adam, Paul. *La Littérature et la guerre.* Paris: G. Crès, 1916.

Adereth, Maxwell. *Commitment in Modern French Literature: A Brief Study of "littérature engagée" in the Works of Péguy, Aragon, and Sartre.* London: Gollancz, 1967.

Barnes, Hazel Estella. *The Literature of Possibility—a Study in Humanistic Existentialism (Sartre, de Beauvoir, Camus).* Lincoln: University of Nebraska Press, 1959.

Bernard, J.-P. A. *Le Parti communiste français et la question littéraire, 1921–1939.* Grenoble: Presses Universitaires de Grenoble, 1972.

Bessière, Jean. *Les Ecrivains engagées.* Collection Idéologies et Sociétés. Paris: Larousse, 1977.

Beugnot, Bernard. *Les Critiques de notre temps et Anouilh.* Collection Les Critiques de notre Temps. Paris: Garnier Frères, 1977.

Bredin, Jean Denis. *L'Affaire.* Paris: Julliard, 1983.

Charles-Brun, Jean. *Le Roman social.* Paris: V. Giard et E. Brière, 1910.

Cobban, Alfred. *A History of Modern France.* 3 vols. Baltimore: Penguin Books, 1957–65.

Combes, Patrick. *La Littérature et le mouvement de Mai 68: Ecriture, mythes, critique, écrivains, 1968–1981.* Paris: Seghers, 1984.

Comminges, Elie de. *Anouilh: Littérature et politique.* Paris: Nizet, 1977.

Coute, David. *Le Communisme et les intellectuels français, 1914–1966.* Paris: Gallimard, 1962.

Curtis, Michael. *Three against the Third Republic.* Princeton: Princeton University Press, 1959.

Curtius, E. R. *Die literarischen Wegbereiter des neuen Frankreich.* Potsdam: Kiepenhauer, 1923.

Daudet, Léon. *Flammes.* Paris: Grasset, 1930.

Debû-Bridel, Jacques. *La Résistance intellectuelle.* Paris: Julliard, 1970.

Delhorbe, Cécile. *L'Affaire Dreyfus et les écrivains français.* Paris: Attinger, 1932.

Dimier, L. *Les Maîtres de la contre-révolution au XIXe siècle.* Paris: Librairie des St.-Pères, 1907.

Dominique, Pierre. *Les Polémistes français depuis 1789.* Paris: La Colombe, 1962.

Drieu la Rochelle, Pierre. *La Comédie de Charleroi.* Paris: Gallimard, 1934.

Droit, Michel. *Le Retour.* Paris: Julliard, 1964.

Field, Frank. *Three French Writers and the Great War: Studies in the Rise of Communism and Fascism.* Cambridge: Cambridge University Press, 1975.

Flower, J. E. *Literature and the Left in France: Society, Politics, and the Novel since the Late Nineteenth Century.* Tottowa, N.J.: Barnes and Noble, 1983.

————. *Writers and Politics in Modern Britain, France, and Germany.* New York and London: Holmes and Meier, 1977.

Garaudy, Roger. *L'Itinéraire d'Aragon.* Collection Vocations, no. 10. Paris: Gallimard, 1961.

Girard, René. *Le Bouc émissaire.* Paris: Grasset, 1982.

Glover, Frederic J. *Drieu La Rochelle and the Fiction of Testimony.* Berkeley and Los Angeles: University of California Press, 1958.

Heller, Gerhard. *Un Allemand à Paris, 1940–1944.* Paris: Seuil, 1981.

Howe, Irving. *Politics and the Novel.* New York: Horizon Press, 1957; New York: Avon Books, 1970.

Krauss, Henning. *Die Praxis der "littérature engagée" im Werk Jean-Paul Sartres.* Heidelberg: Carl Winter Universitätsverlag, 1970.

Lenski, B. A. *Jean Anouilh: Stages in Rebellion.* Atlantic Highlands, N.J.: Humanities Press, 1975.

Levrault, Léon. *La Satire: Evolution du genre.* Paris: Delaplane, 1904.

Loubet del Bayle, Jean-Louis. *Les Non-conformistes des années 30.* Paris: Seuil, 1969.

MacLeod, Alexander. *La Pensée politique de Pierre Drieu La Rochelle.* Publications de la Faculté de Droit et des Sciences économiques, Aix-en-Provence. Paris: Cujas, 1966.

Madaule, Jacques. *Le Nationalisme de Maurice Barrès.* Marseille: Sagittaire, 1943.

Marec, Jean-Paul. *La Ténébreuse Affaire Ben Barka.* Collection Les Grandes Affaires de ce Temps. Paris: Editions des "Presses Noires," 1966.

Matvejevitch, Predag. *Pour une poétique de l'événement.* Edition 10/18. Paris: Union Générale d'Editions, 1979.

Morazé, Charles. *Le Général de Gaulle et la République; ou, La République ne civilise plus.* Paris: Flammarion, 1972.

Nizan, Paul. *Antoine Bloyé.* Paris: Grasset, 1933.

Raimond, Michel. *Le Roman contemporain—Le Signe des temps—Proust, Gide, Bernanos, Mauriac, Céline, Malraux, Aragon.* Paris: SEDES, 1976.

Redfern, W. P. *Paul Nizan: Committed Literature in a Conspirational World.* Princeton: Princeton University Press, 1972.

Rieuneau, Maurice. *Guerre et révolution dans le roman français de 1919 à 1939.* Paris: Kleinsieck, 1974.

Rühle, Jürgen. *Literatur und Revolution: Die Schriftsteller und der Kommunismus.* Cologne and Berlin: Kiepenhauer und Witsch, 1960.

Saint-Auban, Emile de. *L'Idée sociale au théâtre.* Paris: Stock, 1901.

Sartre, Jean-Paul. *Les Mots.* Paris: Gallimard, 1964.

————. *Un Théâtre de situation.* Paris: Gallimard, 1973.

————. *Sartre on Theater.* Translated by Frank Jelinek. Documents assembled, introduced, and annotated by Michel Contat and Michel Rybalka. New York: Pantheon Books, 1976.

Savage, Catherine. *Malraux, Sartre, and Aragon as Political Novelists.* University of Florida Monographs: Humanities, no. 17. Gainesville: University of Florida Press, 1964.

Schalk, David L. *The Spectrum of Political Engagement: Mounier, Benda, Nizan, Brasillach, Sartre.* Princeton: Princeton University Press, 1979.

Seager, Frederic H. *The Boulanger Affair: Political Crossroad of France, 1886–1889.* Ithaca, New York: Cornell University Press, 1969.

Serant, Paul. *Le Romantisme fasciste; ou, L'Oeuvre de quelques écrivains français.* Paris: Fasquelle, 1959.

Serres, Michel. "Entretien avec Michel Serres." *Le Monde,* 15–16 April 1979, 13.

Sorel, Georges. *Réflexions sur la violence.* 3d ed. Paris: M. Rivière, 1912.

Steiner, George. *The Death of Tragedy.* New York: Knopf, 1961.

Sternhell, Zeev. *Maurice Barrès et le nationalisme français.* Paris: Colin, 1972.

Suleiman, Susan Rubin. *Authoritarian Fictions: The Ideological Novel as a Literary Genre.* New York: Columbia University Press, 1983.

Sur, Serge. *La Vie politique en France sous la Ve République.* Paris: Montchrestien, 1977.

Tison-Braun, Micheline. *La Crise de l'humanisme: Le Conflit de l'individu et de la société dans la littérature française moderne.* 2 vols. Paris: Nizet, 1958.

Tucker, William R. *The Fascist Ego: A Political Biography of Robert Brasillach.* Berkeley: University of California Press, 1975.

Vandromme, Pol. *Jean Anouilh: Un Auteur et ses personnages.* Paris: La Table Ronde, 1965.

Weinstein, Leo. "Altered States of Consciousness in Flaubert's *Madame Bovary* and Kafka's *A Country Doctor.*" In *Voices of Consciousness: Essays on Medieval and Modern French Literature in Memory of James D. Powell and Rosemary Hodgin,* edited by Raymond J. Cormier. Philadelphia: Temple University Press, 1977, 215–29.

———. *Hippolyte Taine.* New York: Twayne, 1972.

Worcester, David. *The Art of Satire.* Cambridge: Harvard University Press, 1940.

Wright, Gordon. *France in Modern Times: From the Enlightenment to the Present.* 3d ed. New York and London: W. W. Norton, 1981.

Zeraffa, Michel. *Roman et société.* Paris: Presses Universitaires de France, 1971.

Index